Plate 1 The Glencoul Thrust runs along the prominent sloping shelf on the hillside beyond the loch. Below it, un-moved Cambrian quartzite (forming the prominent cliffs) rests unconformably on Lewisian gneiss of the Foreland. Above it lies Lewisian gneiss. This forms part of the Glencoul Nappe which has been thrust westward over the Foreland sequence. We look north-east from near Kylesku across Loch Glencoul to Aird na Loch (D2820) (*Frontispiece*)

BRITISH GEOLOGICAL SURVEY

British Regional Geology

The Northern Highlands
of Scotland

FOURTH EDITION

G S Johnstone, BSc and
W Mykura, DSc

NOTTINGHAM   BRITISH GEOLOGICAL SURVEY   1989

BRITISH GEOLOGICAL SURVEY

The full range of Survey publications is available from the BGS Sales Desks at Nottingham and Edinburgh; see contact details below or shop online at www.thebgs.co.uk.

The London Information Office maintains a reference collection of BGS publications including maps for consultation.

The Survey publishes an annual catalogue of its maps and other publications; this catalogue is available from any of the BGS Sales Desks.

The British Geological Survey carries out the geological survey of Great Britain and Northern Ireland (the latter is an agency service for the government of Northern Ireland), and of the surrounding continental shelf, as well as its basic research projects. It also undertakes programmes of British technical aid in geology in developing countries as arranged by the Department for International Development and other agencies.

The British Geological Survey is a component body of the Natural Environment Research Council.

Bibliographic reference

JOHNSTONE, G S and MYKURA, W. 1989. *British regional geology: the Northern Highlands of Scotland* (4th edition). (Nottingham: British Geological Survey.)

First published 1936
Second edition 1948
Third edition 1960
Fourth edition 1989
Second impression 1995
Third impression 2003

ISBN 0 85272 465 9

British Geological Survey sales offices

Keyworth, Nottingham NG12 5GG
☎ 0115 936 3100   Fax 0115 936 3200
e-mail: sales@bgs.ac.uk
www.bgs.ac.uk
Online shop: www.geologyshop.com

Murchison House, West Mains Road, Edinburgh EH9 3LA
☎ 0131 667 1000   Fax 0131 668 2683
e-mail: scotsales@bgs.ac.uk

London Information Office at the Natural History Museum (Earth Galleries), Exhibition Road, South Kensington, London SW7 2DE
☎ 020 7589 4090   Fax 020 7584 8270
☎ 020 7942 5344/45
e-mail: bgslondon@bgs.ac.uk

Forde House, Park Five Business Centre, Harrier Way, Sowton, Exeter, Devon EX2 7HU
☎ 01392-445271   Fax 01392-445371

Geological Survey of Northern Ireland, 20 College Gardens, Belfast BT9 6BS
☎ 028-9066 6595   Fax 028-9066 2835

Maclean Building, Crowmarsh Gifford, Wallingford, Oxfordshire OX10 8BB
☎ 01491-838800   Fax 01491-692345

Parent Body

Natural Environment Research Council, Polaris House, North Star Avenue, Swindon, Wiltshire SN2 1EU
☎ 01793-411500   Fax 01793-411501
www.nerc.ac.uk

Contents

Illustrations

Tables

Front Suilven, Sutherland. 'Rocky ridge and boggy hollow' terrain, typical of
Cover the basement Lewisian Gneiss. Suilven is a prominent relict mountain
of flat-lying Torridonian Sandstone which rests unconformably on
Lewisian Gneiss. (D2812)

Plates

For photographs in BGS collections the registered number is given; for photographs in private collections the photographer's name is given.

Foreword to the Fourth Edition

The first edition of the Regional Handbook to the Northern Highlands was published in 1936; for the subsequent editions in 1948 and 1960 the text was updated, but not extensively revised. Since that time there has been a tremendous increase in research into all aspects of the geology of the Northern Highlands and it has become necessary to produce a completely new text. The present handbook gives a fuller treatment of the geology of the Outer Hebrides than the previous editions, and of the deep structures of the crust beneath the Northern Highlands. Unfortunately lack of space has permitted only brief references to the geology of the seas around northern Scotland; it is hoped that this will be treated in more detail in another publication.

The greater part of the handbook was written by Mr G. S. Johnstone, who is the author of Chapters 1, 3, 4, 6, 8, 9, 11, 12, 15, 16, and most of Chapter 7. Dr W. Mykura wrote chapters 10 and 13, Dr J. D. Peacock Chapter 14, and Dr J. R. Mendum Chapter 5. Dr D. J. Fettes wrote most of Chapter 2 and the section on the metamorphic zones in Chapter 7, and Dr D. I. Smith contributed to the writing of Chapters 8, 9, 11 and 13. The account of seismicity (Chapter 15) was written by Drs C. W. A. Browitt and R. M. W. Musson. The handbook was edited by Dr Mykura.

The authors wish to acknowledge the help received from their colleagues in BGS. Dr F. May read the chapters dealing with the Moine and its intrusions, Mr P. J. Brand checked the fossil names appearing in Chapters 4, 10, 12 and 13 and produced the fossil plates (Plates 24 and 25). The block diagram illustrating the palaeogeography of the Helmsdale Boulder Bed (Figure 43) is based on a diagram by Dr C. E. Deegan. Particular thanks are also due to Professor P. E. Brown, who made available his chapter on 'Caledonian and earlier magmatism' prior to its publication in 'The Geology of Scotland' (2nd Edition). Many of the figures in the text are based on ones published previously, and the authors thank the following for permission to use or adapt their diagrams: Dr A. D. Stewart (Figures 8, 10, 11), Dr G. E. Williams (Figure 8), Drs M. P. Coward and J. H. Kim (Figure 12), Drs J. A. Brewer and D. K. Smythe (Figure 13), Dr M. R. W. Johnson (Figure 12), Dr D. Powell (Figure 17), Drs D. Wilson, J. Shepherd and R. I. Harker (Figure 21), Professor I. Parsons (Figure 24), Dr R. N. Donovan (Figure 31), Dr J. M. Speight and others (Figure 36), Dr D. Evans and others (Figure 37), Dr R. Steel (Figure 38), and Dr R. M. Sykes (Figure 40 and 42).

British Geological Survey
Keyworth
Nottingham NG12 5GG

28 March 1989

F. G. LARMINIE, OBE
Director

1 Introduction

BOUNDARIES OF THE AREA

The area dealt with in this book comprises the mainland of Scotland north of the Great Glen, including the Hebridean Islands. Much of the Inner Hebrides, however, consists largely of Tertiary igneous rocks and Mesozoic sediments which are also found in the peninsulas of Ardnamurchan and Morvern. As these areas are described in *British Regional Geology: The Tertiary Volcanic Districts*, only the pre-Mesozoic and post-Tertiary aspects of their geology are dealt with here. The Northern Isles (Orkney and Shetland) are the subject of a separate issue in the series.

No one geographical name adequately covers all the area described in this book. Opinion is divided about calling the mainland part the North-West Highlands, the Northern Highlands, or even, by the insertion of an arbitrary line between Dingwall and Kyle of Lochalsh, about dividing it into the Northern Highlands to the north and the Western Highlands to the south. Authorities could be quoted for each possibility. As none of the names includes either the eastern coastal lowlands or the Western Isles, all must be considered unsatisfactory as titles. The name 'Northern Highlands' has been retained for this book in order to maintain continuity with the previous edition.

An outline map of the region, and of the areas described in the other books in the British Regional Geology series, appears on the back cover.

PHYSICAL FEATURES

Any observer standing on a high mountain within the Northern Highlands, as elsewhere in the Scottish hills, must be impressed by the general uniformity of levels of the summits which surround him. In the distance, with the interference of ridge and valley, individual mountains become lost and the skyline gives the impression of a general plateau-like surface above which occasional notable eminences can be seen (Plate 2). The Highlands, therefore, give the appearance of having been carved out of a generally flat elevated surface — in other words, they appear to represent a dissected peneplain. That this view is too simple has long been appreciated, as many workers in the region have noted groupings of features at various levels which indicate the existence of intermediate erosion surfaces. For instance, George (1966) records three such surfaces in the western part of the mainland and in the Hebrides. These lie at 975 m, 730 m and 440 m above sea level. For other parts of the area, Godard (1965) suggests that five erosion surfaces are present.

To some workers these platforms, from which the local mountains have been carved and to which their summit levels correspond, represent subaerial erosion levels related to periods of stillstand during the upwarping of an original planar surface; to others (notably George, 1966), they suggest platforms of marine erosion. However, whatever the hypothesis favoured, it is now generally accepted that the surfaces were formed after the cessation of the volcanic activity of the Ter-

Plate 2 The accordant summit levels of the southern portion of the Northern Highlands define a former land surface at about 850 m above OD. The craggy ground is typical of the rocks of the Glenfinnan Division of the Moine. We look south-west from Sgurr Thuilm to Glenfinnan and Loch Shiel   (G. S. Johnstone)

tiary igneous period (i.e. during the Miocene–Pliocene) because intrusions of that age (which must have consolidated under considerable cover) are now exposed and are transected by erosion surfaces even at high present-day levels.

It will be seen from Figure 1 that the mountain area of the Northern Highlands is developed on either side of a north–south axis from near Loch Eriboll, through Beinn Dearg and Carn Eighe to Sgurr Dhomhnuill. Along this axis the general level of the summits descends only gradually north and south from Carn Eighe which, at 1183 m, is the highest mountain of the region. Eastwards from the axial line summit levels diminish gently to the north and east coasts; westwards from it, levels are well maintained until near the western seaboard, where the mountains descend steeply to sea level.

This variation in the distribution of elevated land does suggest that, no matter what has been the agent of planation, the late-Tertiary uplift was greatest in the area of the present-day high ground. The present watershed is not far from the axis of the mountain area; straight-running easterly-flowing rivers follow a long course to the sea on the east side of the watershed, and short westerly-flowing torrents descend rapidly to sea level down embayments in the mountain wall to the west. This distribution of drainage has given rise to the suggestion that the rivers reflect an original consequent pattern on either side of the axis of uplift and further, that this pattern was initiated on a surface of undeformed sedimentary rock which formerly covered the Highlands, but has since been completely eroded away from the varied and folded schists which are at present exposed It is possible that only such 'antecedent' drainage development could account for the lack of adjustment of the major streams to the complex geology.

The various hypotheses concerning this theory all contain some difficulties. The most recent, which takes into account those of previous authorities, is by Sissons (1967). He supports the suggestion that the drainage was initiated on a sedimentary cover of Chalk and other Mesozoic rocks which started to rise above sea level prior to the commencement of Tertiary volcanic activity. The drainage pattern would have been well established at the outbreak of volcanicity, and broadly maintained throughout Tertiary times to the present day. On this hypothesis, the stepped benches of the Highland surface would have been formed during the main late-Tertiary uplift, but are essentially features of subaerial erosion related to successively lower relative sea levels. Consequent drainage directions, instituted on either side of the original cover-rock divide, would be maintained more or less by extension of the rivers seawards during each successive emergence. The reader is referred to Sissons' work for a discussion of these theories, and for an extensive bibliography on the subject.

The theories which propose an original divide on cover-rock explain the presence of the major through-valleys which lie across the present watershed of the Northern Highlands by postulating a fortuitous near-coalescene of east-flowing and west-flowing streams. The fact that several have notable straight courses has given rise to the suggestion that the original watershed lay further to the west than at present and that the more active westerly streams have cut back to capture the headwaters of the east-flowing ones, thus causing an eastward migration of the watershed in pre-existing valleys. It may be, however, that some of the valleys are aligned along geological features such as major faults, groups of dykes, or close-set groups of joints of the pervasive east–west set which characterises much of the Northern Highlands. Any of these lines of weakness could cause selective erosion by both east- and west-flowing streams along a common line.

Whatever the origin of the early drainage pattern, the difference in the physiography of the land west and east of the present watershed is most marked. To the east, the original consequent drainage is exemplified by the Strath of

Kildonan, the Loch Shin hollow, Strath Oykell, Strath Conon, and the east – west valleys of the southern Ross and Inverness districts. Subsequent drainage towards the north-east and south-west was developed along the strike of the less resistant rocks, and along north-easterly crush-lines. The most important valleys of this latter system lie along the lines of the Great Glen Fault and the Helmsdale Fault (which skirts the eastern coast of Sutherland). Here erosion was aided by the presence of the relatively weakly resistant sediments of Old Red Sandstone and Mesozoic age, and the broad shallow arms of the sea, (or firths) of Dornoch, Cromarty and Moray represent submerged continuations of these valleys. In the south-east, drainage along the more rapidly deepened Great Glen hollow captured the easterly-flowing rivers of Ardgour which formerly may have reached the North Sea after a long journey across the Grampian Highlands (see Bailey, 1960, fig.1). Capture by subsequent streams is exemplified also in the interior of the region by the rivers Naver and Glas. Valley profiles of the major valleys are on the average gentle; the River Garry, for instance, takes 41 km to fall the 230 m from source to near sea level at Loch Ness (prior to subsequent stream erosion in the Great Glen, it probably took 80 – 100 km to reach the sea). Most valleys have a well developed, smoothly glaciated cross section with post-glacial stream incision confined to relatively localised 'knick-points'. The great lochs which lie in the valley bottoms within the mountain belt are commonly the result of overdeepening by glacial action, possibly, as has already been indicated, along the line of strongly jointed rocks, dykes or, in some cases, shatter-belts.

To the west of the watershed, on the other hand, the streams run swiftly, commonly in gorges incised in the bottom of valleys which, though well-glaciated, are steep-sided and narrow. Sea level (or near to it) is reached at the head of long, narrow, freshwater lochs or fiord-like sea inlets several kilometres from the open waters of the Minch or Sea of the Hebrides. The Carnoch River, companion stream to the Garry (see above) in the same through-valley, descends the 230 m from the watershed to sea level at Loch Nevis in only 8 km. It is clear, therefore that the westerly-flowing streams have cut well back from the mountain wall on the west and have been more active than their easterly equivalents; this is possibly because of the steeper inclination of the original 'consequent' streams, as discussed earlier. Sissons makes the interesting suggestion that the western mountain mountain wall is an exhumed pre-Mesozoic feature. If this is the case then the rapid back-cutting of the western streams could initially be attributed to the relative ease with which cover rocks were stripped. A geologist working in the western part of the Northern Highlands might be forgiven if he attributed the activity of the streams to the fact that, in remote times as at present, the rainfall was the controlling factor. The diminution in precipitation eastwards from the watershed is very marked.

The westward-flowing streams on the mainland thus reach or approach baselevel well within the mountain belt. The freshwater lochs or sea inlets, along which their further course to open water lies, clearly occupy valleys overdeepened by glacial action (Plate 3). For instance, Loch Morar (the surface of which stood at about 10 m above OD prior to hydroelectric modification) has a maximum depth of 310 m, and has only a narrow gravel-crowned rock bar at its present outlet (although the former outlet in the drift-filled Mointeach Mhor channel may have been deeper). The narrow fiord-like sea lochs commonly possess a threshold or sill somewhere along their length separating a steep-walled upper reach from a more open sea reach, with the depth in the upper section much greater than that in the seaward continuation.

Although these lochs were inundated after the withdrawal of the ice, later emergence of the land is indicated by the presence around them of late- or post-

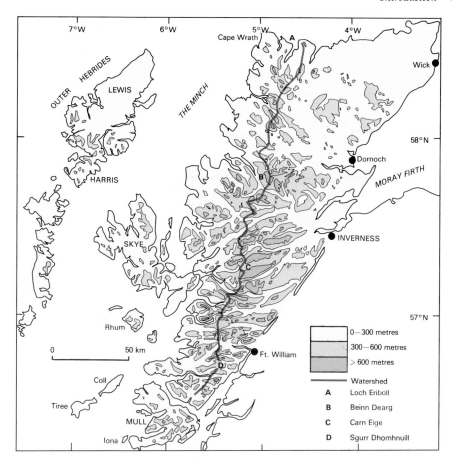

Figure 1 Physiography of the Northern Highlands
(Note: Carn Eige is spelled Carn Eighe on latest maps)

glacial raised beaches. Loch Shiel, now totally land-locked, must at one time have been a 'fiord'; traces of the post-glacial raised beach remain all round its perimeter and shell sand, possibly marine, has been recorded from one locality.

George (1966) extends the area involved in late-Tertiary regional erosion surfaces to include the Long Island (as the Outer Hebrides are sometimes collectively named). This area, composed almost entirely of ancient gneissose rocks, is dominantly low-lying and of low relief, but with isolated hills or massifs rising fairly abruptly from the general level. That there has been considerable late- or post-Tertiary erosion of the area there can be no doubt, as Tertiary dykes are truncated by the the present land surface. It may be, however, that much of the present topography follows an exhumed erosion surface of Lewisian gneiss originally overlain by younger, softer sediments. In its general form it resembles the gneiss pediment below the mountain wall along the western seaboard of the Scottish mainland. On the Long Island, as on the mainland, the intricate pattern of sea inlets clearly indicates a submerged topography. Unlike the mainland there has been no emergence since glacial times; in fact, it is likely that slight submergence has been continuous since that time.

SCENERY

The scenery of the Northern Highlands is related to the geology to a marked degree. In the Outer Hebrides and on the low platform which fringes the mainland coast of western Sutherland, ancient hard gneiss (the Precambrian Lewisian Gneiss) gives rise to a rocky, lochan-dotted terrain (Plate 4). Along the north-west seaboard of the mainland the Torridonian Sandstone forms the mountain wall which has been eroded into steep-sided, often isolated, mountains rising abruptly from the gneiss basement. Further east, along a line from Kyle of Lochalsh to Loch Glencoul the sandstone mountains are capped by glistening white Cambrian quartzite and flanked to the east from place to place with lush grassy areas which mark Cambro-Ordovician limestone outcrops. Further north the tops of some peaks are made of the quartzite resting directly on gneiss. The south-western seaboard, west of the watershed, is made up of wild and remarkably rugged mountains which derive their character from the intensely varied schistose rocks from which they are made. In the more easterly part of the Northern Highlands, however, the stratigraphy is less diverse and the mountains of central Sutherland, Ross and Inverness*, though in places higher than those further west, are less rugged, reflecting the simpler geology. The featureless landscape of Caithness is related to its foundation of limy flagstone and sandstone. Though lacking scenic interest inland it has wild sea-cliffs and stacks on the north and east coasts. The Tertiary igneous areas of the west are either horizontally terraced or ruggedly mountainous depending on whether they are underlain by bedded lavas or intrusive complexes of basic and acid plutonic rock.

Much of the fertile land round Dingwall and Tain owes its presence to spreads of superficial deposits mantling soft sandstone. The prominent hills and knolls in this area mark the outcrops of resistant beds of conglomerate.

SUMMARY OF THE GEOLOGY

The basement rocks of the Northern Highlands consist of gneisses of the Lewisian Complex (Figure 2). They are the products of repeated deformation, metamorphism and migmatisation of early Precambrian crust of uncertain origin, cut by acid and basic igneous intrusions, with some subordinate sedimentary and volcanic rocks. The time interval between the formation of the oldest and youngest rocks of the complex may have been as much as 1200 million years. Two major metamorphic, tectonic and intrusive events can be recognised, separated by a period of crustal tension during which a swarm of tholeiitic dolerite dykes (the Scourie Dykes) was emplaced. The earlier event produced the Scourian Complex, which comprises high-grade (granulite-facies) gneisses of diverse origin, while the later event gave rise to the Laxfordian Complex, in which Scourian rocks have been reconstructed by tectonism and metamorphism to lower-grade (amphibolite-facies) gneisses to a greater or lesser degree. Associated with these 'reworked' gneisses is a suite of granitic intrusions and migmatites.

While Lewisian terrain can be mapped on the basis of these divisions it should be appreciated that the two Complexes do not define chronostratigraphic groups.

---

* Most of the published work in the Northern Highlands uses the former 'Shire' nomenclature for area description. The new major 'Region' divisions are too large for this purpose and the subdivisions of District, which mostly use the old 'Shire' names, cover slightly different areas. Little confusion should arise, however, and 'Shire' terminology is used here.

Plate 3   Loch Hourn is a fiord-like western sea loch, here seen from Sgurr Sgiath Airidh. The hills in the distance are the Cuillins and Red Hills on the Isle of Skye (G. S. Johnstone)

Plate 4   Typical Lewisian scenery is to be seen on North Uist in the Outer Hebrides. The right-hand slope illustrates the dip slope of the Outer Hebrides Thrust Zone. We look northwards to Eaval   (D3196)

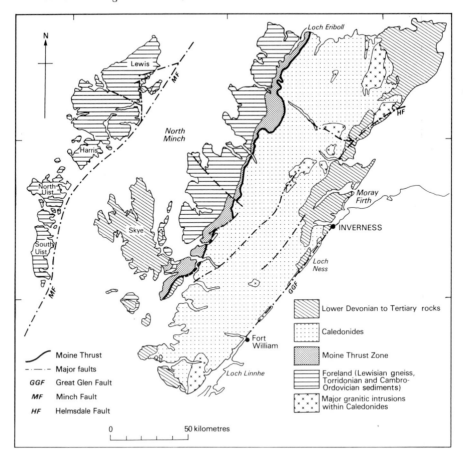

Figure 2   Sketch map showing the main elements of the geology of the Northern Highlands

It is inferred from radiometric age dating, however, that the gneiss-forming process which gave rise to the Scourian Complex took place 2900–2300 Ma (million years) ago (Archaean to Early Proterozoic). There were two major episodes within the Scourian: the Badcallian (c.2800 Ma) and the more localised Inverian (2500 Ma). The Scourie dykes have been dated at about 2400–2200 Ma, the intrusion of the suite being spread over a considerable period of time. The Laxfordian Complex was formed between 2300 Ma and 1700 Ma ago, the main episode being at around 1700 Ma (younger dates of down to 1100 Ma in the Laxfordian Complex probably represent local cooling ages).

After the formation of these basement gneisses the area that is now the Northern Highlands apparently lay on the south-eastern* margin of a large continental mass which included most of present-day Greenland and the Laurentian Shield of north-east Canada. About 1000 Ma ago, after a prolonged period of uplift and erosion the deep-seated Lewisian gneiss was exposed on a land surface. It formed

---

* When referring to ancient rocks which have existed through periods of plate movement and relative polar shift, compass directions given in the text refer to their present situation unless otherwise stated.

moderately hilly country of up to 400 m relief with gentle slopes and fairly extensive areas of flat, knolly terrain between groups of hills. To the north-west lay higher ground traversed by large rivers. To the south-east may have lain NNE-trending lacustrine rift-basins, the precursors of a major ocean—the Iapetus—which later developed as Laurentia and Baltica (the south-eastern continent); gradually drew apart.

On this hilly surface, and in the basins between the uplifted areas, a great thickness of fluviatile and lacustrine red beds accumulated, comprising mainly arkosic sandstones and conglomerates with subordinate shales and some scree preserved as breccia banked up against former hillslopes. With some grey sandstones and grey, probably lacustrine, shales these beds make up the 'Torridonian' rocks, a late Precambrian succession of Riphaean age. This essentially unmetamorphosed sequence contains a notable angular unconformity, which separates the Stoer Group, (deposited at about 1000 Ma) from the overlying, more extensively developed Torridon Group, (750–800 Ma). There is a considerable disparity between the palaeomagnetic orientations of the rocks above and below the unconformity, although the environment of deposition did not change greatly. This disparity suggests that the unconformity itself represents a considerable time gap.

Some distance to the east of these terrestrial accumulations a thick sequence of sandstones and shales was laid down in shallow seas. Unlike the Torridonian rocks, however, they have undergone deformation and metamorphism and are now represented mainly by psammitic, semipelitic and pelitic gneisses and schists. They make up the Moine Succession which may in part be the shallow-water marine, or estuarine, equivalent of the continental Torridonian rocks. An interpretation of isotopic ages from pegmatites and metamorphic minerals in the Moines of the Northern Highlands suggests that most of the rocks were metamorphosed at c.750 Ma (during the Morarian episode, whose status as an orogenic event is uncertain) and some have been involved in the earlier Grenvillian Orogeny (c.1100 Ma). It was at one time considered that a depositional age of more than 1000 Ma implies that the Moine rocks are too old to be equivalent to the Torridonian, but the most recent age proposed for the Stoer Group (see above and p. 34) has again revived this possibility.

In the Grampians south of the Great Glen, rocks long held to be Moines show only Caledonian or 'Grampian' (c.500 Ma) deformation (see below) and these 'young' Moines may also be present in the Northern Highlands, although no unconformity has been detected. Some workers, however, hold that a group of younger Moines overlies a Grenvillian basement in parts of the area.

In the North-West Highlands the Torridonian rocks underwent a period of gentle tilting and considerable erosion prior to a marine incursion which laid down basal Cambrian strata on a peneplaned surface. Baltica and Laurentia were separated by the developing Iapetus Ocean by this time, and the Cambrian quartzites, shales and limestones (which extend upwards into the Ordovician) are shallow-water marginal shelf deposits of the Iapetus Ocean. As these Cambrian beds were separated by the Iapetus from their equivalents in England and Wales they contain a fauna allied to that of North America, not that of Europe.

To the south of the Northern Highlands, elongate basins on the continental margin of the Iapetus Ocean received vast quantities of sediment. As the continents approached each other again in Ordovician times, the basement and overlying sedimentary rocks along the continental margins were folded and metamorphosed to rise in a mountain belt which stretched from what is now East Greenland and Scandinavia through the British Isles to the east coast of America. To this mountain belt the name Caledonides has been applied, and the process of mountain building which gave rise to it is termed the Caledonian Orogeny*. This orogeny is generally taken to have commenced in post-Cambrian pre-Silurian times (c.500 Ma).

In the Northern Highlands the Caledonian belt is sharply limited, and the rocks of the region are divided into two associations of fundamentally different geological structure. To the east of a line extending from Loch Eriboll to the Sound of Iona the Caledonides comprise mainly metamorphic Moine strata within which appear small, but significant, inliers of the Lewisian basement entirely reconstructed by the effects of the Caledonian Orogeny (and earlier Grenvillian and Morarian events). To the west of this line the Lewisian basement, with its cover of Torridonian and Cambro-Ordovician strata, has remained virtually unmoved from Laxfordian times onwards. This stable block constitutes a foreland. The Caledonides have been pushed westwards over the foreland along a network of low angle thrusts which forms the Moine Thrust Zone, so named after the most important single thrust plane in the group. The mechanism which gave rise to this overthrusting was the eventual collision of the Laurentian and Baltic plates, much further to the south-east. This collision resulted in compressive forces being directed upwards and outwards away from their line of junction, through some of the thrust sheets along the Moine Thrust Zone may have been emplaced by gravity sliding as part of the general process.

An orogenic belt such as the Caledonides, which results from the mechanism of continental collision, is commonly accompanied by intense igneous activity. The Northern Highlands contain many intrusions of acid and basic dykes, sheets and plutons collectively referred to as the Caledonian Igneous Suite. These intrusions can be assigned to groups which are pre-tectonic, syn-tectonic and post-tectonic with respect to the main Caledonian deformation. Certain of the pre-tectonic intrusions in the Northern Highlands in fact may not be associated with the Caledonian Orogeny; they could belong to an earlier magmatic episode.

Laurentia and Baltica welded together to form a new continental mass, within which the Caledonides were subjected to erosion. The resulting debris was deposited in intermontane, possibly fault-bounded, basins as thick accumulations of conglomerate, sandstone and siltstone laid down in alluvial fans, on the flood plains of rivers, and in lakes. These deposits are now known as the Old Red Sandstone and they are mainly found on the east side of the Northern Highlands. In several respects these rocks resemble the earlier Torridonian strata, and are analogous to the Alpine Molasse, i.e. they are typical of the degradation products of an uplifted mountain belt. It is probable that they never completely covered the degraded Caledonian mountains. They did, however, fill in the through-valley of the ancient Great Glen and adjacent hollows.

The Caledonian Orogeny is generally taken to have terminated prior to the deposition of the Middle Old Red Sandstone, but in the Northern Highlands late movements continued into Middle Devonian times.

The Northern Highlands (and the adjacent Grampians) are traversed by several faults trending NE–SW and a lesser (although also important) number of fractures with the complementary NW–SE orientation. The faults show considerable sinistral (NE–SW suite) and dextral (NW–SE suite) displacement up to and including the Middle Old Red Sandstone, although it is becoming clear that some faults have a long history of pre- and post-ORS movement, of which the present apparent strike-slip displacement is the end result. Of the faults, that

---

* The term Caledonian Orogeny is also commonly used to refer to the *period* over which the *process* took place.

along the Great Glen is the most important, although the direction and amount of movement along it are in dispute.

A small outlier of Carboniferous strata is found on the north-east shore of the Sound of Mull in Morvern, apparently lying directly on Moine rocks. These fluvial and deltaic deposits were probably laid down in one of the ephemeral basins on the continental margin of a Highland massif which at that time bounded the Midland Valley trough.

There followed, in late Carboniferous to early Permian times, the intrusion of an important suite of dykes, mainly of camptonite and monchiquite; the dykes form several almost discrete swarms whose members trend mainly E–W. A few volcanic vents have also been identified and the igneous activity seems to be related to a period of crustal tension; this was possibly a precursor of that later event responsible for the opening of the Atlantic Ocean.

Mesozoic rocks, comprising mainly Triassic and Jurassic strata, are found on the eastern and western seaboards of the Northern Highlands. In the west they were deposited directly on the Precambrian rocks of both Foreland and Caledonides. Thick sequences are found in asymmetrical west-tilted, fault-bounded basins ('half-grabens') in what is now the Minch and the Sea of the Hebrides. The Minch Fault, which lies close offshore along the eastern edge of the Outer Isles, is a boundary of one basin; the Camasunary Fault, seen onshore in Skye, is another. On the western mainland, however, only small outcrops of these rocks are found. (For descriptions of the extensive outcrops in the Inner Hebrides the reader should refer to the companion handbook, *The Tertiary Volcanic Districts*.) The Helmsdale Fault on the east coast of Sutherland and, further south along the coast of Cromarty, the Great Glen Fault limit the landward extension of the Mesozoic strata which occupy the Moray Firth Basin.

During Triassic times a relatively arid climate prevailed, and red sandstones and conglomerates were deposited in alluvial cones and on the plains of ephemeral rivers. Later, during the Jurassic, the basins were inundated by the sea and the deposition of shallow-water marine and estuarine sandstones, siltstones and limestones was eventually followed by the deposition of deep water shales, which are the source rocks of most of the North Sea oil. A seam of coal at Brora was formed during a period of emergence, and later the spectacular Helmsdale Boulder Bed was laid down as a series of submarine fans along the foot of the active Helmsdale Fault scarp.

It is likely that the subsiding fault-bounded basins in which the thick Hebridean Mesozoic sequences accumulated resulted from tensional stresses which heralded the break-up of the supercontinent formed by the fusion of the Laurentian and Baltic shields during the Caledonian Orogeny. The tension within this continental crust produced a number of fractures and half grabens, such as the Mid-North Sea Viking graben and the troughs in the Hebridean Sea. They were all sites of early 'failed' Atlantic spreading centres. The final successful rift took place in late Cretaceous times somewhat further west along the Mid-Atlantic Ridge. Ocean spreading from this fissure at an average rate of 2 cm per annum has created the Atlantic Ocean, separating the present outcrop of Lewisian gneiss in the Northern Highlands from its parent Laurentia.

During the Mesozoic the Highland massif was an area of low relief, and in Cretaceous times it may even have been completely covered by a shallow sea. The Hebridean region was the main locus of the Tertiary igneous activity which took place mainly in Palaeocene times (50–60 Ma ago). During this period basaltic plateau lavas accumulated over the Inner Hebrides and the adjacent mainland to a thickness of many thousands of feet. This outpouring of lava was followed by the eruption of central volcanoes; their eroded roots form the Cuillins of Skye and

Rhum, and the hills of Ardnamurchan, Mull and St Kilda. Other volcanic centres have been discovered under the sea at the Blackstones Bank, SW of Mull, and in the Malin Basin, NW of Malin Head. Swarms of NW-trending basalt and dolerite dykes are aligned on (though they do not necessarily emanate from) the Skye, Rhum and Mull centres and cut the older rocks of the North-West Highlands and the Outer Hebrides.

After the cessation of the Tertiary igneous activity there was a renewed period of uplift and erosion (as described on p.163). The ice sheets, and more especially the later valley glaciers, of the Pleistocene glacial period (c.1 million to 10 000 years ago) modified the river valley profiles; they are largely responsible for the detail of the present-day topography. Isostatic adjustments of land and sea levels due to the melting of the ice sheets gave rise to a fringe of raised beach deposits around the coast, as the land (in general) emerged from the sea. Areas of submerged topography are found marginally, in the Outer Hebrides.

2 Lewisian

The Lewisian Complex is a residual fragment of the ancient Laurentian continental mass, the southern extension of which is now buried under the metasediments of the Scottish Highlands. The gneisses of the Lewisian Complex represent a long and varied part of the earth's history. They bear evidence of having been formed then repeatedly deformed, often deep within the earth's crust, over a period of nearly 1800 Ma.

The greater part of the complex probably formed in the late Archean, around 2900–2700 Ma. During this time the earth's crust was relatively hot and mobile and, in consequence, the rocks were subjected to repeated deformation accompanying high-grade metamorphism. Subsequently, in the early Proterozoic c.2600–2400 Ma, the crust became cooler and more rigid; deformation was confined to more linear structures with generally lower grade metamorphism. Repeated deformation of this type continued intermittently until c.1100 Ma, the last deformation producing low-grade brittle structures. By this time the rocks had been uplifted, probably to near their present level, where they formed the basement on which the Torridonian and Moine sedimentary assemblages were deposited. During the late Proterozoic, the eastern Lewisian underlying the Moine was involved in the Grenvillian (c.1100 Ma), Morarian (c.750 Ma) and Caledonian (c.450 Ma) tectonothermal events.

In the following account the Lewisian is considered under two main headings relating to its present structural state (Figure 3), namely, the Lewisian Foreland, covering all the gneisses lying west of, and within, the Moine Thrust Zone, and the Lewisian Inliers, which are basement gneisses which have been thoroughly reworked by the later (Grenvillian etc.) tectonothemal events, and are now seen as tectonically-introduced slices and bands within the Moine.

FORELAND LEWISIAN: THE MAINLAND

The Lewisian Complex of North-West Scotland was formally divided by Sutton and Watson (1951), following the lines of regional variations outlined by Peach and others (1907). Sutton and Watson defined a central region (Figure 4) in which the predominant rocks are granular pyroxene gneisses (granulites); these were deformed and altered at considerable depth during an Archaean metamorphic episode, which they termed Scourian. The central region is flanked to the north and south by areas in which gneisses were strongly deformed during a later (early-Proterozoic) metamorphic episode, which they termed Laxfordian. The distinction between gneisses affected only by the Scourian episode of metamorphism and those reworked by the later Laxfordian metamorphism was largely made by reference to a suite of dykes — the Scourie dykes. These dykes cut across the gneissose banding and structures within the Scourian area, but are deformed and metamorphosed within the Laxfordian areas. Sutton and and Watson suggested that there was a considerable time gap between the Scourian and Laxfordian, and therefore gave them the status of major divisions of the Lewisian Complex.

Within the Scourian, Sutton and Watson (1969) subsequently defined an early and a late event. The early episode was regarded as the main gneiss-forming event accompanied by granulite-facies metamorphism. The late episode was marked by the production of steep linear deformation belts trending NW-SE, associated with retrograde amphibolite-facies metamorphism. Park (1970) gave this division a more formal status by proposing the term Badcallian for the early Scourian events and Inverian for the later ones. Park also suggested that the Inverian episode was closer in deformational style to the succeeding Laxfordian than to the preceding Badcallian, and suggested that the Badcallian and Inverian divisions should be accorded major status.

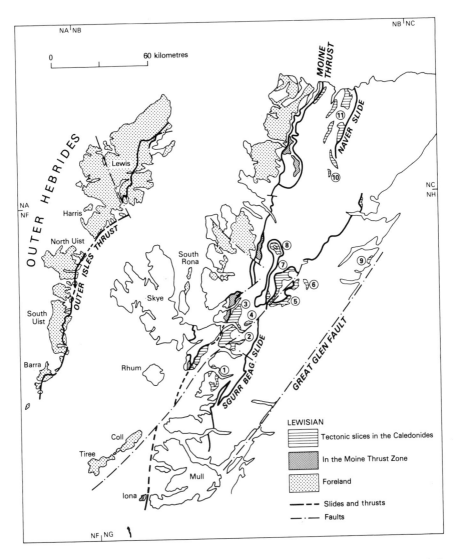

Figure 3   Major structural divisions of the Lewisian rocks of the Northern Highlands
The inliers east of the Moine Thrust are; **1** Morar   **2** Glenelg   **3** Attadale   **4** Coire nan Gall   **5** Strathfarrar–Monar   **6** Orrin   **7** Scardroy   **8** Fannich   **9** Rosemarkie
10 Shin   **11** Sutherland Group

Central region

The Central Scourian region stretches from Loch Laxford to Loch Broom (Figure 4); it consists predominantly of banded gneisses with a variety of basic and ultrabasic inclusions. The gneisses are coarsely banded with alternating acid and mafic layers. Granulite-facies gneisses are common; they have two pyroxenes, brown hornblende and plagioclase assemblages. In areas of retrograde metamorphism the pyroxenes are progressively replaced by hornblende and biotite.

Ultrabasic rocks occur in small bodies ranging from a few centimetres across to several tens of metres. The smaller bodies are generally concentrations of hornblende and biotite. The larger bodies show a considerable variation, including pyroxenites and dunites. The minerals may include olivine, pyroxene, hornblende, garnet and spinel and are commonly arranged to define a rough banding.

Basic rocks are relatively abundant and vary from tiny lenses to large masses which may be tens of metres thick and traceable for several kilometres along the strike. They generally contain pyroxene-hornblende-plagioclase assemblages. In many cases the minerals are arranged in well defined bands with an overall compositional variation within the body from ultramafic to anorthosite. The basic bodies frequently concentrate in zones, of which one of the most notable lies south of Loch Laxford. It is 2 km wide and stretches in a NW–SE direction for over 10 km. According to Davies (1974) the zone occupies a complex syncline within which the basic rocks are associated with a series of brown-weathering schists, believed to be metasediments.

All of these rocks were subjected to the deformation and high-grade metamorphism of the early Scourian (Badcallian). The deformation associated with this metamorphism appears to have been very 'fluid' with major structures seldom persisting for any great distance. The subsequent Inverian deformation, however, occurred in more rigid gneisses with structures confined to near-vertical NW–SE belts. One of the most important of these is the Lochinver Antiform (Sheraton and others, 1973), which stretches from Loch Inver inland for up to 10 km (Figure 4). This fold has a steep, strongly deformed north-east limb (Canisp shear belt) and gentle south-west limb. Retrogression of the pyroxene gneisses is largely controlled by these structures, being greatest in the highly deformed belts.

Several workers (e.g. Tarney and others, 1972; Holland and Lambert, 1975) have shown that the gneisses are characteristically depleted in many lighter elements (K, Rb, Nb, Th, U). They have also shown that the retrogressive effects of the Inverian were essentially isochemical and did not destroy the characteristic chemistry of the Scourian.

Considerable controversy exists on the origin of the Scourian gneisses. Sutton and Watson (1951) originally considered the complex to be a supracrustal sequence. Sheraton and others (1973) and Bowes and others (1971) suggested that it was largely a dacite-andesite volcanic sequence with intercalated sediments; Tarney and others (1972) suggested that it was part of the crust depleted in lighter elements by mantle degassing, and Holland and Lambert (1975) proposed a model where the crust was built up through a process of 'under-plating' by upper mantle melts, the supracrustal rocks being tectonically incorporated subsequently. On balance it is probable that the bulk of the gneisses were formed from the addition of calc-alkaline igneous rocks into or onto a supracrustal sedimentary sequence. The proportion of intrusive to extrusive material is, however, uncertain (see Watson, 1983). Watson (1975) proposed that the rocks on which the supracrustal sequence was deposited should be defined as the Pre-Scourian Complex. How extensive such rocks are, or even whether they are present at all, is uncertain.

Work on Rb-Sr and Sm-Nd systematics (Hamilton and others, 1979) suggests that the calc-alkaline parents of the gneisses separated from the mantle at c.2900 Ma, approximately 200 Ma before the main high-grade Badcallian metamorphism (Pidgeon and Bowes, 1972). Scourian pegmatites, generally taken as marking the onset of Inverian events, give dates of 2500–2400 Ma.

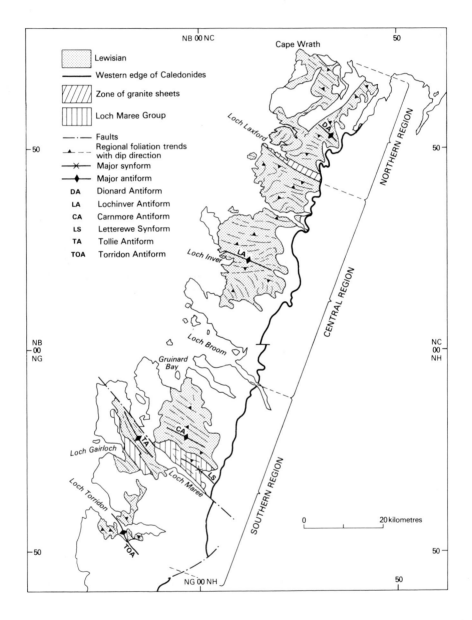

Figure 4   Lewisian rocks of the North-West Highlands (after Park, 1973; Sheraton and others, 1973).

The Central region corresponds to the area dominated by Scourian effects, with only weak or localised Laxfordian reworking. The Northern and Southern regions correspond to the Laxfordian belts

Scourie dyke suite

Cutting the heterogeneous gneiss complex of the Scourian is a suite of basic and ultrabasic dykes collectively termed the Scourie Dykes. The dykes are discordant to the foliation in the host gneisses; they are steep sided, and can be traced for considerable distances (up to 15 km), the basics trending NW – SE, the ultrabasics near E – W. Many dykes have apophyses and fine-grained margins. Although most of the dolerites retain igneous minerals, they all show evidence of amphibolite-facies metamorphism, the degree of amphibolitisation usually increasing from the centre to the margins of the dyke. The ultrabasic rocks are dominantly picrites and olivine gabbros. Like the dolerites they frequently show evidence of amphibolitisation, the degree of alteration being greatest at the margins.

O'Hara (1961; 1962) and Tarney (1973) suggested that the textures of the dykes indicate that they were intruded into hot country rocks, the ambient temperatures inducing autometamorphism. Tarney also suggested that the metamorphism of the dykes was probably controlled by aqueous fluids moving upwards along Inverian shear zones during the waning stages of Inverian metamorphism. He also believes that the trend of the dykes was controlled by pre-existing Inverian structures (Plate 5). He cites evidence of minor Laxfordian shearing affecting the dykes of the Scourian block, the geometry of the Laxfordian deformation being largly controlled by pre-existing Inverian structures.

The dykes cut amphibolite-facies gneisses and are largely undeformed. They must, therefore, post-date the main Inverian events. It is generally accepted that the dykes were emplaced over a relatively short time span between 2400 – 2200 Ma; the basic varieties are earlier than the ultrabasic dykes.

Northern region

The Northern region, or Northern Laxfordian area, stretches from Loch Laxford to Cape Wrath (Figure 4). The area is characterised by relatively uniform acid biotite-hornblende gneisses with a variety of basic and ultrabasic lenses and sheets. Pegmatitic and granitic veins, lenses and sheets are common, giving the gneisses a migmatitic appearance. These veins increase in number southwards culminating in the Loch Laxford granitic zone at the southern boundary of the complex. The ultrabasic bodies are characteristically composed of hornblende and biotite with more subordinate olivine and pyroxene, whereas the basic varieties may contain garnet, plagioclase and minor amounts of clinopyroxene. Chemically the Laxfordian is much richer in the lighter elements than the Scourian.

Many of the basic sheets are regarded as the deformed and metamorphic equivalents of the Scourie dyke suite. Bowes and Khoury (1965) have argued that there is more than one period of post-Scourian basic dyke intrusion, and that basic dykes can be seen cutting structures produced by Laxfordian deformation. This view has, however, been widely challenged and discussed in the geological literature (e.g. Park, 1970; Park and Cresswell, 1972).

The characteristic trend of the Laxfordian foliation is NW – SE. At the southern edge of the zone the foliation dips steeply to the south-west; further north, the dip decreases and the foliation is disposed in a series of rolling folds. In Strath Dionard the regional dip reverses across the major Dionard Antiform (Figure 4); north of it the dip is to the north-east, with the foliation arranged in a series of rolling folds. The dip steepens at the southern end of the Kyle of Durness, and from there northwards to the coast the foliation has a near vertical attitude (see Park, 1973, fig.70).

Relationship of the Central region to the Northern region

Considerable controversy exists on the relationship between the Central (Scourian) region and the Northern (Laxfordian) region. Sutton and Watson (1951) regarded the Laxfordian as Scourian gneiss which was strongly metamorphosed and migmatised. The limit of Laxfordian reworking, the Laxford Front, is marked by the Laxford granite zone, the product of metasomatism and migmatisation from depth. One of the main lines of evidence for this contention is the apparently transitional contact between the two areas, with a progressive amphibolitisation of the pyroxene gneisses and the progressive deformation of the Scourie dykes. Sutton and Watson recognised a series of zones within this transitional area. These comprise the Scourie zone of pyroxene gneiss; the Claisfearn zone of partially amphibolitised gneiss; the Foindle zone of completely amphibolitised gneiss; the Badnabay zone of pegmatite and granite-rich gneiss; and the Laxford zone of biotite-hornblende gneiss. The boundary between the Foindle and Badnabay zones is coincident with the Ben Stack Line, defined by Peach and others (1907) as separating the Central and Northern regions.

This cogenetic concept of the two areas was strongly challenged by Bowes (1978) who suggested that the Laxfordian represented a supracrustal sequence (the Rhiconich Group of Dash, 1967) deposited on the gneissose Scourian basement. Bowes also suggested (1969; Bowes and Khoury, 1965) that certain discordant basic dykes were intra-Laxfordian, thus weakening the use of the Scourie dykes as a time marker. Isotopic data presented by Moorbath and others (1969) indicates that both the Scourian and Laxfordian suffered uranium depletion in the Archean, and therefore both regions were in existence at that time. This argues strongly against Bowes' model. Chemical work, by Holland and Lambert (1973) and Sheraton and others (1973), suggests that the Scourian and Laxfordian areas have quite distinctive chemistries and, even allowing for the possible roles of migmatisation and metasomatism, the two assemblages could not be cogenetic.

Holland and Lambert (1973) suggested that the Laxfordian is a supracrustal sequence laid down on the Scourian basement. This view was strengthened by Bott and others (1972) who suggested, on geophysical grounds, that the dense Archean gneisses of the Scourian block underlay the lighter Laxfordian gneisses. They also stated that the granites at Loch Laxford could not have been generated at depth and introduced to the Laxfordian, but rather that they were the product of local melting of the biotite gneisses. This view has been challenged by Beach and others (1974), who argue that the geometry of deformation across the Laxford Front indicates that the Laxfordian was moved upwards against the Scourian block. Davies (1978) argues that the Laxfordian Front was initiated as a tectonic break in late Badcallian times and acted as a progressive dextral transcurrent displacement during the Inverian and Laxfordian deformations.

Recently, Davies and Watson (1977) have described banded basic gneisses from the Laxfordian area. They regard these rocks as equivalent to the banded basics of the Scourian block. Since the latter can be shown to predate most of the early Badcallian events, it follows that the Laxfordian region must also predate these events. They argue that the chemical differences between the two areas were in existence at the end of the Badcallian.

Opinion is obviously divided. Whatever the origin of the two gneiss groups, both the Laxfordian and Scourian assemblages appear to have been in existence at the end of the Badcallian, although with characteristically different chemistries. The concept of the Laxford Front as a tectonothermal front is valid in the original Sutton and Watson (1951) sense, with the progressive effects of Laxfordian deformation and metamorphism increasing northwards across the transition zone. The coincidence of this front with the original boundary between the two groups suggests that the pre-existing nature of the complexes controlled the position of the front of Laxford deformation.

Southern region

The Southern region, or Southern Laxfordian belt, stretches from Loch Broom to Loch Torridon (Figure 4); the area is more varied than the Northern region. Between Loch Broom and Loch Gairloch the rocks are hornblende-biotite gneisses with many basic and ultrabasic knots and lenses. The mineralogy is consistent with the amphibolite facies, although small patches of pyroxene gneiss have been reported from Gruinard Bay and Creag Mhor Thollaidh (Park, 1970). These gneisses, however, lack the pegmatite and granite veining and the general migmatitic character of the rocks of the northern Laxfordian belt. In the area between Gairloch and Loch Torridon migmatitic gneisses are much more common.

   This region contains two major belts of supracrustal rocks which together constitute the Loch Maree Group. The eastern belt lies in a synformal structure on the north-east side of Loch Maree. Hornblende-biotite gneisses lie above and below the supracrustals, but both contacts are highly tectonised, with local development of mylonite. The western belt runs south-eastwards from Gairloch. It is flanked by biotite gneisses and, like the eastern belt, has highly tectonised contacts. The rocks of the Loch Maree Group consist mainly of thick basic sheets, generally of hornblende schist or hornblende-chlorite schist, and a series of interleaved schists including garnet-mica schist, semipelite and siliceous schists. Calc-silicates also occur in association with limestone and dolomite. Small bands of kyanite-mica schist lie in the hornblende-biotite gneiss to the north of the Loch Maree Group. These bands apparently pass laterally into the gneiss.

   The basic sheets and dykes are believed to be the equivalent of the Scourie dykes. They are generally in the state of foliated amphibolites. Discordant contacts are seen throughout the area but are particularly common in the region south of Gruinard bay. The general trend of the foliation is NW–SE. It is disposed in a series of major folds, from north-east to south-west (Figure 4); the most important are the Carnmore Antiform, Letterewe (Loch Maree) Synform, Tollie (Thollaidh) Antiform and Torridon Antiform. Sutton and Watson (1969) considered these folds to be of Laxfordian age, but Park and Cresswell (1973) argue that most of the major structures of the area were largely formed in the Inverian, and that the succeeding Laxfordian deformation, and the structure and trend of the dykes, were generally controlled by these pre-existing Inverian structures.

   Laxfordian metamorphism was generally of amphibolite-facies grade. A late phase of retrogressive metamorphism, possibly associated with pegmatite intrusion, affected the gneisses, producing chlorite-muscovite-microcline assemblages (Park, 1970). The last phase of activity to affect the rocks of this area was the production of brittle zones marked by the presence of pseudotachylite and ultramylonite. These are considered by Park (1970) to be essentially post-Laxfordian and pre-Torridonian. Moorbath and Park (1972), using K-Ar measurements, give a date of 1700–1500 Ma for the main amphibolite facies metamorphism of the Laxfordian. They place the retrogressive phase at c.1400 Ma and the late-stage cataclasis at c.1150 Ma. Bickerman and others (1975) give Rb-Sr whole rock dates of 1975 Ma as the main Laxfordian metamorphism, 1745 Ma for the late pegmatites and suggest that the 1500 Ma K-Ar mineral date of Moorbath and Park (1972) reflects cooling of the rocks associated with uplift. Lyon and others (1973) dating rocks from South Rona found no evidence of dates younger than c.1700 Ma, and suggested that this represented the end of the Laxfordian. This conclusion has, however, been challenged by Park (*in* Lyon and others, 1973) who considered the 1700 Ma dates as early Laxfordian.

Relationship of the Southern region to the Central Region

Sutton and Watson (1951) regarded the area between Gruinard Bay and Loch Maree as a transitional zone from the Scourian to the Laxfordian. The lack of migmatisation, the presence of deformed but cross-cutting dykes and the few relict patches of pyroxene gneiss all provided supporting evidence. The gneisses in the south around Loch Torridon were regarded by them as examples of thoroughly reworked Laxfordian gneisses.

Holland and Lambert (1973, fig.2) recognised several distinct geochemical assemblages in the southern region. These include the Gruinard assemblage stretching roughly from Loch Broom to Loch Gairloch, the Gairloch assemblage covering the rocks of the Loch Maree Series, and the Laxford assemblage in the area between Loch Gairloch and Loch Torridon. The Gruinard assemblage has the same chemical characteristics as the Scourian rocks of the Central region and is therefore classed as metamorphosed equivalent of the Scourian Complex. Holland and Lambert's data thus support Sutton and Watson's model for a transition. However, Holland and Lambert regard the Laxford assemblage as chemically quite distinct from the Scourian, and equivalent to the rocks of the Northern region. This supports the conclusion of Bowes (1972) that the Northern and Southern Laxfordian assemblages are chemically similar and distinct from the Scourian.

Isotopic age data from the area of Torridon, Gairloch and Gruinard Bay (Moorbath and others, 1969; Moorbath and Park, 1972) show that both the Gruinard and Laxford assemblages (*sensu* Holland and Lambert, 1973) were subjected to a high-grade metamorphism at c.2900 Ma, and were thus both in existence at that time. The origin of the rocks of the Southern region between Loch Gairloch and Loch Torridon is therefore uncertain, but it is almost certainly the same as that of the Northern region.

Gneisses in the Gruinard Bay – Loch Maree area are cogenetic with those of the central (Scourian) region, although they have been fairly throughly reworked in the Proterozoic. They could therefore be equally regarded as a part of the Scourian Complex or the South Laxfordian Complex.

The age of the Loch Maree Group is problematical. The rocks are probably deformed by Inverian structures but appear to post-date the main gneissification events of the Badcallian. Most workers would therefore place them as post-Badcallian and pre-Inverian. Bickerman and others (1975), however, suggested from isotopic evidence that the Group was deposited 2200 – 2000 Ma ago, which would place it as post-Inverian and pre-Laxfordian. The strips of kyanite gneiss just north of the Loch Maree Group grade into the surrounding gneiss and are therefore considered to have a pre-Badcallian age. This would make them equivalent to the supracrustals seen in the Scourian region (p. 19). This conclusion is supported by Bickerman and his colleagues whose isotopic data indicate that the kyanite gneisses were subjected to the main Badcallian events.

FORELAND LEWISIAN: THE HEBRIDES

South Rona and Raasay

Lewisian rocks outcrop in South Rona and the northern tip of Raasay (Figure 3).

They are biotite-hornblende gneisses, locally migmatitic, with basic and ultrabasic bands, lenses and clots. The gneisses are very similar to the Laxfordian rocks around Loch Torridon and are generally considered to be part of the same assemblage. The generalised trend of the foliation is NW–SE, the dip is highly variable. It is steep in the north of Rona but becomes nearer horizontal in the south. It is relatively steep in Raasay.

Lyon and others (1973) obtained a whole rock Rb-Sr isochron of 2790 ± 210 Ma from the gneisses, which supported the view (see p. 19) that the Laxfordian assemblage is of relative antiquity and has been subjected at least to part of the Badcallian metamorphism. They also dated a granite sheet, emplaced at a late stage in the structural history of the rocks, at 1680 ± 170 Ma and suggested that this recorded an event very close to the end of the Laxfordian. This date is considerably older than that suggested by Moorbath and Park for the mainland (see p.19). Park (*in* Lyon and others, 1973) has, however, argued that Laxfordian deformation persisted for much longer on the mainland than on Rona, the late deformation dying out southwards.

Rhum

Small outcrops of Lewisian gneiss outcrop within the main ring fault of the Tertiary igneous complex on Rhum. The main rock type is biotite-hornblende gneiss. The original minerals have been considerably modified by thermal metamorphism, notably in the growth of pyroxene and clouding in plagioclase. A Rb-Sr whole rock age of 1880 ± 40 Ma has been obtained from the rock, suggesting significant Laxfordian effects.

Tiree and Coll

In Tiree and Coll the main rock type is biotite-hornblende gneiss, locally migmatitic, with various basic and ultrabasic inclusions. In south-west Tiree the gneiss is pyroxene-bearing, whereas in north-east Coll it is highly sheared and retrograded (Drury, 1972). Metasediment bands are particularly abundant in these islands. They contain garnet-biotite schists, siliceous schists, and a variety of calc-silicate impure calcareous rocks. Among the purer marbles is the Tiree marble, which has a generally pink appearance; it has been used as an ornamental stone.

In western Tiree the pyroxene gneisses are cut by a series of sharp-edged basic dykes with two-pyroxene and hornblende assemblages. In eastern Tiree and Coll these dykes have amphibolite facies assemblages with, in some cases, clinopyroxene and garnet; they are strongly deformed, although they still retain some discordant contacts (Westbrook, 1972; Drury, 1972). The gneissose foliation on Coll and Tiree is disposed in a monoclinal synform (Drury, 1972) whose axial trace runs N–S. The greater part of Coll lies on the gently inclined limb of this structure; the foliation varies around NE–SW and dips moderately to the south-east. Western Coll and Tiree lie on the steep limb of the synform, the foliation striking roughly N–S with nearly vertical dips.

A simple history of the area can be given as follows: a period of high-grade granulite-facies metamorphism; intrusion of basic dykes; deformation associated with amphibolite-facies metamorphism; and late deformation and localised greenschist-facies metamorphism. Correlation with other Lewisian areas is uncertain. Westbrook (1972) correlated the basic dykes with the Scourie dykes and regarded the history of events in eastern Tiree as roughly the same as that of the Outer Hebrides. Drury (1974), however, noting the two-pyroxene assemblage in the dykes, suggested that they predate the granulite-facies metamorphism, which he regards as the equivalent of the Scourian. The amphibolite-facies metamorphism he referred to the Inverian; the Scourie dyke swarm and Laxfordian deformation he regarded as largely absent in the area. However, high-grade assemblages are found in the probable equivalents of the Scourie dykes in the Outer Hebrides (see below), although the dykes only intrude amphibolite-facies gneisses. There it is argued (p.25) that the high-grade assemblages relate to relatively dry conditions in the dykes and not to regional granulite-facies metamorphism. It is, therefore, possible that the dykes of Coll and Tiree do postdate the main granulite-facies metamorphism, and that Westbrook's correlations are correct.

Iona

Iona consists of biotite-hornblende gneiss with some interleaved metasediments. The gneisses are cut by a series of amphibolite dykes, which may be members of the Scourie dyke suite. The metasediments include garnet-mica schists, psammites and the well known Iona marble. The marble forms a narrow (6–8 m) band in the south of the island; it is white with a green serpentinous mottle. Also noteworthy is the 'white rock', a conspicuous band of feldspathic rock up to 400 m wide, which runs northwards from the south coast for some 2 km. Associated with the white rock in two localities are broad bands of magnetite rock, the origin of which is uncertain.

The foliation throughout Iona is very variable, but generally strikes NE–SW with dips to the SE. The rocks have been affected by movements on the Moine Thrust Zone.

The Outer Hebrides

The Outer Hebrides, sometimes collectively known as 'the Long Island', consist almost entirely of Lewisian gneiss; as such they constitute by far the largest area of such rocks in the British Isles. The term Lewisian was proposed by Macculloch (1819) from the predominance of the gneiss in the Isle of Lewis.

The islands consist of a mixed group of biotite gneiss and hornblende-biotite-quartzofeldspathic gneiss with a variety of basic and ultrabasic inclusions, the latter collectively termed the Older Basics and Ultrabasics (Figure 5). Pyroxene-bearing gneiss is found in a small area on the east coast of South Uist and more extensively on the east coast of Barra. The area as a whole is broadly equivalent to the Laxfordian zones of the mainland. The gneiss is believed to have been derived from a complex suite of largely calc-alkaline igneous parents intruded in the period 2800–2900 Ma (Moorbath and others, 1975), the rocks being subsequently deformed and migmatised during the Scourian event (c.2600–2700 Ma). The metamorphic grade of the gneiss during the Scourian is not thought to have exceeded the amphibolite facies over most of the area. Granulite-facies conditions were attained only to the south and east, as evidenced by the pyroxene gneiss and the extreme depletion of uranium which occurred in South Uist at that time (Moorbath and others, 1975), this latter feature being typical of high-grade gneiss terrains.

Lying within the gneiss are a group of exotic lithologies believed to be

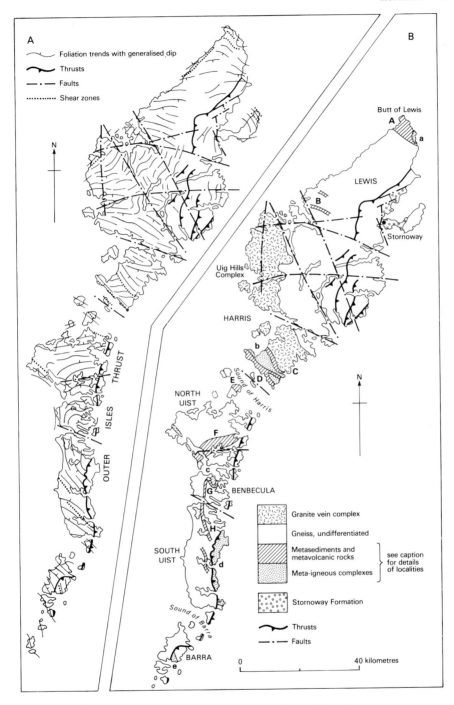

Figure 5 Diagrammatic maps of the geology of the Outer Hebrides

The left-hand map **A** shows the main structural features; the right-hand map **B** shows the main lithological units (after Fettes and others, in press)

Outcrops of metasedimentary and metavolcanic rocks are; **A** Ness **B** Laxavat **C** Langavat **D** Leverburgh **E** Sound of Harris **F** North Uist **G** Benbecula **H** South Uist

Outcrops of meta-igneous complexes are; **a** Ness **b** South Harris **c** Market Stance **d** Corodale gneiss **e** Barra

supracrustal sequence of metasediments and metavolcanic rocks. These are found as isolated occurrences throughout the islands (Figure 5B) but reach their largest and most varied development in the Langavat and Leverburgh Belts which flank the South Harris Igneous Complex and with it form the South Harris Complex (Figure 6). These major belts contain a mixture of pelitic schist, locally graphitic, quartzite, marble and finely banded amphibolite. Elsewhere the supracrustal sequence is commonly represented by garnet-biotite schist, which is locally kyanite- or sillimanite-bearing. The extent of the sequence is masked by the long history of deformation and metamorphism; in consequence only the more exotic lithologies can be readily identified. There are, at a number of localities, finely striped hornblende-bearing gneisses and quartzose gneisses of uncertain parentage and affinity.

Areally associated with this supracrustal sequence, and believed to be of broadly the same age, there is a suite of characteristically banded basic rocks. Occurrences of the suite are largely confined to the southern isles, although the anorthosite at Ness in the north of Lewis (Watson, 1969) is believed to be part of the group. These basics show compositional banding on a centimetre to metre scale, the composition of individual bands ranging from ultramafic to felsic. Although the mineralogy and textures are now entirely metamorphic, the banding is believed to reflect original igneous layering. Chemically these rocks are similar to modern tholeiites.

The supracrustal sequence and associated banded basics are thought to be broadly equivalent to those of the Scourian region of the mainland (p. 15) and the kyanite-gneiss north of Loch Maree (p. 19). They are believed to be the oldest rocks of the Outer Hebrides, having been intruded by the igneous parents of the gneisses; this igneous event was so extensive that the earlier rocks survive only as subordinate relics.

A group of late-Scourian intrusives dated at c.2600 Ma, has been extensively recognised in South Uist and Barra. Although possibly present throughout the islands, this group is best seen in areas where the effects of the subsequent Laxfordian event are least. The group consists of an older set of microdiorites, monzodiorites and diorites, and a younger set of potash-rich granites, monzonites and pegmatites. The two sets are separated by a phase of deformation; subsequent deformation of late-Scourian age also affects the younger group of intrusions. These two deformational phases may be broadly equivalent to the Inverian of the mainland.

The Inverian or its equivalent is also marked in the Outer Hebrides by the development of regional scale shear zones with a dominant NW–SE trend (Figure 5A). During the waning stages of this event the gneisses were intruded by a suite of basic dykes collectively termed the Younger Basics. These are believed to be broadly equivalent to the Scourie dykes of the mainland, although some workers (Taft, 1978; Hopgood and Bowes, 1972) have argued that the Younger Basics represent a series of intrusive events of different ages. The suite consists of picrites, norites and dolerites, the dolerites being by far the most abundant. Where they have not been extensively deformed by later events the dykes have a generalised W–NNW trend. In common with their mainland equivalents, the dykes show evidence of having been intruded into a hot and tectonically active crust, although the shear zones appear to have been less active and to have exerted less control on the style of intrusion than on the mainland. The dykes exhibit a range of metamorphic textures and mineralogies, ranging from subophitic and equigranular assemblages of the granulite facies to highly schistose lower amphibolite assemblages. The high-grade assemblages, generally now found in the cores of the larger dykes, relate to recrystallisation associated with intrusion into hot crust, their higher grade (relative to the mainland dykes) indicating deeper levels of intrusion. Although the dyke assemblages are consistent with granulite-facies conditions it is believed that the ambient pressures and temperatures of the host rocks were only typical of the upper amphibolite facies, and that the dykes recrystallised in relatively dry conditions.

The South Harris Igneous Complex (Figure 6) is roughly the same age (c.2200 Ma, Cliff and others, 1983) as the Younger Basics. It consists of a number of plutonic masses and related dykes which are, in order of intrusion from oldest to youngest, of gabbro, anorthosite, norite, and diorite. The mineralogy and tex-tures are now almost wholly metamorphic, although the chemistry still defines ig-neous trends. The suite is thought to have resulted from progressively deeper magma generation from one or more olivine tholeiite parent magmas. The early gabbros and anorthosite represent gravity-layered rocks with tholeiitic trends, whereas the diorite and norite plutons have calc-alkaline trends. The final product of the Complex was the intrusion of minor, thin (2 – 50 cm) shoshonite dykes. The

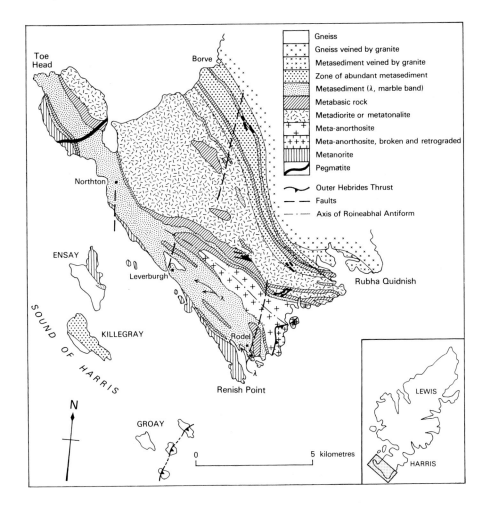

Figure 6   Map of the South Harris Complex which comprises the South Harris Igneous Complex of metabasic rocks and the marginal belts of metasediments.

rocks show assemblages consistent with the granulite facies, which are believed to have resulted from recrystallisation following intrusion into the hot lower crust.

The eastern half of South Uist is composed of a massive meta-igneous body termed the Corodale Gneiss (Coward, 1972) which is everywhere in thrust contact with the other gneisses. The gneiss is dioritic in overall composition but shows evidence of igneous layering, the more mafic bands containing pyroxene- and garnet-bearing assemblages. The body has been regarded as broadly equivalent to the South Harris Igneous Complex (Coward, 1972) but is cut by a number of basic dykes, which have been correlated with the Younger Basic suite. If this latter correlation is correct then the gneiss may be older than the South Harris Complex.

The gneisses and intrusive rocks of the Outer Hebrides were variably deformed during the polyphasal deformation and metamorphism of the Laxfordian, which attained its maximum development in the period 1700–1800 Ma. The major folds of the Laxfordian have determined the present regional trends of the gneiss foliation (Figure 5A). The regional foliation in central Lewis is relatively flat, relating to major folds with subhorizontal axial planes, whereas in the southern isles and South Harris the dominant folds belong to a later set which have nearly vertical axial planes trending NW-SE. The orientation of the Laxfordian folds is believed to have been partly controlled by the pre-existing Inverian and Scourian structural and metamorphic pattern. The degree of Laxfordian deformation or reworking of the gneisses varies considerably and on all scales throughout the islands, from areas of low reworking (marked by cross-cutting Younger Basics with high-grade pyroxene-garnet-bearing assemblages) to areas of high reworking (with a markedly planar foliation and concordant, thoroughly recrystallised Younger Basics). The metamorphic grade during the various phases of the Laxfordian appears to have been entirely within the amphibolite facies. Locally remobilisation and recrystallisation of the gneiss occurs, and the rock loses its gneissose foliation.

The end of the Laxfordian was marked by the intrusion of a suite of thick granitic veins, lenses and sheets at c.1700 Ma. Although found at a number of localities, by far the greatest abundance of granite is in western Harris and Lewis where it constitutes the Uig Hills Complex. In this area the granite forms a complex network of veins and sheets ranging in thickness from centimetres to hundreds of metres. The centre of the complex is marked by the development of porphyritic granite, whereas the marginal zone is characterised by the relative abundance of leucogranite. Although the complex is associated in part with highly recrystallised and remobilised gneiss, the granites are not believed to be partial melts from the local gneiss. The granites show evidence of late-stage cataclasis, and several veins have highly mylonitic centres. These and other features are though to indicate the inception of regional thrusting (see below) before the later granite veins were fully consolidated (Fettes and others, in press).

The host gneisses to the granite also characteristically show evidence of widespread brittle structures and mylonite development, although to a lesser degree of intensity than the granites. Farther east deformation increases with typically ultramylonite and then pseudotachylite being found. The increasing deformation culminates in a major shallow ESE-dipping thrust zone running down the east seaboard—The Outer Isles (or Hebrides) Thrust. In Lewis, this thrust is marked by a wide zone of cataclastic gneiss and small thrusts with pseudotachylite, but further south it develops as a more discrete thrust plane. In the thrust zone the pseudotachylite development is overprinted by a later phase of lower greenschist-facies mylonite production and associated hydrous retrogression of the gneiss. Fettes and others (in press) have argued that the pseudotachylite development related to late Laxfordian movements, the greenschist-grade mylonites marking reactivation of the thrust during the Caledonian. Some workers (e.g. Sibson, 1977) however, have argued that the development of mylonite and pseudotachylite are both essentially Caledonian. They also postulate that any pseudotachylite production of late-Laxfordian age is relatively minor, and equivalent to the pseudotachylite belts of the mainland (p. 19).

LEWISIAN INLIERS EAST OF THE MOINE THRUST

The original surveyors of the Geological Survey recognised Lewisian rocks within the Caledonian orogenic belt (Figure 3). Most of these, according to the fashion of the times, were believed to represent complex upfolds (inliers) of autochthonous basement. Later structural reinterpretation of some of these Lewisian-like out-crops gave rise to speculation that they could be integral parts of the Moine Suc-cession (Sutton and Watson, 1953). However, it is now generally accepted that they are Lewisian rocks lying within the Moines, either as attenuated isoclinal cores or as thrust slices (or both). The folding and thrusting which resulted in the emplacement of the Lewisian sheets may be of late Precambrian age, but all the inliers are to a greater or lesser extent affected by Caledonian folding and metamorphism (see Figure 3). Their structure has been studied by, amongst others, Sutton and Watson (1953; 1955), Ramsay (1958) and Tobisch and others (1970).

In the west, near the Moine Thrust, the inliers may be parautochthonous, in the sense that they are either folds or thrust sheets in contact with Lewisian base-ment which directly underlies basal Moine strata. This basement, however, may have been transported for a considerable distance on the Moine Thrust. Within the central part of the Northern Highland Moines, and well within the orogenic belt, a group of inliers rest directly on the major structural break formed by the Sgurr Beag Slide; they appear to be essentially allochthonous. Between the Moine Thrust Belt and the Sgurr Beag Slide lie numerous Lewisian inliers. In the south these are found as small thrust slivers ranging downward to a few tens of metres in length, but in the north they form larger areas of thrust and folded Lewisian rocks which may be several kilometres long. The distinction between allochthonous and parautochthonous is possibly only of significance insofar as it indicates remoteness from the basement and the degree of strain necessary to emplace a Lewisian sheet at a given level (see Rathbone and Harris, 1979).

In the parautochthonous inliers near the Moine Thrust the Lewisian is represented by two facies, a 'Western Lewisian' with a character similar to that of the adjacent Foreland Lewisian, and an 'Eastern Lewisian', which differs in hav-ing a higher proportion of metabasic rocks and sedimentary gneisses, including types not represented (or scarce) in the metasediments of the Foreland, such as graphite schist, calc-silicate rock and marble. This eastern facies is dominant in the allochthonous slices within the Moine, suggesting that the Lewisian basement further east is significantly different from that found in the Foreland. Moreover, Watson and Dunning (1979) cite evidence of the chemistry of crust-derived Caledonian plutons to suggest that the basement underlying the Caledonides also contained a higher proportion of granites.

The largest of the parautochthonous inliers is that of Glenelg – Attadale (Ram-say, 1958b; Barber and May, 1976). This inlier contains both 'Western' and 'Eastern' Lewisian rocks separated, in Attadale, by a narrow zone of tectonic schist containing both Lewisian and Moine components, and in Glenelg by a nar-row zone of mixed, probably interfolded, rocks. The rocks of the Western Lewisian have Scourian affinities and show little, if any, Laxfordian effects—or at least none clearly separable from the later Caledonian overprint, which becomes more marked eastwards. Both Eastern and Western gneisses have a pre-Caledonian deformation history and the movements along the Moine Thrust appear to be the fourth (D_4) of the six phases of deformation recognised in the inlier. The inlier is the only one where a basal conglomerate indicates a non-tectonic transition from the Lewisian to the overlying Moine. The conglomerate is considerably deformed.

The Morar Inlier (Figures 3, 16 and 17) comprises hornblende gneiss and amphibolite (Plate 6). It has been interpreted as Lewisian interleaved with basal Moine strata by folding and thrusting (Richey and Kennedy, 1939; Kennedy, 1955; Ramsay and Spring, 1962). This interleaved sequence was folded in Caledonian times into a large antiformal structure, the Morar Anticline.

East of those two parautochthanous inliers lie several minor slices—some only metres to centimetres thick—which lie on thrusts; their platy fabric can be traced into the Moine rocks for long distances beyond the limit of Lewisian outcrop. Larger areas of mixed Moine and Lewisian rocks, in part infolded and in part thrust, are found in Coire nan Gall (Clifford, 1958) and the Saddle area (Simony, 1973). Hornblendic or biotitic schists are the common rock types of these enclaves, contrasting with the gneisses of the adjacent Moines. Along the Sgurr Beag Slide, Lewisian rocks are found in the south as tiny slices of basic gneisses (e.g. near Loch Hourn) and as larger, but still minor, masses of hornblende gneiss, amphibolite and marble in Glen Shiel. It has been inferred (Tanner and others, 1972) that the major inliers of Central Ross-shire further north also lie immediately above the Sgurr Beag Slide (or possibly slide complex). These major inliers (of Strathfarrar–Monar, Glen Orrin, Scardroy, etc.) are of 'Eastern' type, comprising feldspathic gneisses and various hornblende gneisses, with hornblende schists, ultrabasic rocks, marbles, calc-silicate rocks and some graphitic schists. The Fannich Inlier is now interpreted (Tanner and others, 1972) as lying on the Sgurr Beag Slide below a klippe of Glenfinnan Division schists; this suggestion has received recent support from the trace element studies of the pelitic rocks (Winchester and others, 1981).

Between central Ross and the north coast several major and minor slices of Lewisian rock lie to the west of the inferred continuation of the Sgurr Beag Slide. Amongst these, the minor outcrops were taken in places to be Moine rocks of unusual aspect but are now recognised as thrust lenticles (e.g. Peacock, 1975). Major Lewisian masses with abundant basic gneisses are found in folded and thrust slices in Sutherland. Some of these have previously been interpreted as Moine basics of pre- to early-Caledonian age. More recent work by Moorhouse and Moorhouse (1979) has distinguished geochemically between the basics of Moine and Lewisian age. The major Lewisian enclaves of Sutherland are those of Loch Naver, Borgie, Tongue, Bettyhill and Mudale; they are known as the Sutherland Group, with the Strathy Complex on the north coast. The Strathy Complex consists of a grey quartzose gneiss with subordinate amphibole-bearing gneiss, amphibolite and marble. It is of unusual aspect, both for Lewisian and Moine rocks. Moorhouse and Moorhouse (1983) discuss the possibility that it is a much modified part of the Laxfordian Lewisian basement, including originally dacitic supracrustal igneous rock.

Adjacent to the Great Glen Fault at Cromarty and Rosemarkie, two inliers of Moine rocks protrude through the Old Red Sandstone sediments of Easter Ross. In the southerly inlier, that of Rosemarkie, the Moine rocks are intimately associated with hornblende gneisses which Rathbone and Harris (1980) consider to be part of the underlying Lewisian basement.

Plate 5 Scourie dykes intrude a late Scourian shear zone in Lewisian gneiss. The gneiss to the left of the dyke still retains a largely Scourian fabric. Aird Fenish, West Lewis (D1570)

Plate 6 The typical lithology of a Lewisian inlier affected by Caledonian metamorphism and deformation. The darkest material is hornblende gneiss, and the paler material is quartz-feldspar and hornblende-biotite-quartz-feldspar gneiss. Ardnamurach Inlier, south shore of Loch Nevis (G. S. Johnstone)

3 Torridonian

In late Precambrian times (1000–750 Ma) the eroded land surface of Lewisian gneiss of the North-West Highlands was covered by a thick accumulation of sediments which, in the area of the Caledonian Foreland, have never been deformed or regionally metamorphosed. It is possible that these sediments represent the last of several cycles of deposition and erosion since the gneisses first formed a land surface; within them there is a major unconformity, representing a long time-gap. The late Precambrian sediments are, in turn, unconformably overlain by Lower Cambrian strata.

The name 'Torridon Sandstone' was introduced by Nicol (1866), but sandstone, though the dominant rock type, is only one of several lithologies to be found. For this reason the rocks are usually collectively termed 'the Torridonian', a term coined by Geikie (*in* Peach and Horne, 1892). The name is derived from the Torridon area of the North-West Highlands, where mountains carved from the rocks of the sequence form some of the most spectacular scenery in the British Isles (Plate 7). Precipices of deeply eroded, generally flat-bedded strata rise 600–900 m, often from a valley floor in which the underlying gneiss is exposed. Individual peaks and ridges are commonly capped by small outliers of Cambrian quartzite, well to the west of its main outcrop. North of the type area, the Torridonian sandstone mountains become isolated, giving rise to characteristic 'inselberg' or 'island mountain' terrain; this is at its most spectacular in Assynt (Plate 8). There, the sandstone forms long narrow ridges separated by broad valleys of gneiss. Viewed from the east or west several of the mountains appear as tower-like, isolated masses, often with precipitous walls through which a way to the summit is not easily made.

Within the Northern Highlands the Torridonian (Figure 7) comprises, for the greater part, an assemblage of terrestrial sedimentary rocks. These are commonly reddish or reddish brown, laid down under fluviatile and, more rarely, shallow lacustrine conditions, with local accumulations of scree-breccias on or near the contacts with the Lewisian land surface. Certain grey-facies rocks were formerly taken to be marine, but Stewart and Parker (1979), by a study of palaeosalinity indicators, showed that this is unlikely to be the case. The great thickness of terrestrial deposits, and the palaeoenvironment indicators they contain, suggest that the rocks accumulated in subsiding basins which were probably fault-determined. Stewart (1982) considers that these basins were in the form of NNE-trending rifts cutting the Archaean and early Proterozoic crust, the rifts marking an early stage in the development of what later became the Iapetus Ocean separating Laurentia from Baltica. On this hypothesis the grey-facies shales, in broad terms, are distal representatives of proximally-deposited red beds in each rift (Figure 8). Direct evidence for the presence and extent of the rifts is obscured by later thrusting within the succession, and the over-riding of the Moine Nappe.

It should be clearly understood that the Torridonian is not a 'System'. In common with late Proterozoic sediments elsewhere, comparative studies have not reached the stage where it can be correlated world-wide. Nonetheless some comparisons have been made of its nannofossil content of acritarchs and cryptarchs (Diver and Peat, 1979), as several of the grey-shale beds of the Torridonian have a

Plate 7   The Torridonian mountains typically show horizontal bedding in sandstone, producing alternate vertical cliffs and near-horizontal ledges. Beinn Alligain (right) and Beinn Dearg are seen from Beinn Bhreac, with part of the Liathach ridge in background (W. Mykura)

Plate 8 Beyond typical terrain of the Lewisian foreland north-east of Stoer we see relict mountains of Torridonian Sandstone—from left to right, Canisp, Suilven, Cul Mor, Cul Beag, Stac Pollaidh, seen from the north-west (D2819)

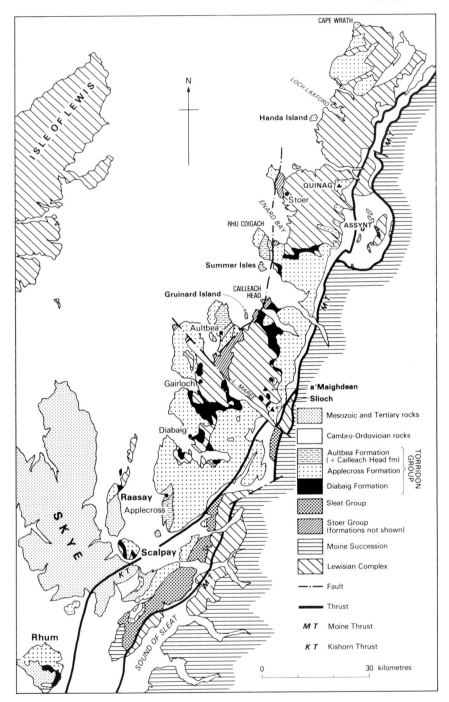

Figure 7 Distribution of groups and formations of the Torridonian (with an outline of Cambrian, Mesozoic and Tertiary rocks)

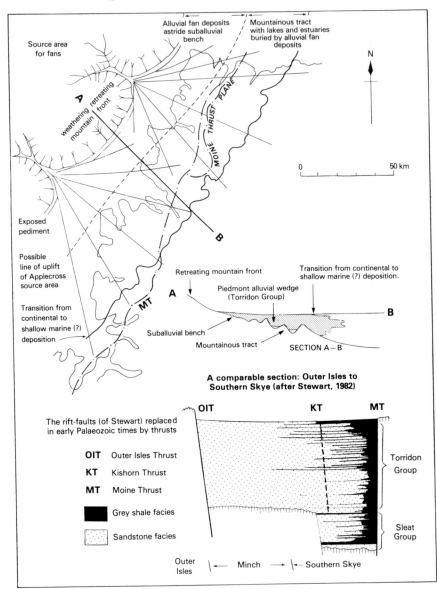

Figure 8   A hypothetical interpretation of the palaeogeography of the Torridon and Sleat Groups within a rift basin (after Williams, 1969; and Stewart, 1982)

large and varied assemblage (e.g. Zhang, 1982). These fossils indicate that the rocks can be correlated with the Upper Riphaean of the Russian classification.

It was formerly thought that the Torridonian rocks were laid down during one continuous period of deposition. It has now been established (e.g. Gracie and Stewart, 1977) that one notable unconformity exists within the sequence. Below it the rocks (termed the Stoer Group) have a radiometric (Rb-Sr isochron) age of c.960 Ma (Moorbath, 1969) and a palaeomagnetic age inferred to be about 1100 Ma (Smith and others, 1983). Above the unconformity the rocks on the mainland comprise the Torridon Group; their isotopic age is c.770 Ma and they have a palaeomagnetic age of c.1040 Ma. The palaeolatitude of the 'Upper' and 'Lower' Torridonian differs by some 45°.

Prior to the deposition of the Torridon Group, the Stoer Group was tilted to the north-west by up to 30° and extensively eroded, so that over much of the area the Torridon Group now rests directly on basement gneisses. It is thus clear that the regional sub-Torridonian surface is composite, comprising a pre-Stoer Group surface which was further modified during the long period of erosion between the deposition of the Stoer and Torridon Groups. How extensive this modification was is not yet known. Taken as a whole, however, the sub-Torridonian land surface was gently undulating in north-west Sutherland, but south of the mountain Quinag it became more irregular and locally had a high relief. Striking examples of Torridonian-filled valleys can be seen at Quinag, a'Mhaighdean and Slioch (Figure 9) where hills of gneiss rise 400 m, 300 m and 600 m respectively above the pre-Torridonian valley floors. Pre-Torridonian valleys in the gneiss can be traced for some distance; the present drainage in south Assynt and north-west of Loch Maree may well follow lines established in pre-Torridonian times. Williams (1969) suggested that the relatively flat surface of the gneiss in north-west Sutherland is part of a large 'suballuvial bench', a planated piedmont surface lying below a retreating front of gneiss mountains (which lay to the west of the Minch) and from which most of the Torridonian sediments were derived. Sedimentary structures and current-bedding directions suggest that these were deposited in coalescing fans formed by E- to SE-flowing streams (Figure 8). On Stewart's hypothesis (above) these fans debouched over the western margin of the steadily subsiding rift-valley.

The Torridonian is absent from the Outer Hebrides, although its presence under the waters of the Minch has been shown by Chesher and Lawson (1983). According to the rift hypothesis of Stewart, the western bounding fault of the basin of deposiion was in the position of the present Outer Isles Thrust, and the eastern fault was in the position of the 'root' of the Moine Thrust (now concealed under the Moine Nappe), both faults being reactivated as thrusts in Caledonian times. If this interpretation is true, Torridonian strata may never have covered the Outer Hebrides in great thickness.

Table 1   Subdivisions of the Torridonian rocks

Groups	Formations, etc.	Thickness (m)
Torridon Group	Cailleach Head Formation	750 +
	Aultbea Formation	up to 2500
	Applecross Formation	up to 3000
	Diabaig Formation	0 – c.500
Sleat Group (formerly part of Diabaig Group)	Kinloch Formation	900 – 1400
	Beinn na Seamraig Formation	1200 – 1500
	Loch na Dal Formation	800
	Rubha Guail Formation	c.100
Unconformity on Foreland below Torridon Group		
Stoer Group	(No formation subdivision)	2000 +

The Torridon and Sleat Groups make up the 'Upper Torridonian' of Smith and others (1983). The 'Lower Torridonian' comprises only the Stoer Group.

For the geographical distribution of the Groups, see Figure 7.

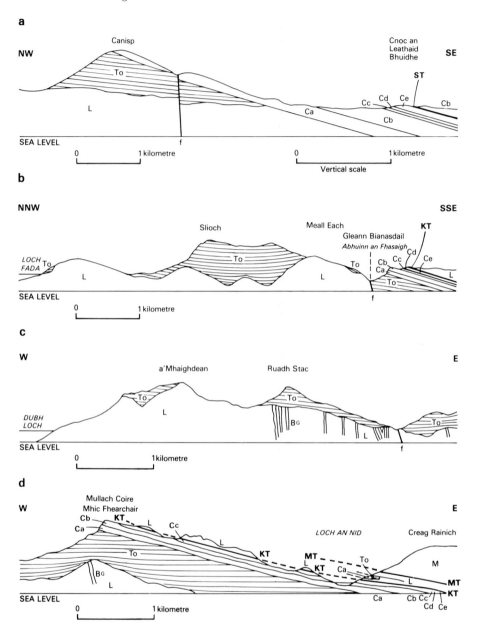

Figure 9   Sections illustrating the unconformity of the Torridonian on Lewisian gneiss and the overstep of the Cambrian across the Torridonian on to the Lewisian

a Canisp to Cnoc an Leathaid Bhuidhe   **b** Loch Fada across Slioch to Gleann Bianasdail   **c, d** A'Mhaighdean by Mullach Coire Mhic Fhearchair to Creag Rainich

L Lewisian gneiss   **B**^{G} Basic dykes in gneiss   **M** Moinian schists   **To** Torridonian sandstone
C Cambrian   **Ca** Basal Quartzite   **Cb** Pipe Rock   **Cc** Fucoid Beds
              Cd Serpulite Grit   **Ce** Durness Limestone
MT Moine Thrust   **KT** Kinlochewe Thrust   **ST** Sole Thrust   **f** fault

Following the researches of the original surveyors (Peach and others, 1907) it was long held that the Torridonian comprised three main divisions—the Diabaig, Applecross and Aultbea groups (in ascending order); a fourth group—the Cailleach Head Group—was of doubtful status, as it was only seen in faulted contact with the Aultbea Group. The recognition of the intra-Torridonian unconformity and the reallocation of former Diabaig Group rocks in the Sleat of Skye to a separate group (the Sleat Group) has resulted (see Table 1) in the formal redefinition of the groups by Stewart (1969, and 1975).

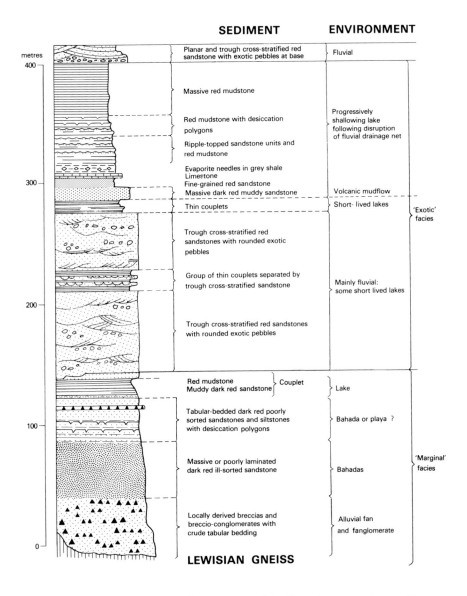

Figure 10 Graphic log of part of type section of the Stoer Group at Stoer, with suggested environments of deposition (after Stewart, *in* Barber and others, 1978)

'LOWER TORRIDONIAN'

Stoer Group

The Stoer Group was first recognised as lying beneath an unconformity at Enard Bay (Stewart, 1966a; Gracie and Stewart, 1967), and rocks of the Group were eventually shown to have a widespread, although not areally extensive, outcrop. The name was formalised by Stewart (1969).

The Group consists of unmetamorphosed red beds, over 2 km thick, resting on a land surface of Lewisian gneiss with up to 400 m relief. Stewart (1975) recognised a lower 'marginal' facies and an upper 'exotic' facies (Figure 10). The former contains breccia conglomerates, planar and cross-bedded sandstones, and rare, playa-lake sediments with thin limestones. This facies is interpreted as a fanglomerate deposit. The 'exotic' facies contains locally cross-bedded red sandstones and mudstones. It contains rounded pebbles of gneiss and quartzite which are not found in the underlying basement gneiss. This facies is thought to be of fluvial origin, with sediments derived from both a westerly and, locally, south-easterly source. One important horizon within the exotic facies—the Stac Fhada Member—contains volcanic debris, glassy shards and accretionary lapilli; it is considered to be a volcanic mudflow (Lawson, 1972) derived from the east. If this is taken as a time-plane, then the variations in thickness of the 'exotic' facies indicate that the basin of deposition was deepest in the Loch Maree area, where the sediments beneath the volcanic horizon are thickest. In Stoer Bay, nannofossils have been obtained from limestone by Downie (1962), and from grey shale by Cloud and Germs (1971).

'UPPER TORRIDONIAN'

Sleat Group

Rocks of the Sleat Group, which are only found within the Kishorn Nappe on the island of Skye and adjacent mainland, were first described by Clough (*in* Peach and others, 1907), and the subdivisions which he established are still accepted. More recent workers (Stewart, 1969; Sutton and Watson, 1964) are agreed, however, that Clough's estimates of the thickness of the various groups are too low; the thicknesses given in this account follow Sutton and Watson. The formation names are based on localities in Skye, but have also been applied to the equivalent beds in the Kyle of Lochalsh and Kishorn areas. The Rubha Guail Formation (c.100 m—formerly the 'Epidotic Grit Formation') is made up mainly of coarse 'gritty' or pebbly sandstone with abundant fragments and pebbles of epidote and epidotised feldspar, thought to be derived from the weathering of the underlying Lewisian gneiss. Trough cross-bedding is common. There are occasional bands of purple and green shale. The Loch na Dal Formation (800 m—formerly Loch na Dal Beds) comprises dark grey siltstones and sandy shales with bands of coarse sandstone and some calcareous lenticles. The Beinn na Seamraig Formation (1200–1500 m—formerly Beinn na Seamraig Grits) consists mainly of current-bedded sandstones or 'fine grained grits' with thin bands of grey laminated siltstone and sandstone. The Kinloch Formation (900–1400 m—formerly Kinloch Beds) is made up of dark grey siltstones, grey and buff sandstones and 'fine grits' with thin calcareous lenticles. Cross-bedding is rare.

Sutton and Watson point out that while the above grouping of strata into formations is valid on the basis of field characteristics, it depends as much on the variations of the proportions of lithologies common to several groups as it does on the presence, within any group, of a distinctive rock type.

Unlike the rocks of the Torridon Group the dominant colour of the Sleat Group sediments is grey or buff; they were formerly considered to be littoral or lagoonal deposits. As mentioned earlier, Stewart and Parker now consider them to have been laid down in a freshwater environment, the grey shales possibly representing distal fluvial or lacustrine deposits. The predominant grey colour of the sandstone could be due to the alteration of hematite to magnetite during Caledonian metamorphism, the effects of which can be seen in the Loch Alsh Syncline where the Torridonian rocks reach the lower greenschist facies. Within the Kishorn Nappe of Skye (Figure 7) the Sleat Group is followed conformably by Torridon Group strata. Stewart (1969; 1982) discusses reasons for ascribing the Sleat and Stoer Groups to completely separate stratigraphical units.

Torridon Group

The Torridon Group is the typical 'Torridonian Sandstone'. It is up to 7 km thick and comprises unmetamorphosed red beds with subordinate grey shales (Figure 11). Where it lies unconformably on Lewisian rocks, its basal beds are commonly

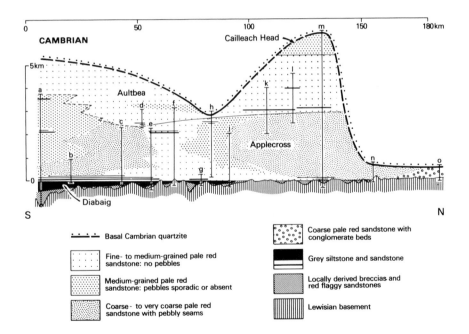

Figure 11 Generalised section through the Torridonian from Rhum to Cape Wrath, mainly based on the sections: **a** Rhum **b** Soay **c** Scalpay **d** Toscaig **e** Raasay **f** Shieldaig to Applecross **g** Diabaig **h** Torridon **j** Gairloch **k** Aultbea **l** Summer Isles **m** Stathkanaird to Rubha Coigeach and Cailleach Head **n** Quinag **o** Cape Wrath

Named rock units are formations of the Torridon group (the Sleat Formation of Skye is not shown) (After Stewart, 1975)

fanglomerates, fossil screes and sandstones which can be seen filling old pre-Torridonian valleys and even small clefts in the Lewisian basement; spectacular examples are to be seen in the area south of a'Mhaighdean, east of the Fionn Loch. These basal beds pass upwards and laterally into grey shales which are thin or absent in the north but become thicker and more widespread south of Gairloch to form the redefined Diabaig Formation of Stewart (1975). This formation reaches its maximum thickness in Rhum and Scalpay (c.500 m). The Diabaig shales were formerly thought to be of marine origin, but are now more generally accepted as lacustrine. In Sleat the passage between the rocks of the Kinloch and Applecross Formations is marked by intercalcation with, lateral passage to, shales of 'Diabaig' type.

The Applecross Formation comprises over 2500 m of fluvial, strongly cross-bedded, red-brown to pale red arkosic sandstone and pebbly sandstone, locally with conglomerate. During the deposition of the group the source area lay to the west, with two major alluvial fans spreading south-eastwards from a mountainous source area, the eastern margin of which occupied most of the present-day Outer Hebrides (Figure 8). Stewart (1982) suggested that the fans accumulated at the base of a fault along the east side of the present Outer Hebrides and that the cyclic nature of the sequence indicates periodic rejuvenation of the fault movements. The pebble content of the rocks (including quartzite, jasper, and feldspar porphyry) cannot be matched with the lithology of the Lewisian at present exposed in the Outer Isles; this indicates a provenance in a higher level of basement than that now exposed. The rocks providing the clasts could either have been entirely eroded away or, alternatively, lie to the west of the present Outer Hebrides.

The Aultbea Formation consists of red, cross-bedded, fine- to medium-grained arkosic sandstone which reaches 2500 m in Coigach. Like the Applecross Formation, it is of fluvial origin and its source area was to the WNW. Unlike the Applecross, however, pebbly sandstone and conglomerate horizons are sparse. The sandstones are interbedded with thin shales which have occasional sun cracks and rain pits. Stewart (1969 and 1975) shows a degree of diachronism between the upper part of the Applecross and lower part of the Aultbea Formation and this is confirmed by the palaeomagnetic studies of Smith and others (1982).

The position of the Cailleach Head Formation is not fully proved, as it is not seen in unfaulted contact with the (presumed) underlying Aultbea Formation*. Its outcrop is confined to the tip of the peninsula between Loch Broom and Little Loch Broom, where it is at least 750 m thick. It consists of a sequence of cycles each of grey shale grading upwards into red sandstone.

A whole rock Rb/Sr isochron from shales near the bottom of the Applecross Formation gave an age of c.770 Ma (Moorbath, 1969). The Upper Torridonian time sequence of pole positions coincides with the Laurentian polar wandering path at about 1040 Ma according to Smith and others (1983).

Teall (*in* Peach and others, 1907) was the first to record possible organic remains in the Torridonian. He recorded minute spherical bodies and fibres within black phosphate nodules in the Cailleach Head Formation near Loch Broom. Nannofossils have since been recorded in several black shales within the Torridon Group (Naumova and Pavlovsky, 1961; Sutton, 1962; Diver and Peat, 1979). Zhang (1982) has given a detailed description of a nannofossil assemblage from Aultbea Formation shales on the Summer Isles. These fossils belong to the

---

* Dr W. Diver reports the presence of beds ascribed to the Cailleach Head Formation conformably overlying Aultbea Formation sediments on Gruinard Island (personal communication, 1983).

sphaeromorphic acritarchs and cryptarchs, and include the sheaths of filamentous cyanobacteria. They are believed to indicate an Upper Riphean age.

The Torridonian strata and basement gneisses were tilted westward and planated prior to the deposition of the lower Cambrian rocks, the planar surface itself being tilted in post-Cambrian times to incline as much as 20° to the east, with the underlying Torridonian rocks more or less recovering their original horizontal disposition.

4 Cambrian and Ordovician

In the time interval (c.200 Ma) between the deposition of the Torridonian rocks and the Cambrian there was a period of crustal warping during which the Precambrian rocks of what is now the Caledonian Foreland were arched into large folds. Considerable erosion followed this folding and several hundreds of metres of Torridonian rocks were removed in places to lay bare the underlying Lewisian gneiss. By the beginning of Cambrian times the erosion had produced a remarkably flat surface passing across hard gneiss and softer sandstone alike; this may have been formed by marine erosion or as a subaerial peneplain. Cambrian sediments were deposited on this surface as it progressively and gently subsided to form the floor of a shelf sea. This shelf lay on the south-east side of the continental mass which bounded the Iapetus Ocean on its north-western side and, as a result, the fauna of the Cambro-Ordovician rocks of the North-West Highlands resembles that of the North American Province—the Beekmantown (Canadian) Fauna of older accounts. It shows a marked contrast to that found in the rocks of similar age in England and Wales, which were laid down close to the south shore of the Iapetus.

Cambro-Ordovician strata now lie on the Caledonian Foreland and within the Moine Thrust Belt along a narrow zone from Durness to Skye (see Figure 7). They are overlain by metamorphic rocks of the Moine Nappe which were pushed westward along the Moine Thrust itself.

The long-accustomed names given by the original surveyors (Peach and others, 1907) to the Cambro-Ordovician rocks were revised, first by Swett (1969) and later by the Stratigraphical Committee of the Geological Society (Cowie and others, 1972; Williams and others, 1972). The names currently in use are given in Table 2. A further modification proposed by Palmer and others (1980) is also incorporated.

Swett's account of the depositional and diagenetic history of the Cambro-Ordovician rocks of the North-West Highlands is the most comprehensive modern synthesis available but the memoir by Peach and others (1907) still remains the best for locality descriptions. The formation thicknesses in Table 2 are based on Cowie and others (1972) and Williams and others (1972); they differ to some degree from those of Swett.

The junction between the Cambrian and Ordovician systems lies within the Durness Group—a sequence of carbonate rocks which have significant features in common throughout their thickness. Over the years there has been much discussion about how much of the Group is Cambrian (and, if so, what part of the Cambrian) and how much of it is Ordovician. Recently the question seems to have been settled by the recognition by Palmer and others (1980) of a major erosion surface between the Sailmhor (Lower Cambrian) and Sangomore (Arenig) Formations (see Table 2). This erosion surface seems to represent a time interval equivalent to the Middle and Upper Cambrian.

Eriboll Sandstone Group

This Group consists predominantly of hard white quartzite which forms a con-

Table 2 Subdivisions of the Cambrian and Ordovician rocks

Peach and others, 1907	Swett, 1969	Cowie and others, 1972 / Williams and others, 1972	Thickness (m)	Palmer and others, 1980
Calcareous Series (Durness Limestone)	**Durness Carbonate Formation**	**Durness Group**		**Upper Durness Group**
VII Durine Group	Durine member	Durine Formation	186	(Ordovician)
VI Croisaphuill Group	Croisaphuill member	Croisaphuill Formation	145	
V Balnakeil Group	Balnakeil member	Balnakeil Formation	307	Unconformity
IV Sangomore Group	Sangomore member	Sangomore Formation	90–180	
III Sailmhor Group	Sailmhor member	Sailmhor Formation	100–170	**Lower Durness Group**
II Eilean Dubh Group	Eilean Dubh member	Eilean Dubh Formation	120–200	(Lower Cambrian)
I Ghrudaidh Group	Ghrudaidh member	Ghrudaidh Formation	60	
Middle Series	**An t'Sron Formation**	**(An t'Stron Group)***		
Upper Zone (Serpulite Grit)	Salterella Grit member	Salterella Grit Formation	5–15	
Lower Zone (Fucoid Beds)	Fucoid Beds member	Fucoid Beds Formation	12–27	
Arenaceous Series	**Eriboll Sandstone Formation**	**(Eriboll Sandstone Group)***		
Upper Zone (Pipe Rock) Subzone V Subzone IV Subzone III Subzone II Subzone I Lower Zone	Pipe Rock member (subzones no longer divisable – see text)	Pipe Rock Formation	76–100	
False-bedded Quartzite	False-bedded Quartzite member	False-bedded Quartzite Formation		

* Group name not given in Stratigraphical Committee reports (Cowie and others, 1972; Williams and others, 1972)

spicous feature of the landscape of the North-West Highlands. The quartzite has the composition of orthoquartzite with subordinate subarkose and arkose. It comprises a lower False-bedded Quartzite Formation and an upper Pipe Rock Formation. The False-bedded Quartzite, as its name implies, is conspicuously cross-bedded. It commonly has a pebbly base 0.3 to 3.9 m in thickness. The pebbles are well rounded and consist of quartzite, feldspar and felsite, set in a cream or greenish matrix. The overlying quartzite is made up of sets, 8 cm to 1 m thick, with mainly tubular cross-bedding and bimodal current directions. These features suggest a shallow water, subtidal or intertidal environment. Only in one place have trace fossils (annelid tubes) been found.

The Pipe Rock Formation is also quartzitic, but lacks cross-bedding. Its name is derived from the abundant vertical pipes which are 3 – 15 mm in diameter and up to 1 m long (Plate 9). These are the casts of suspension-feeding organisms. One form of pipes is represented by straight, subcylindrical, unbranched tubes normal to the bedding. These are called *Skolithus*. In another form the tubes pass upwards into a 'stacked funnel' arrangement, which appears on the bedding planes as concentric rings (Plate 10; the 'Trumpet Pipes' of the older descriptions). These are called *Monocraterion*. Hallam and Swett (1966) considered the two forms to be produced by the same organism, the different structures resulting from differences in the response to burrowing in sand of varying thixotropic properties. They found that the zonation of the Pipe Rock established by the older surveyors (which in part depended on the presence of Trumpet Pipes and in part on the size and frequency of the skolithid tubes) could not be followed in practice, so this well known zonation has now been abandoned.

The Eriboll Sandstone Group is remarkably uniform in thickness (it is slightly thicker in the southern area of its outcrop), suggesting to Swett (1969) either that the deposit is tabular, as might be expected with a gradual transgression, or that its outcrop trends more or less parallel to the strandline of a wedge-shaped deposit.

An t'Sron Group

The group derives its name from the promontory An t'Sron on the east shore of Loch Eriboll. It comprises a lower Fucoid Beds Formation and an upper Salterella Grit Formation.

The Fucoid Beds Formation consists of dolomitic siltstone with some dolomitic shale and sandstone, some layers of dolomite, and rare pisolitic ironstones. The beds were originally named Fucoid Beds because the abundant trace fossils which they contain were mistakenly identified as seaweed markings (fucoids). These are now considered to be flattened (?) annelid burrows, termed *Planolites*, but the old name has been retained. They were found by the early surveyors to contain *Olenellus lapworthi* at one horizon, and several new occurrences of this tribolite have been recorded by Brand (1965). In addition to the trilobites *Olenellus* and *Olenelloides*, an assemblage of *Hyolithes sp.*, *Salterella sp.*, a few brachiopods, echinodermata indet. and trace fossils has been recorded (Plate 25, p.153). The fauna indicates a late Lower Cambrian (*Bonnia – Olenellus* zone) age, and provides the only valid index fossils within the Cambrian sequence of the North-West Highlands (Cowie and McNamara, 1978).

The Fucoid Beds have an abnormally high content of potash (Bowie and others, 1966) and are considered to have an economic potential (p.179). The potash is contained in finely divided adularia feldspar. It is considered by Swett (1966) to be due to authigenic enrichment by migrating K_2O derived from the Durness Group carbonates.

Plate 9 The Pipe Rock Formation of the Eriboll Sandstone Group (Cambrian) is to be seen in a road cutting at Skiag Bridge, north shore of Loch Assynt. The vertical pipes (pale) in the locally reddened quartzite were made by burrowing worms (*Skolithus*) (W. Mykura)

Plate 10 The horizontal bedding-plane surface of Cambrian Pipe Rock shows the worm tubes (pipes) in plan. Lochan Gainmheach outflow, near Kylesku (G. S. Johnstone)

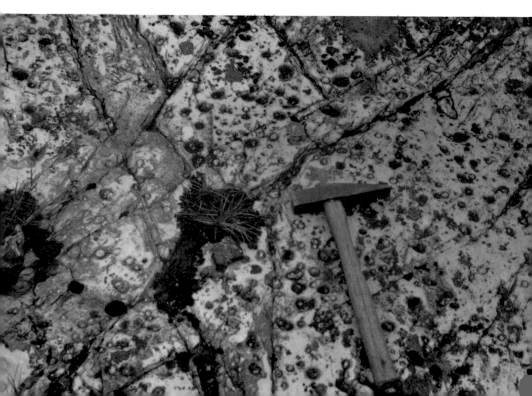

Plate 11 Cambro-Ordovician limestone, part of the Durness Group, forms Stronechrubie cliff, south of Inchnadamph. The lower three-quarters of the cliff is made up of rocks of the Ghrudaidh Formation (pale grey). The topmost part (less than a quarter of the whole) of the cliff is a thrust and imbricated mass of limestones of the Eilean Dubh Formation   (C6)

Plate 12 Moine psammitic granulite. Moderately thick flags of Loch Eil Psammite, Glen Suileag, Loch Eil. The rocks show the gentle undulations characteristic of much (but not all) of the Loch Eil Division   (C4220)

The Salterella Grit Formation comprises beds of orthoquartzite, with some arkosic grits and dolomitic sandstones. Interleaved shales at the base of the formation contain *Olenellus lapworthi* and, in the upper part, dolomitic sandstones have layers full of *Salterella*. As this fossil was originally identified as *Serpulites*, the old name for the formation was the 'Serpulite Grit'.

Durness Group

Formerly, but inaccurately, referred to as the Durness Limestone, the Group comprises limestone, dolomitic limestone, calcareous dolostone and dolostone (i.e. fine-grained carbonate rock, grading from pure limestone to pure dolomite), with a few minor variants such as cherty limestone; there are chert nodules and bands at some horizons (Plate 11). Peach and others (1907) divided the 'Durness Formation' into seven 'groups' and, although Swett (1969) notes that these divisions are indistinct and poorly defined, they form the basis of the 'Formations' nomenclature of Cowie and others (1972) given in Table 2.

To account for the dolomitic beds, which form a variable part of the sequence, Swett (1969) considers that the presence of dolomitised fossils, dolomitised oolite and dolomite replacement of secondary chert nodules suggests authigenic dolomitisation of limestone, although he does not exclude the possibility that some of the Durness Group sequence comprises primary dolomite.

The Ghrudaidh Formation consists of generally dark, lead-coloured and mottled dolomite with *Salterella sp.* in the lower 10 m. There are some oolitic horizons formed of dolomite, calcite and, more rarely, silica in the middle of the sequence. The Eilean Dubh Formation consists of fine-grained flaggy argillaceous 'dolomite' and limestone with many stromatolitic algal bands. Some horizons exhibit small-scale cross lamination, scour structures and load casts, and there are thin lenticular mud flake conglomerates. The Sailmhor Formation comprises massive mottled granular 'dolomite'. The spectacular dark grey and white mottling has led to the use of the term 'Leopard Rock' for the formation. The mottling is possibly due to differential dolomitisation of branching trace-fossil burrow systems (Palmer and others, 1980). Another characterisic of this formation is the extensive development of chert, both as nodules and as finely laminated layers. A fauna of gastropods, cephalopods and trilobites which was recorded at one locality within the formation is of Tremadoc age. Palmer and others (1980) were unable to confirm its presence and, reviewing the evidence, feel that it may represent a fissure-filling by material which was deposited above a major unconformity. The macrofaunal content of these lower three formations suggests that they are of Lower Cambrian age, and Brasier (1966) recorded diagnostic Lower Cambrian microfossils from a chert band near the base of the Eilean Dubh Formation.

Palmer and others (1980) have identified a major break between the Sailmhor Formation and the overlying Sangomore Formation. In Balnakeil Bay, west of Durness, the top of the Sailmhor Formation is considered to represent a karst surface. Solution cavities extending downwards from this surface are filled with breccia which can be traced downwards as far as the Eilean Dubh Formation in places. As the four formations above this unconformity contain Ordovician (including Tremadoc) fossils, it is inferred that Middle and Upper Cambrian rocks are not represented in the Durness Group, which is, accordingly, divided into an Upper and Lower Durness Group (see Table 2) with the break at the base of Sangomore Formation.

The Sangomore Formation comprises fine, granular dolomites with cream or pink limestones near the top and chert bands near the base. Only one macrofossil locality has been found (Palmer and others, 1980) with *Murchisonia sp.*, *Pleurotomaria sp.* and *Orthoceras sp.* (suggesting Lower Cambrian – Tremadoc age). The Balnakeil Formation comprises dark and light grey 'dolomites', limestones and impure layers with chert nodules, while the Croisaphuill Formation is made up of black and dark grey 'dolomites' and white limestone. These formations have a fauna of brachiopods, gastropods, cephalopods and trilobites of Arenig age (Williams and others, 1972). The overlying Durine Formation of fine-grained light grey 'dolomites' and limestones contains gastropods and is also thought to contain conodonts of Llanvirn age (although they may in fact come from the upper part of the Croisaphuill Formation).

MOINE THRUST ZONE

This zone of thrusting, associated with folding and low-grade metamorphism, forms a narrow but continuous belt stretching south-south-west from Loch Eriboll on the north coast to Skye (and probably to the Sound of Iona). Its outcrop width varies from a few hundred metres near Ullapool to 19 km in Skye. In the Assynt region north of Ullapool, the thrust zone, there 11 km wide, is particularly well exposed in a broad open antiformal culmination termed the Assynt Window. North of Assynt the thrust zone is 2 to 5 km wide. The thrust zone dips very gently ESE and delimits the Moine. East of it, all pre-Devonian rocks in the Scottish Highlands were folded and metamorphosed during the Caledonian Orogeny.

The thrusts and the 'Zone of Complication'

Within the thrust zone there are several major individual thrust planes. Although some are continuous along the exposed length of the thrust zone (e.g. Moine Thrust), they are more generally restricted to specific areas. The most important dislocation is the Moine Thrust itself which, with the exception of the Sleat Peninsula of Skye, marks the western limit of rocks of the Moine assemblage. The thrust is now commonly marked by a well defined low angle fault with local crushing and brecciation, for example, at Creagan road, Loch Eriboll (Soper and Wilkinson, 1975), and the Sleat Peninsula, Skye. This late fault truncates earlier folds, thrusts and mylonite zones in the thrust zone around Knockan (between Elphin and Ullapool). North of Kinlochewe the Moine Thrust coincides with an earlier zone of thrust movement marked by extensive mylonites at the base of the Moine Nappe.

Below the Moine Thrust *sensu stricto* lies what was termed by the original surveyors (Peach and others, 1907) a 'Zone of Complication' within which are several thrust-bound nappes stacked one above another. The zone comprises a sequence of thrust, overfolded and faulted Cambrian–Ordovician sediments, Torridonian sediments and Lewisian gneiss. The major lower thrusts in the northern part of the zone are preferentially localised in the Fucoid Beds and Lower Cambrian quartzites whereas south of Assynt, where Torridonian rocks are present, shales of the Diabaig Formation have acted as planes of weakness and provided a locus for thrusting. Because each thrust transports overlying rocks to the WNW they move generally older rocks from deeper levels to lie on younger strata; thus inversions of stratigraphical order are common. Overturned and recumbent folds and minor thrusts add to the complications. Later tilting has given the thrust planes a regional, gentle easterly dip (11–15°); in detail, they may be considerably folded, locally discontinuous, and intersect one another.

The original surveyors from the Geological Survey carefully mapped the structures of the Moine Thrust Zone and described and documented this geometry in considerable detail (Peach and others, 1907). Because the Moine Thrust in southern Assynt prominently cuts down to the west across the underlying Ben More Nappe, the thrust sequence was generally interpreted to imply that higher thrusts overlap lower ones, and that the first thrust to develop was the lowest and most westerly structure (generally the Sole Thrust). This was in contradiction to the early experimental work of Cadell (1889), who showed that thrusts developed progressively towards the foreland carrying pre-existing thrust slices 'piggyback'. Work in connection with the search for oil in the foothills of the Rocky Mountains of Canada (by Bally and others, 1966, and, more notably, by Dahlstrom, 1970) has carefully defined the geometry of many thrust structures. This work, which incorporated both seismic interpretation and much exploratory drilling, resulted in the establishement of a series of tenets or 'thrust rules' which particularly apply to a foreland-directed thrust sequence involving bedded units.

It has long been recognised that thrust faults are concave upwards and cut structurally up-section in their direction of transport; in a bedded sequence they typically have a staircase trajectory. In the less competent or weak horizons the thrust forms near horizontal *flats* which are separated by steeper (typically dipping about 25°) *ramps* where the thrust cuts up section in a more competent horizon. As the thrust rocks move up the ramp an antiform is formed in these overlying units. The rocks and structures which overlie a thrust surface are said to be in the hangingwall; conversely, those below lie in the footwall. After initial development of a thrust with a staircase trajectory, further thrust movement is commonly taken up by the generation of a new ramp ahead of, and below, the existing ramp. Continued thrusting movement thus takes place largely along pre-existing flats, but with progressive footwall ramp collapse. When a new ramp forms, a lensoid thrust-bounded mass termed a *horse* is created and this is then incorporated into the hangingwall of the thrust. The development of multiple horses creates an imbricated sequence with individual slices or horses stacked up like tiles on a roof. This structure is termed a *duplex* and is bounded by an upper roof thrust and lower floor thrust. As a duplex is formed, the beds within the horses and the early-formed thrusts are progressively steepened (commonly to near vertical) and an antiformal culmination develops in the units of the hangingwall.

Ramps generally have a strike near to 90° to the thrust transport direction, but may also lie oblique, or even parallel (lateral ramps), to the direction of thrusting. A lateral ramp may pass into a tear fault, such a structure providing a good indication of the direction of transport within the thrust belt. For a fuller description of the geometry of thrust zones, the reader is referred to R. W. H. Butler (1982a).

The application of these rules to the Moine Thrust Zone, even though basement gneisses are involved, seems to be validated by the observed geometry (McClay and Coward, 1981; Elliot and Johnson, 1980; R. W. H. Butler, 1982b; Coward and Kim, 1981). The thrust sequence must thus be reinterpreted with the lower and younger thrusts transporting the older and higher thrusts to the west-north-west in a piggyback fashion. The Sole Thrust is then the latest structure and in many areas the Moine Thrust is the earliest. Many of the fold structures within the thrust zone can be related to underlying ramps, and culminations are the high level manifestation of thick duplexes beneath.

Figure 12 gives examples of several types of structures seen within the Moine Thrust Zone. The scale of the structures is considerably smaller than those described in North America, possibly because of the relatively thinly bedded nature of the Cambro-Ordovician sequence. The sections shown are all examples of *balanced* cross-sections, with those in Figures 12b and c lying in the plane of thrust movement. The term 'balanced' was introduced by Dahlstrom (1969) to describe sections which can be restored to their undeformed state to give a

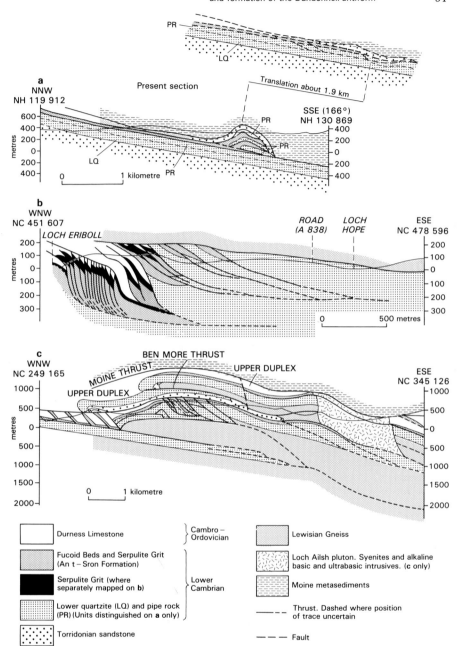

Figure 12 Balanced cross-sections through the Moine Thrust Zone

a Through the Dundonnell Antiform perpendicular to its axis and oblique to the direction of thrusting; the partially restored section above shows the position of the units prior to thrust formation (from Elliot and Johnson, 1980)

b Through the imbricated Cambro-Ordovician sequence below the Arnaboll Thrust, ESE of Loch Eriboll (modified after Coward and Kim, 1981); the section is parallel to the direction of thrusting

c Across the southern part of the Assynt Window, showing the Ben More and Moine Thrusts. Note that the present upper levels of the thrust zone (formerly deeper crustal levels) contain recumbently folded Lewisian gneiss and Torridonian sandstone (modified after Elliot and Johnson, 1980)

coherent stratigraphy and acceptable thrust fault trajectories, with both being compatible with adjoining data. Section balancing enables estimates of the amount of translation to be made. The average dip of the basal thrust can also be reconstructed, based on the introduction and translation of, for example, Lewisian gneiss into the imbricated Cambrian sequence. Coward (1983) estimates the true dip of the Moine Thrust Zone to be less than 3° using this method.

Figure 12a shows a simple stacking sequence near Dundonnell, with the overlying Moine Thrust folded by accretion of underlying horses at a particular locality. It is important to realise tha the Moine Thrust is the earliest structure with thrusts becoming progressively younger downwards. Figure 12b illustrates a classic imbricated Lower Cambrian to Ordovician sequence typical of the Sole Nappe, here seen on the east side of Loch Eriboll. The overlying Arnaboll Thrust has carried Lewisian gneiss over this sequence, with imbrication taking place as the active thrust 'front' migrated westward by ramp collapse. A small klippe (or outlier) of this thrust is seen adjacent to the section line. Figure 12c shows a more complex section in Assynt. Here recumbent folding has occurred in the deeper levels of the Moine Thrust Zone; this interfolded Lewisian gneiss and basal Torridonian sandstone and conglomerate now constitute part of the Ben More Nappe.

In Assynt and locally elsewhere evidence for low-angle extensional faulting is seen. Coward (1982) has described a section of the Glencoul and Sole Nappes within which late-stage WNW downsection movement has occurred in what he termed a 'surge zone'. Coward (1983, fig.7) has also illustrated the well known truncation and downsection movement of the Moine Thrust across underlying imbricated Cambrian–Ordovician rocks near Elphin (South Assynt). He suggested that such movements occurred late in the history of the Moine Thrust Zone and were a manifestation of gravitational spreading, which in turn resulted from uplift of the central part of the Caledonide Orogenic Belt and intrusion of large volumes of granitic magma.

In Cambrian and Torridonian strata of the foreland lying west of the Sole Thrust and strictly outside the Moine Thrust Zone, repetitive reverse faults may pass downwards into large open-to-tight asymmetrical folds verging to the west-north-west.

The basal or Sole Thrust is best seen in the Assynt region; further south in the Coulin Forest area and in Skye the western limit of thrusting is more poorly defined. The Sole Thrust lies within Cambrian quartzites around Loch Eriboll but climbs in Assynt to lie within the Fucoid Beds. South of Assynt the basal thrust is generally within the Diabaig Formation of the Torridonian. The Sole Nappe generally comprises imbricated Cambro-Ordovician units but, as Lewisian gneisses are also present, the basal thrust must lie in structurally lower horizons further east (see Figure 12c).

In northern Assynt the overlying Glencoul Thrust has also cut down into the Lewisian gneiss 'basement' and up to 500 m of internally little-modified gneiss and associated Cambro-Ordovician cover are thrust and imbricated over Cambro-Ordovician and Torridonian units (Frontispiece). Further north, east of Loch Eriboll, the Arnaboll Nappe occupies a similar position. There nappes wedge out along the strike of the thrust zone, with the structurally higher Moine Thrust then lying directly on the imbricated Cambrian of the Sole Nappe. The Glencoul Nappe dies out near Inchnadamph (Bailey, 1934) and the overlying Ben More Nappe (which contains Cambrian, Torridonian and Lewisian rocks) is prominent in southern Assynt.

Further south, the Kinlochewe and Kishorn thrusts translate folded Torridonian and Cambrian units and Lewisian gneiss to the west-north-west. Stratigraphical inversions are particularly notable in these more southern nappes, a prime example occurring around Kyle of Lochalsh where locally metamorphosed and schistose Torridonian sandstones and grits are folded into a large recumbent fold, the Lochalsh Syncline. This structure, which lies in the Kishorn Nappe, closes to the east-south-east and its upper limb is transected by the overlying Moine, Balmacara and Tarskavaig Thrusts.

Locally, small nappes occur above the Arnaboll, Ben More and Kishorn nappes (e.g. Balmacara Nappe), but in general the Moine Thrust lies structurally above. On the Sleat Peninsula of Skye a sequence of greenschist-grade schistose grits and phyllites, with affinities to both Torridonian and Moine rocks, constitute a large part of the Tarskavaig Nappe (Bailey, 1955; Cheeney and Matthews, 1965). This nappe lies on the Tarskavaig Thrust, which overlies the Kishorn Nappe and is in turn truncated by the Moine Thrust.

Within the Moine Thrust Zone north of Kinlochewe thin mylonites (see the following section) are common along the thrusts; particularly good examples are seen along the Glencoul and Arnaboll Thrusts. Considerable internal deformation and bedding-plane shearing also occur in many of the imbricated nappe sequences. In Assynt, Torridonian rocks near the Ben More Thrust are strongly deformed and lineated. Conglomerate pebbles in the basal Torridonian are flattened and stretched, and in some areas they become fractured as the thrust plane is approached. Skolithid pipes in the Lower Cambrian Pipe Rock commonly become distorted and bent over in the direction of thrust movement (McLeish, 1971) and in the mylonites themselves at the Stack of Glencoul they are reduced to white ribbons, near-parallel to the mylonitic foliations (Wilkinson and others, 1975; Coward, 1983). Lewisian gneiss, although locally sheared, fractured and even mylonitised during Caledonian deformation and metamorphism, is not generally penetratively deformed.

In contrast, south of Kinlochewe the Lewisian gneiss and Torridonian units are moderately to strongly mylonitised, and the distinction between Lewisian gneiss in the Moine Thrust Zone and mylonitic Lewisian inliers in the lowermost part of the Moines is unclear. Immediately below the Moine Thrust in Lochalsh there is a thick development of mylonitised rocks within the Balmacara and Sgurr Beag Nappes (Barber, 1965). North of Loch Carron similar rocks occur in the Kishorn Nappe (Johnson, 1960). To both the north and the south, late reactivation of the Moine Thrust causes it to overstep the rocks in the 'Zone of Complication'.

Mylonites

Mylonites were first described from the Loch Eriboll district by Lapworth (1885) who noted that they had formed by thrusting along narrow planar zones. Mylonite is a hard, very fine-grained, commonly laminated and platy rock formed by intense ductile deformation, and resulting in marked grain-size reduction and recrystallisation of the parent rock type. It forms under moderate hydrostatic pressure at depths below about 5 km in the earth's crust in response to locally high initial strain rates, commonly associated with shearing. It should be emphasised that mylonites are dominantly a product of ductile deformation mechanisms and not a result of grinding, although recent work has suggested that brittle failure also may take place during mylonitisation (White and others, 1980). Mylonites are present along the length of the Moine Thrust Zone but show their maximum development in the basal part of the Moine Nappe in the Loch Eriboll area, where they are 600–800 m thick. They are derived dominantly from Moine and Lewisian rocks in the north and from Lewisian and subsidiary Torridonian rocks in the south. The mylonites show a colour banding which in parts is extremely closely spaced, particularly where the parent rock was a banded Lewisian gneiss. The mylonites of the Moine Nappe show evidence of lower greenschist-facies metamorphism and three episodes of small-scale folding subsequent to the formation of the mylonite fabric. They are generally white, quartz-rich or dark, grey-green, chlorite-phengite-rich varieties. The dark type is termed 'oyster-shell' rock because of its field appearance. The mylonites grade gradually upwards into impure Moine psammites of greenschist facies.

In thin sections of mylonite, feldspars are seen to be fractured and fragmented, quartz has recrystallised to aggregates of much smaller grains (commonly with irregular grain boundaries) and biotite has been largely retrograded to chlorite. Pale-green muscovite, presumably with a high iron content (phengite), and epidote-clinozoisite are both commonly developed. Rarely, remnant yellowish biotite is found. Recrystallisation has largely obscured original mylonitic textures.

As the thrust zone is traced southwards into the Lochcarron–Lochalsh area (Johnson, 1960; Barber, 1965) the character of the mylonite changes. South of Kinlochewe the Moine rocks directly above the Moine Thrust show platy, recrystallised fabrics, but are only rarely totally reconstituted into mylonites. Lewisian rocks above the Moine Thrust are interleaved with the Moine sequence and, in part, still retain original structures and fabrics (although these are strongly modified by Caledonian deformation and metamorphism). The great development of mylonites occurs in Lewisian rocks below the Moine Thrust in the 'Zone of Complication' (see the previous section).

Age of the Moine Thrust Zone

It is difficult to date the earliest movement in the Moine Thrust Zone. At the Stack of Glencoul, Lower Cambrian Pipe Rock is strongly mylonitised and directly underlies mylonites derived from Moine and Lewisian rocks. This Pipe Rock mylonite has been interpreted by Christie (1963), and Soper and Wilkinson (1975) as being the same generation as the Moine mylonites, inferring that the main mylonitisation post-dated the deposition of the Cambro-Ordovician sequence. However, Coward (1983) has recently interpreted the highly strained pipes as being a product of ductile extensional strain, possibly a product of the later stages of movement on the Moine Thrust Zone.

There is abundant evidence for shear-dominated deformation in the lower parts of the Moines themselves. Ductile thrusts and slide zones are common and may relate to the mylonites and mylonitic schists which directly overlie the Moine Thrust. The Moine Thrust Zone has acted as the western margin to the Caledonian orogenic zone and has most probably been active over a considerable time period. As each phase of movement is in part superimposed on earlier phases it partly destroys evidence of such movements. The age of the earliest movements may well be linked to the overall orogenic history of the Moines; some of the mylonites may be of Precambrian age.

Work on the Loch Borralan and Loch Ailsh syenites has been summarised by Parsons (1972; 1979); he concluded that the Loch Ailsh body was emplaced prior to the main movements on the Ben More Thrust but the Borralan body was emplaced at the same time as the movements. Van Breemen and others (1979a) have dated the intrusion of the Loch Borralan complex at 430 ± 4 Ma using U-Pb methods on zircons.

The younger age limit of movement on the Moine Thrust Zone can be inferred from the occurrence of a thick lamphrophyre sill emplaced along the Moine Thrust in the central part of the Sleat Peninsula of Skye. The intrusion is commonly broken and converted to clay gouge by late fault movements probably of late-Caledonian or Tertiary age. The lamphrophyre is a member of the suites associated with the Ratagan and Ross of Mull Granites. Beckinsale and Obradovich (1973) obtained K-Ar ages of 423 ± 4 Ma from biotite and 416 ± 4 Ma from amphibole of the Ross of Mull Granite. They also obtained a single K-Ar biotite age of 406 ± 10 Ma from a minette dyke cutting the granite. Beckinsale and Obradovich also suggested that the form of the Ross of Mull Granite intrusion was controlled by a pre-existing thrust structure in the Sound of Iona which they correlated with the Moine Thrust. Thus major thrust movement along the Moine Thrust Zone appears to have terminated before 420 Ma (Mid-Silurian).

Amount of translation across the thrust zone

McClay and Coward (1981) infer from stretching lineations and the general trends of imbricate and tear faults that overall thrust movement across the Moine Thrust Zone is towards 290° (WNW). The occurrence of Moine rocks at Faraid Head near Durness implies that at least 11 km of movement has taken place along the Moine Thrust, and Clough (*in* Peach and others, 1907) and Bailey (1934) both showed that a minimum displacement of 20 km to the west-north-west has occurred along the Glencoul Thrust in Assynt. There is a complex relationship between thrusting in the 'Zone of Complication' and the Alkaline Complex of the Assynt area (p.103). The recent use of balanced-section techniques has shown that minimum estimates of translation may be obtained from the thickness of imbricated sequences in individual duplexes. Thus Butler (1982b) showed that the Coneamheall Duplex, 4 km SW of Loch Eriboll, had a pre-shortening width of 27 km compared with 6 km at present. Elliot and Johnson (1980) revised the values of Clough and other workers in the Loch More area of the Moine Thrust Zone; they calculated the minimum amount of translation that had taken place in the thrust zone beneath the Loch More Klippe as 43 km, and that the minimum slip across the whole Moine Thrust Zone here totalled 77 km. By analogy with other major thrust belts of the world it is likely that total translation across the Moine Thrust Zone was at least 100 km.

OUTER ISLES THRUST ZONE

Approximately parallel to the Moine Thrust Zone but about 85 km to the west lies the Outer Isles Thrust Zone (see Figure 3). This dips moderately ESE (Plate 4). The western margin of the thrust zone extends from Tolsta in northern Lewis to the Isle of Sandray, south of Barra, and it forms the eastern seaboard of North and South Uist and parts of South Harris. It is particularly well exposed in the Park district of Lewis, in South Uist and on the Isles of Eriskay and Barra. The eastern limit of the thrust zone lies beneath the waters of the Minch and in part probably terminates against the Minch Fault. In South Uist granulite-facies metadiorite (Corodale Gneiss) lies above the thrust, and in Barra some pyroxene-bearing acid gneisses also locally lie above the thrust. With these exceptions the thrust does not define a lithological boundary but lies within the heterogeneous Lewisian gneiss complex.

The major thrust plane is marked by a 1–10 m thick zone of pseudotachylite and cataclasite. Pseudotachylite is a black or dark grey, glassy material which develops as a result of frictional heating during 'stick-slip' faulting at moderate depths in the earth's crust (see Sibson, 1975). The glass is generally devitrified, giving an extremely fine-grained rock with relict features of melting (e.g. microlites, intrusive veins, fine-grained margins). Cataclasite is a cohesive, non-foliated, finely comminuted crush rock in which individual fragments are commonly microscopic (less than 1 mm) or even submicroscopic. In many areas this basal fault product is overlain by a thick pseudotachylite-gneiss breccia, notably in South Uist and Eriskay where up to 100 m are seen. Pseudotachylite is particularly abundant in the Outer Isles Thrust Zone and also occurs west of the thrust plane in either localised linear zones (e.g. in North Uist) or as wide diffuse zones in the gneiss (e.g. in Barra). Sparse examples also occur along the western seaboard of the Outer Isles.

The effects of subsequent lower greenschist-facies retrograde metamorphism and associated mylonite development are seen in parts of the thrust zone, particularly in North Uist and Lewis. Mylonite develops in narrow shear zones at moderate crustal depths and requires sufficient fluid to promote mineral reactions, recrystallisation and ductile deformation mechanisms, whereas pseudotachylite and cataclasite are dominantly products of brittle deformation in dry rock and are formed by melting and comminution respectively. The mylonite zones developed either subparallel to the relict gneissic banding, generally dipping moderately SE, or in zones dipping gently to moderately E, discordant to the gneissic banding. The age of the main pseudotachylite formation is thought to be late Laxfordian (Fettes and others, in press; but see Sibson, 1975) but the mylonite formation and related retrograde metamorphism are probably of Caledonian age. The pseudotachylite zones may correlate in age with the NW- to W-trending, subvertical pre-Torridonian crush zones found in Foreland Lewisian gneiss on the mainland of Scotland (e.g. Park, 1961).

GEOPHYSICAL DATA

Recent deep seismic reflection profiling has been carried out in the Pentland Firth extending west from the Orkney Isles to north of the Isle of Lewis (Figure 13b). The traverse was designed to determine the subsurface profile of the Moine and Outer Isles Thrusts (hence its name MOIST), the depth to the Mohorovičić Discontinuity (or Moho: the base of the continental crust) and the nature of any other major reflectors in the crustal section. In the light of spectacular results from similar work in the Appalachians (COCORP), summarised by Ando and others (1983) and Cook and others (1979), Brewer and Smythe (1984) have interpreted the major seismic reflectors from the MOIST traverse and presented crustal models. These models, which trace major tectonic structures through the crust, also take into account seismic reflection data from oil companies working in the

Figure 13   The MOIST deep seismic reflection profile

a Interpretation of the principal seismic reflectors on the MOIST traverse. Dipping reflectors lie in their approximately correct spatial location. To convert two-way time in seconds to approximate depth in kilometres multiply it by three (after Brewer and Smythe, 1984)

b Map showing the elements of the geology of northern Scotland with the location of the deep crustal geophysical traverses

c Geological interpretation of the eastern part of the MOIST deep seismic reflection profile (B–C) also using data from along strike. Note that the depth conversion assumes constant crustal wave velocity (6 km/s) exaggerating the depths of sedimentary basins by a factor of 1.5 to 2 (after Brewer and Smythe, 1984)

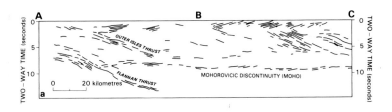

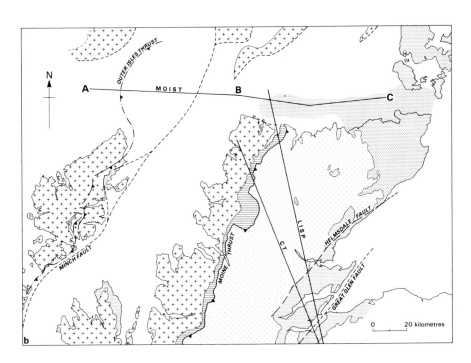

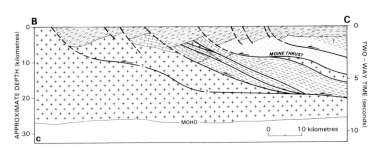

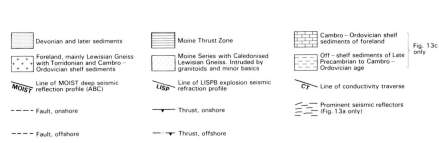

area. They are also constrained by the existing seismic refraction data from the LISPB profile (Bamford and others, 1978) and the results of an electrical conductivity traverse by Hutton and others (1980).

The interpreted MOIST profile is shown on Figure 13a; the preferred geological interpretation of Brewer and Smythe is in Figure 13c. The seismic reflection data show clearly that in its western part the Outer Isles Thrust forms a planar discontinuity dipping about 25° to the east. It has apparently been reactivated as a listric (curved) normal fault in connection with the formation of Mesozoic and possibly Torridonian fault-controlled basins. The overall offset of reflections across the thrust is only 2 to 3 km. About 6 km below the Outer Isles Thrust and subparallel to it, a further strong reflector termed the Flannan Thrust has been recognised. This feature displaces the Moho which, on the MOIST section, is normally constant at a depth of around 26 km. If these reflectors represent tectonic structures of Caledonian age, and there is strong evidence of extensive Caledonian mylonitisation in the Outer Hebrides (Sibson, 1977; Fettes and others, in press), then it appears that the foreland to the orogenic belt did not remain a rigid unfractured block. Thus the 'rules' of thrust development noted earlier in this section may well apply to the complete crustal section, with the basal detachment lying in a low-velocity zone in the upper mantle, and ramps corresponding to the interpreted major thrust features such as the Outer Isles and Flannan thrusts. Displacement along such ramps cannot be large, however, as unrealistic crustal thickening would result.

The eastern part of the MOIST traverse (Figure 13c) contains a sequence of shallow, westerly-dipping reflectors which are interpreted as Devonian and Permo-Triassic red beds by Brewer and Smythe. These beds are affected by a series of easterly-dipping listric normal faults which appear to be sited above a series of shallow, easterly-dipping reflectors (discontinuities) in the underlying Moines. Hence the late normal faulting has apparently utilised the earlier thrust planes. The Moine Thrust itself is identified tentatively as a reflector dipping up to 25° E below which a layered sequence is present. As shown on Figure 13c, Brewer and Smythe interpret these units to be part of an off-shelf sedimentary sequence (?Dalradian) overlain by the Cambro-Ordovician units and overthrust by the Moines.

However, as discussed by Coward (1983), there are problems in interpreting the position of the Moine Thrust within the crust, in particular the distribution of ramps and flats. There is a lack of correlation in dip and outcrop position of the various units between the MOIST profile and the onshore geology of North Sutherland. This has been explained by invoking either a lateral ramp and/or tear fault running approximately east–west immediately offshore.

MODELS FOR MOINE AND OUTER ISLES THRUST ZONES DEVELOPMENT

There has recently been renewed interest about which events fashioned the north-west margin of the Caledonides in Scotland. The concepts of 'piggyback' thrusting and balanced sections, in concert with the new geophysical data, all constrain models of development of the Moine Thrust Zone.

Coward (1983) has noted that the main thrusts appear, overall, to climb stratigraphy westwards with a dip of about 3° over at least 25 km. If estimates of total translation on the thrust zone are near correct, then foreland may underlie almost all of the Northern Highlands. However, the seismic reflection work off the north coast (MOIST) has indicated major thrust features commonly dipping about 25° to the east. The Outer Isles Thrust and the newly recognised Flannan Thrust (which apparently cuts the Moho) both affect the whole crustal section and imply that at least some Caledonian deformation apparently affected a large part of the western Foreland. If such a dip were valid for the Moine Thrust Zone on the mainland then high-grade metamorphic rocks should have been upthrust if translation exceeded 70 km, as seems probable.

Stewart (1982) has suggested that a Torridonian basin about 80 km wide extended between bounding faults near the present positions of the Outer Isles and Moine Thrusts. He envisaged that the eastern fault formed the locus for thrusting during the Caledonian Orogeny (see Chapter 3 and Figure 8). There is no evidence from the Torridonian in the Moine Thrust Zone for any eastward termination of the sequence, merely for planation prior to deposition of the Cambrian. There are also insuperable difficulties in reconciling the geometry of a Moine Thrust which steepens to near vertical 25 to 30 km east of its current outcrop if amounts of translation exceed 70 km. Soper and Barber (1982) used the LISPB deep seismic refraction data (Bamford and others, 1978) and conductivity data (Hutton and others, 1980) to suggest a stepped crustal profile. They modelled major changes in geophysical properties which they correlated with the presence of the Moine Thrust Zone extending down to the Moho with a curved profile dipping about 25° east. They envisaged the 'Zone of Complication' of the Moine Thrust Zone as largely a product of late-stage thrusting with about 30 km of westward translation, earlier movement being taken up on the Moine mylonites and within slide zones in the Moines themselves. Soper and Barber cite other larger-scale examples of deep crustal duplex structures from various orogenic belts and interpret this Caledonian margin similarly. Coward (1983) reviews the evidence from Moine Thrust Zone and related rocks and, like Soper and Barber, favours a two-stage evolution of the Moine Thrust Zone. He proposes that late-stage low-angle extensional movement was responsible for reactivation of the Moine Thrust and for its widespread, locally downcutting, extensional movements. The main compressional thrust profile must extend eastwards at an angle of about 3° for approximately 35 km (cf. Soper and Barber, c.25 km), and possibly up to 70 km, before a steep ramp occurs. The role of the MOIST data in the light of this latter model is discussed in the previous section.

Although during the past decades considerable advances have been made with regard to the geometry and deep-level structure of the Moine Thust Zone, it can be seen that the nature of this orogenic margin still presents considerable problems.

6 Moine Succession

The Moine Succession, which takes its name from the peninsula of a'Mhoine (the Peat Bog) in northern Sutherland, is a group of metasedimentary strata, the oldest of which may have been deposited on the Lewisian basement between 1500 and 1025 Ma ago (Brook and others, 1976) and whose youngest members, on current definition (Johnstone, 1975), pass upwards in the Grampian Highlands into Dalradian strata, whose base is taken to be around 700 Ma. Isotope ages suggest that the succession comprises two groups of rocks. One has been subjected to two late-Proterozoic tectonothermal events (the Grenvillian Orogeny at c.1000 Ma and the Morarian episode at c.750 Ma), and overprinted by the Caledonian Orogeny; the other has only been affected by the latter event. Harris and others (1978) consider that those 'younger' Moines are best referred to the Dalradian Supergroup.

Within the Northern Highlands, Moine rocks are found only east of the Moine Thrust, but in southern Skye a small outcrop of 'Tarskavaig Moines' lies within the thrust zone. They are intermediate in character between the metasediments of the overlying Moine Nappe and the Torridonian rocks of the underlying Kishorn Nappe (Figure 14).

The general equivalence of the Moine and Torridonian successions has been proposed, rejected and, more recently, again considered as a possibility.

LITHOLOGY

The Moine rocks comprise a limited number of lithological types, representing a metamorphosed series of arenaceous and argillaceous sediments containing a very minor proportion of calcareous and dolomitic material; beds of limestone are extremely rare. The present mineral composition and condition of the rocks depends upon their metamorphic grade and the extent to which they have been migmatised.

Psammitic schists and granulites

These vary from quartzose schists to massive or flaggy grey quartz-feldspar 'granulites' with rare quartzites. The granulite is so called because of the granoblastic, equigranular texture of its principal minerals, not because of any association with the granulite facies of metamorphism.

By far the dominant type is the psammitic (sandy) granulite, representing sandstones, locally pebbly, in which the constituent minerals are quartz, feldspar (typically potash feldspar and sodic plagioclase) and a variable, though small, proportion of mica (which can be muscovite or biotite, or both). Garnet is a common, though inconspicuous, constituent, and zoisite or epidote, apatite, zircon, sphene and iron ore occur as accessories, some being abundant in certain groups. In the typical granulite the micas are dispersed and, although they may show a pronounced orientation, the rock as a whole is not schistose; it is commonly quite massive. In certain areas thin pelitic bands (probably representing original bedding planes) are sufficiently schistose and closely spaced to impart a pronounced flaggy aspect to the rock, which tends to split along these micaceous surfaces. In other localities flags of similar appearance result from the fissility imparted by more or less micaceous laminae developed along cleavage surfaces, which are usually axial planar to the dominant folds of the area.

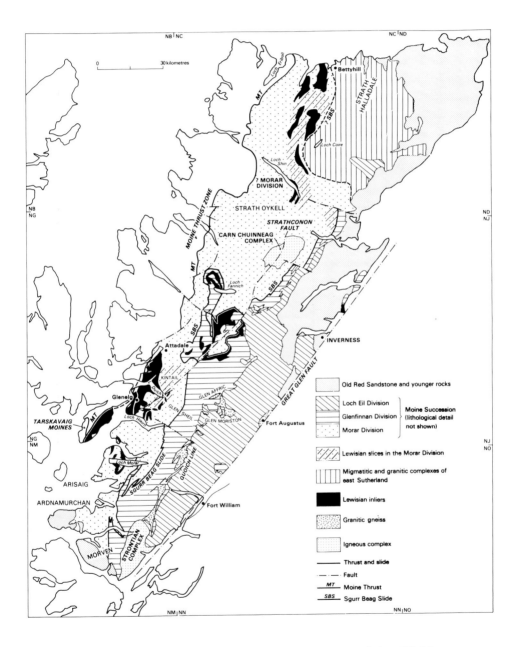

Figure 14 Distribution of Moine rocks in the Northern Highlands (modified from Johnstone, 1975)

Cross-bedding can be seen from place to place and is well displayed in areas which have escaped intense tectonic deformation, especially in the western part of the district around Morar and Arisaig (Richey and Kennedy, 1939). In that area too, numerous pebbly bands can be found with grains up to 8 mm across and, rarely, even up to 25 mm. Elsewhere in the outcrop pebbly bands are uncommon.

Undoubted conglomerates are rare. They have been recorded as a basal conglomerate of Moine overlying the Lewisian basement at Attadale on the south shore of Loch Carron (see p.28); in a uniquely preserved area of low deformation around the Carn Chuinneag pluton in Ross-shire (p.92); and in the north of Sutherland, west of the Kyle of Tongue at Strathan (Mendum, 1976). In the last area there are many excellent exposures; the thick lenses of conglomerate have quartzite pebbles (originally possibly as much as 20 cm across) and rarer granite pebbles. The rock here has been so strongly deformed that individual pebbles have been reduced to thin discs, and the original nature of the beds is barely recognisable. In several exposures it now resembles a *lit-par-lit* gneiss.

In certain areas, and especially in some groups thought to represent stratigraphical units, heavy mineral bands are developed. These are up to 15 mm thick, and some of the minerals (including zircon, garnet, sphene, epidote, allanite, ilmenite and magnetite) retain their original detrital form. A conspicuous development of these bands is found in the Lower Morar Psammite (see p.68 and Table 3). Biotite-sphene schists (which may also represent metamorphosed placer concentrations) have been recorded, especially from the Upper Morar Psammite of Ardnamurchan (Butler, 1962).

Throughout most of the Northern Highlands the Moine psammites show little megascopic variation resulting from changes in regional metamorphism. Recrystallisation of a quartzofeldspathic sandstone under grades of metamorphism up to amphibolite facies results in a very similar quartzofeldspathic metasandstone (psammitic granulite). It seems unlikely that the commonly-occurring granulite of the Moines is other than a metamorphosed sandstone, even though recrystallisation of the larger pebbles in the pebbly bands of Morar is progressive for a few kilometres eastward from the assumed position of the Moine Thrust, and the resultant granulation of these pebbles under strain and rising temperature when traced eastwards into the area of more intense deformation and metamorphism can produce a rock of even-grained 'sandy' appearance. Slightly deformed cross-bedding and the sparse occurrence of almost non-deformed pebbles well within the Moine outcrop suggest that the medium-grained, even texture of the rocks reflects that of the original sediment.

The remarkable deformation of the Sutherland conglomerates referred to above does, however, indicate that care must be exercised in the interpretation of any section. It cannot be assumed, either, that the apparent bedding of the Moine psammites is everywhere an original feature. The flagginess can result from the reduplication of bedding in isoclinal folds, accentuated (as already mentioned) by the development of a new schistosity parallel to the axial planes of the folds. Langford (1980) attributes much planar banding in the Moines east of Attadale to extreme flattening of the limbs of folds.

The psammitic granulite normally remains unaffected by the regional migmatisation found in adjacent pelitic rocks (see below). Certain bands seem, however, to be liable to develop augen and lits (elongate pods) of quartz and microline. Such susceptible bands are commonly feldspathic and often micaceous, sometimes, but not always, approaching semipelite in composition. These *lit-par-lit* or augen psammites are referred to as psammitic gneiss (Clough, 1910). The quartzofeldspathic lits rarely exceed 10 cm in width and usually have a conspicuous biotite selvedge (see Chapter 8).

Semipelitic schists and granulites

With increase in mica content, both muscovite and biotite, the psammitic granulites pass into semipelites. While the increase in mica content is usually taken to reflect the higher clay-to-sand ratio of the original sediment, it could be a function of the composition of the sand grains making up the rock and their alteration by diagenetic and metamorphic processes. Semipelites are commonly fissile with a pronounced foliation of more or less micaceous layers which show a well

Table 3   Summary of lithological characters of Moine formations of western Inverness-shire

---

Loch Eil Division

| Loch Eil Psammite | Variably quartzose psammitic granulite (locally a micaceous 'salt and pepper' type) with very subordinate bands of pelitic and semipelitic schist. Calc-silicate ribs and lenticles present throughout, and locally abundant |

Glenfinnan Division

| Glenfinnan Striped Schist | Banded siliceous granulite (locally quartzite) and pelitic gneiss. Pods or lenses of amphibolite and calc-silicate granulite |
| Lochailort Pelite | Pelitic gneiss, with subordinate psammitic or semipelitic stripes. Amphibolite and calc-silicate lenses are usually present |

Sgurr Beag Slide with Lewisian slices

Morar Division

Upper Morar Psammite	Dominantly psammitic granulite, pebbly in west, with common semipelitic bands. Calc-silicate ribs present throughout
Morar (Striped and Pelitic) Schist	A dominantly pelitic assemblage locally divided into: a rhythmically striped and banded pelite, semipelitic schists and micaceous psammitic rocks with abundant calc-silicate ribs b pelitic schist with some subordinate semipelitic stripes c laminated grey, semipelitic and micaceous granulites, locally with thin siliceous and calc-silicate ribs
Lower Morar Psammite	Micaceous and siliceous psammitic granulite, pebbly in west; subordinate semipelitic rocks developed locally and more thickly towards the top. Calc-silicate ribs rare except towards the top; heavy-mineral bands present, but most common near the base
Basal Pelite	Dominantly pelitic and semipelitic schists, thinly banded with psammite. Apparently typified by abundant contorted veins. May be tectonically mixed 'slide' schist

~~~~~~~~~~~~~~~ Unconformity ~~~~~~~~~~~~~~~

Lewisian gneiss

developed schistosity. More massive varieties with uniformly distributed mica and a less pronounced schistosity are also found. Where they have both muscovite and biotite those rocks commonly have a 'pepper and salt' speckled appearance. Semipelitic rocks show all gradations between psammites on the one hand and pelitic rocks on the other and, because of this, the extent to which they have been separated from these types during mapping depends somewhat on subjective interpretation. Like the psammites (above) and the pelites (described below) the rocks become *lit-par-lit* gneisses on migmatisation.

Pelitic schists

These are metamorphosed shales or siltstones. Felts of muscovite and deep brown biotite form the bulk of the rocks, which appear black or silvery depending on the predominant mica determining the foliation surface. Feldspar and quartz are the other main constituents. Over much of the Moine outcrop in the Northern Highlands, however, these schists lie within the area of migmatisation and are represented by quartz-feldspar(oligoclase)-biotite gneisses which show a pronounced foliation on account of the segregation of quartzofeldspathic bands and lenticles. In the areas of more intense migmatisation it can be impossible to decide whether the host-rock was originally a pelite or semipelite (Plate 17).

The pelitic rocks contain additional minerals according to the grade of metamorphism. Garnet-bearing varieties are almost universal, as by far the greater part of the Northern Highlands Moine outcrop lies above the greenschist-facies of metamorphism (Chapter 7). Sillimanite-, kyanite- and staurolite-bearing schists are found, the latter two being sparse (a function of whole-rock composition rather than metamorphic grade). The former presence of sillimanite is commonly indicated by knots of muscovite nucleated on retrogressive shimmer aggregate. Within the area of migmatisation, 'books' of well formed muscovite up to 2 cm across give a spangly aspect to the rock.

Striped and banded schists

These comprise groups of rocks made up of psammite (commonly quartzitic) and pelite in alternate bands and laminae too thin to be individually mapped, the bands being 3 cm or so to several metres in thickness (Plate 13). These schists represent alternating sand and mud deposition and are especially common in the rocks of the Glenfinnan Division. They, too, give rise to *lit-par-lit* gneisses when migmatised.

Calc-silicate rocks and marbles

In all the above rock types, but especially in the psammites and semipelites, there are some thin discontinuous ribs and lenticles of calc-silicate minerals (plagioclase feldspar, epidote, zoisite, hornblende, pyroxene, garnet). The actual minerals present at a particular locality depend partly on the chemical composition of the rock (notably the CaO/Al_2O_3 ratio) and partly on the metamorphic grade. These ribs, which may be up to 30 cm thick, are quantitatively insignificant but are characteristic of certain stratigraphic formations (see Table 3 and Figure 15) and their mineralogy forms the basis of metamorphic zonation in the psammitic rocks (see Chapter 7).

They are white or dark grey compact rocks, speckled with red garnet and usual-

Plate 13 Striped and banded schist of the Glenfinnan Division. 0.5 km upstream from Glenfinnan Viaduct. Bands of psammitic granulite alternate with pelitic/semipelitic schist. There is some migmatisation of the more pelitic bands   (G. S. Johnstone)

Plate 14 Moine topography of the Morar Division. The knolly terrain is typical of the southern part of the Morar Division (Upper Psammite) of the Moine. The peak on the right (out of cloud), An Stac, lies in the Glenfinnan Division. The view is to the north-east from Loch Ailort   (G. S. Johnstone)

ly with a visible green calc-silicate mineral. Banding occurs frequently as a result of the parallel disposition of garnetiferous, hornblendic and biotitic layers; all the minerals are granoblastic except hornblende, which tends to assume a poikiloblastic habit. In some of the semipelitic schists the ribs form part of a rhythmic unit comprising semipelite → psammite → calc-silicate rib → psammite → semipelite. The calc-silicates in most of these rhythmic units probably represent original marly bands; others, however, particularly the scattered and discontinuous occurrences, probably represent calcareous concretions in the original sediments. Epidotic bands and epidosites (which carry pyroxene or amphibole) have been recorded among the pelitic schists but are not common.

Marbles which apparently form integral parts of the Moine succession are extremely rare. At Rebeg and Blairnahenachrie (10 km and 6 km WSW of Inverness) crystalline limestones are associated with hornblende schists; they vary from pure-white or pink coarsely crystalline marbles to calc-silicate rocks. The rocks of these areas have riebeckite, a soda-rich amphibole, associated with them. Marbles and calc-silicate rocks are found on the east side of the Glendessary Complex (Figure 22), well within the Moine outcrop. In Ardgour rather similar rocks lie close to the Glen Scaddle Complex (Figure 19). In this area, however, the adjacent rocks include mica schists and black schists which resemble Dalradian strata of the Appin Group, and abut on the Great Glen Fault. The true stratigraphic affinities of these marbles are thus uncertain and will be further discussed on p. 72.

STRATIGRAPHY

Elucidation of the stratigraphy of the Moine over most of its outcrop is a matter of considerable difficulty, due to lack of good marker bands or distinctive sedimentary criteria, tectonic thinning, and change in aspect of the rock as the result of various degrees of metamorphism and migmatisation. Nevertheless a grouping of strata into the Morar Division, the Glenfinnan Division and Loch Eil Division (proposed by Johnstone and others, 1969) has proved useful (Table 3 and Figure 15). The divisions are based on regional associations of rocks of similar lithological type and structural aspect. The extent to which they represent a stratigraphical sequence is not proven and is the subject of current research. The tripartite grouping based on the West Highlands holds good over much of the Northern Highlands. North-west of a line joining Strath Carron and the Dornoch Firth, however, the incoming of numerous slices or infolds of Lewisian rocks, and the presence of migmatite and granitic complexes which obscure the original nature of the strata, renders the recognition of the Glenfinnan and Loch Eil divisions problematical.

Morar Division

A succession was worked out in the type area of Morar by Richey and Kennedy (1939) for the rocks which now form this division, and this forms the basis (with modifications) of the present stratigraphy of the division throughout the whole area. The three Formations are the Lower Morar Psammite, the Morar Schist (itself divided into three in the type area) and the Upper Morar Psammite. The lithological characteristics of these formations (and of those making up the other divisions in the the south-west part of the Northern Highlands) are given in Table 3. Alternative names used by previous workers are given in Figure 15.

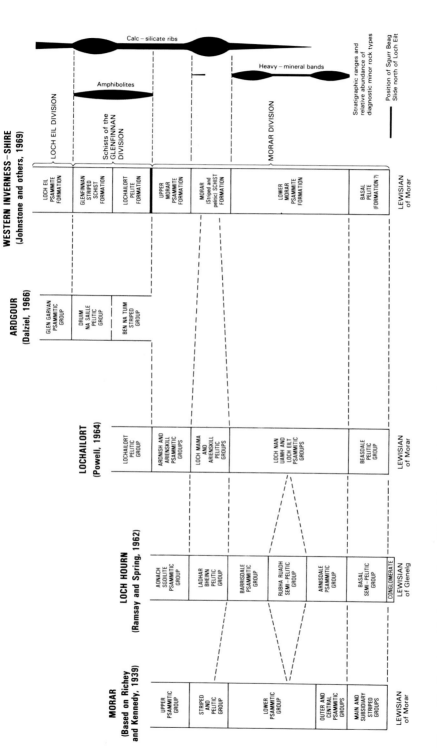

Figure 15 Stratigraphical successions of the Moine rocks in western Inverness-shire (after Johnstone and others, 1969)

In addition to these three formations, a Basal Pelite is usually found below the Lower Morar Psammite. The true status of this 'formation' is not yet certain. It is probably a stratigraphical unit but its variable composition suggests that it may be in part a tectonic *mélange* of basal Moine strata and slices of underlying Lewisian basement. It is commonly characterised by the presence of numerous thin deformed quartz veins.

The succession can be followed on either side of the Morar Anticline (Figure 16). The centre of this structure is a tectonic window into a more complex structural level with   which the Lower Morar Psammite can be seen to overlie infolded or thrust Lewisian strata (Kennedy, 1955; Poole, 1966). The Lower Morar Psammite between Attadale and the Coire nan Gall Lewisian inlier (p.28) comprises a pale (lower) and dark (upper) division made out with difficulty in a zone of multiple sliding. These divisions probably respectively represent the Arnisdale psammite and Rubha Ruadh semipelite of the Loch Hourn area (Figure 15), but north of Kintail the sequence of the Morar Division becomes less clear. This is in part because of a probable facies change of the upper part of the Lower Morar Psammite to a more mixed psammitic–semipelitic assemblage and, in part, due to the cut-out of the higher groups of the Division by a major slide or slide zone—the Sgurr Beag Slide—a feature which is taken as the boundary between the Glenfinnan and Morar divisions (Table 3).

Between Kintail and Strath Oykell, however, the current state of knowledge suggests that the Moine rocks attributed to the Morar Division are essentially Lower Morar Psammite, with attenuated representatives of the higher groups around the north side of the Fannich inlier of Lewisian. It is unlikely, however, that the Morar strata in this area form a simple succession, because projecting into them from the north there is a complex series of thrust Lewisian slices traceable from the north coast down to, and past, the south end of Loch Shin. Langford (1980) considers that, east of Attadale, the apparently uniform sedimentary sequence is strongly folded, with laminar or platy zones representing what may be the continuation of the slides or sheared infolds, which are responsible for the interbanding of Lewisian rocks in the Kintail area. If this is so, then the 'zone of Lewisian slices' (see below, and Figure 14) of the north could be structurally equivalent to the tectonic interbanding in Kintail.

North of Loch Shin no subdivision of the Moine rocks is possible with the present state of knowledge. West of a line from the Kyle of Tongue to Lairg, the rocks are mainly psammites, which in places are pebbly and feldspathic; they resemble much of the Lower Morar Psammite to the south, but Soper and Barber (1982) consider that some could be 'young' Moines, equivalent in age to the Grampian Group of the Dalradian. The conglomerate of Strathan has already been referred to. East of the Tongue–Lairg line, however, the country appears to be formed of interleaved slices of Moine and Lewisian basement (Mendum, 1979) and includes rock types unknown in the south. Of these, the gneisses of Strathy appear to be of higher metamorphic grade than any recorded elsewhere in the Moines (Harrison and Moorhouse, 1976) but are unlike Lewisian gneiss.

Glenfinnan Division

In contrast to the massive units which make up the Formations of the Morar Division, the Glenfinnan Division typically comprises an assemblage of pelitic schists and striped and banded rocks. Thick psammites are found from place to place but do not form identifiable 'Formations'.

Indeed no clear stratigraphic units can be identified in the Glenfinnan Division,

Plate 15 The rugged terrain typical of the Glenfinnan Division of the Moine gives way at the extreme right of the picture to smooth-weathering slopes underlain by the intrusive syenitic rocks of the Glendessary Complex. The horizontal line above the river is a 'Parallel Road' of an ephemeral glacial lake. Strathan area, Glendessary (G. S. Johnstone)

although in the Glenfinnan – Loch Ailort area itself two distinct rock formations are the Lochailort Pelite (Powell, 1964), composed dominantly of mica schist and the Glenfinnan Schist, the typical striped and banded rocks of the Division as a whole (for other names used in other areas see Figure 15). It is a matter of great difficulty to decide whether the broader pelite bands of the Division are facies variants of the Glenfinnan Schist, or whether they are infolds of, for example, the Lochailort Pelite.

Between Glen Moriston and Glen Affric the Division contains major psammitic units, while around the Glendessary Complex at the head of Loch Arkaig other thick siliceous psammites are present (and marbles are found within the complex itself). The stratigraphical status of these psammites depends on the structural interpretation of the area, as this is not clear everywhere. The allocation of the psammites is similarly uncertain; they could even be attributed to the Loch Eil Psammite of the adjacent division (see below). It is this kind of uncertainty which has given rise to the suspicion that the 'Divisions' of the Moines may be as much structural zones as a stratigraphical sequence (Johnstone and others, 1969; Roberts and Harris, 1983).

The Glenfinnan Division is bounded in the west by the Sgurr Beag Slide (Figure 14). South of Loch Hourn the slide separates pelitic or striped rocks typical of the Glenfinnan association from Morar Division rocks (Tanner and others, 1970) but, in central Ross-shire, broad outcrops of Lewisian strata are interfolded or interleaved with psammitic Moine rocks, and lie between the Divisions in places. These Lewisian – Moine complexes are taken to lie either above the Sgurr Beag Slide or within a zone of slides which separates the Divisions. Whatever the explanation, it seems that the pelites and striped rocks of the Glenfinnan association lie either in direct stratigraphic contact with Lewisian basement or are only separated from it by a relatively minor basal psammitic group. Where there are no large outcrops of Lewisian along the Sgurr Beag Slide zone this psammite persists as a typically gneissic rock whose gneissosity may be the result of the metamorphic effects associated with sliding. It is locally referred to as the Reidh Psammite, although its continuity along the slide as a single formation is questionable. (Similar gneissic psammites accompany the thrust slices of Lewisian rock within the Morar Division of Kintail.)

The rocks of the Glenfinnan Division are commonly highly deformed (Plate 16). In the striped lithology this deformation has, in places, resulted in the break-up of the psammitic bands in a mobile pelitic matrix. Curvilinear fold axes (which show no evidence of having been formed by repeated folding) are common, and highly elongate basin-and-dome structures are characteristic (p. 78). Much of the Division lies within the area of regional migmatite complexes in which *lit-par-lit* banded gneisses are developed (p. 88). Calc-silicate lenses are common and the rocks of the Division locally have numerous pods of coarse garnetiferous hornblende schist. Their occurrence helps to distinguish the Glenfinnan pelites from those of the Morar Division where, in the type area, such features are not seen. Winchester (1976) however, reports that hornblende schists do occur with increasing frequency in rocks of the Morar Division northwards towards Sutherland; he notes that these are geochemically different from the ones found in the Glenfinnan Division of the area around the Fannich Forest.

Northwards from Glen Affric the Glenfinnan Division is, as already described, separated from Morar-type rocks by large and small inliers of Lewisian gneiss, including the major inliers of Monar, Scardroy and Fannich (see p. 28). It contains fairly thick psammite units, in places strongly cross-bedded which, for want of contrary evidence, are taken to be variants of the Glenfinnan stratigraphical succession. Glenfinnan Division rocks with marginal Lewisian slivers along a pos-

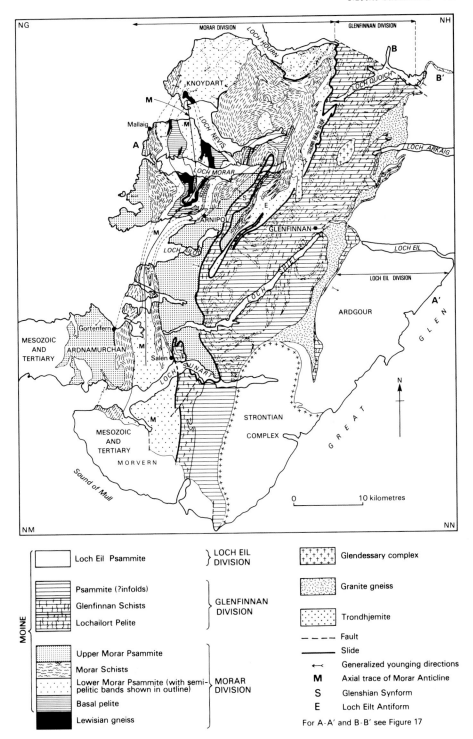

Figure 16 Geological sketch map of the Morar, Glenfinnan and Loch Eil areas (after Johnstone and others, 1969)

sible extension of the Sgurr Beag Slide have been mapped just north of the Dornoch Firth. Further north their identity is lost in the migmatite complexes of Strath Halladale and Loch Coire (p. 90).

Loch Eil Division

Although local subdivision is possible (e.g. Strachan, 1982), the rocks of this division are usually referred to a single formation, the Loch Eil Psammite. This is a quartzofeldspathic granulite which can vary with increased biotite content to a 'pepper-and-salt' type and also, by diminished feldspar, to a quartzite. It is notably quartzitic along its junction with the Glenfinnan rocks south of Loch Eil. Some zones are characterised by thin pelitic bands.

The Loch Eil Psammite strongly resembles parts of the Upper Morar Psammite, both in its general aspect and in its content of calc-silicate lenses. Cross-bedding is present from place to place, but is much less common than in the Morar rocks; its relative scarcity could be attributed to obliteration due to the higher degree of deformation suffered by the Loch Eil rocks, which are commonly flaggy.

It has been pointed out that the grouping of the Moines into divisions is not entirely on a stratigraphical basis; however the Loch Eil Psammite, on the evidence of well preserved cross-bedding, certainly appears to be younger than the adjacent Glenfinnan Division pelites. Roberts and Harris (1983) state that there is a stratigraphical passage between the two at Loch Quoich and, in the Glen Cannich area, BGS surveyors hold that there is no sharp separation of the rocks of the two divisions. In Ardgour, Stoker (1983) also suggests a stratigraphical passage between rocks of Glenfinnan and 'Loch Eil' types through an intermediate passage zone with mappable lithological subdivisions. Near Achnacarry, at the east end of Loch Arkaig, an area of striped schists has been tentatively assigned to an upfold of Glenfinnan rocks.

Rocks of uncertain affinity

The marbles of Blairnahenachrie, Rebeg, Glendessary and Ardgour have already been referred to (p.66); in the Ardgour area, they are associated with black schists and other pelites of Dalradian aspect. A similar assemblage uncharacteristic of the Moine rocks is found in the Glen Urquhart area, near Drumnadrochit (Rock, 1985). Other limestones are found at Kirkton (5 km W of Inverness) and South Clunes (12 km WSW of Inverness). The possibility that these rocks (with the quartzite of Scaraben) are of Dalradian or other non-Moine affinity is under current examination (Rock, in press).

The Tarskavaig Moines

Although by definition the Moine rocks are found 'east or south-east of the Caledonian Front Thrust belt' (Johnstone, 1975), within the thrust belt itself, between the Kishorn Thrust and the Moine Thrust in the Sleat peninsula of Skye, a minor thrust-bounded nappe—the Tarskavaig Nappe—contains strata intermediate in character between the little-altered Torridonian rocks of the Kishorn Nappe and the overlying Moines above the Moine Thrust (Clough, 1910; Bailey, 1955; Cheeney and Matthews, 1965). Various correlations have been made between these Tarskavaig Moines and the Torridonian and Moine rocks, but bed-for-bed matching in nappes of uncertain displacement must always be speculative.

These rocks reach the garnet grade of metamorphism and comprise three 'groups' (Cheeney and Matthews, 1965), of which the upper and lower are mainly psammites and the middle group mixed psammitic, semipelitic and pelitic rocks. Pebbly beds are common and the rocks show varying degrees of granulation and deformation. Although less deformed that the immediately adjacent Moines above the Moine Thrust, they seem to have much in common with the pebbly psammites of Mull, west Ardnamurchan and west Morar. Cheeney and Matthews note, however, that they may never have been affected by the 'very early' folds of the Mainland. The possibility that they represent 'Young Moines' equivalent to the Grampian Group (Dalradian) of Harris and others (1978) must thus be considered.

7   Structure and metamorphism within the Northern Highlands Caledonides

STRUCTURE

Most of the Moine rocks of the Northern Highlands had apparently already been deformed and metamorphosed by 740 Ma, when a suite of concordant pegmatites was emplaced (van Breemen and others, 1974). The pegmatites were evidently formed during a period of migmatisation which produced *lit-par-lit* gneisses from the more schistose rocks (see Chapter 8). This period was part of a tectonothermal event to which the name Morarian (Lambert, 1969) has been applied. The host rocks of these migmatites, however, may be schists formed during an even earlier episode at about 1100 Ma (Brook and others, 1976) during the period to which the name 'Grenville Orogeny' has been given in North America. Much research in recent years has gone into the nature and extent of these pre-Caledonian episodes of the Northern Highlands and there is still some doubt as to whether two such distinct events did in fact take place.

The Morarian pegmatites were themselves folded, and in places foliated, by later phases of deformation generally agreed to be Caledonian in age (comparable folds affect the 560 Ma old Carn Chuinneag intrusion, p. 94) and the initial pre-Caledonian metamorphic pattern has been overprinted by Caledonian metamorphism.

The pre-Caledonian structural and metamorphic features seem to be lacking from the Moine rocks of the far north-western part of the area (Soper and Wilkinson, 1975). It has been a matter for conjecture whether this is due either to the presence of a pre-Caledonian tectonic front trending obliquely across the Northern Highlands, to the north-west of which only Caledonian effects are seen, or to the rocks of the north-western area being 'young' Moines deposited after the Morarian Orogeny, and thus equivalent to the Lower Dalradian (Grampian Group) south of the Great Glen, which was laid down on a pre-Caledonian basement of 'old' Moines. In either case, as no sharp change is readily apparent on the ground, the junction has been concealed or modified by complex tectonism. Recent research seems to indicate that pre-Caledonian structures are present throughout the north-western area.

Despite intensive study of local fold histories and structural styles within the Caledonides of the Northern Highlands, no unified picture of the overall tectonics has emerged. Fold sequences from different areas are numbered differently and have not been satisfactorily correlated; some workers recognise three or four phases of folding, others as many as six. Broadly speaking, however, the fold phases can be related to the sequence given in Table 4. This is taken from Mendum (1979), to whose paper reference should be made for more detailed descriptions and further references.

In the sequence indicated in Table 4, D_2 is considered to be the first Caledonian phase, in agreement with the sequence affecting Carn Chuinneag and the Morarian pegmatites of Lochaber. However, in Knoydart this appears to be the D_3 of Powell (1974), while in Lochaber Powell and others (1981) also recognise two phases of pre-Caledonian deformation. D_2 of the table is a 'complex and multiple phase' wherein D_2 slide zones can be folded by tight folds similar to D_2

Table 4   Structural sequence in the Moine

	Deposition and formation of the sedimentary structures, local soft sediment folding and boudinage. Minor cleavage formation
D_1	Large- to small-scale tight folds. Associated strong axial-planar fabric. Nappe structures in Glenelg-Knoydart area showing E vergence NNE-trending axes. Possible local thrusting. Deformation apparently limited in extent
D_2	Ubiquitous thrusting (sliding) to W or WNW. Associated close-to-isoclinal, commonly reclined, large- to small-scale folds. Axes generally plunge gently E to S. Widely developed axial-planar schistosity, dipping moderately to gently E to SE. Mylonite formation in Moine Thrust Zone
D_3	Widespread open to tight folds on all scales, best developed in Glenfinnan Division rocks. Axial planes generally trend N, but with marked variation of axial plunge. In pelites, rare axial plane cleavage; more generally, coaxial crenulations. Minor sliding
D_4	Large-scale open folds, in parts monoclinal. Crenulations with locally developed cleavage; commonly in conjugate sets. Variable axial planes. In the Moine Thrust Zone box and kink folds developed. Major brittle movements in lower part of the Moine Thrust Zone involving foreland units

structures elsewhere as part of a continuous process; almost collinear fabrics can be superimposed (Johnstone *in* van Breeman and others, 1974).

D_1 is everywhere pre-Caledonian. During this episode Lewisian and Moine rocks were repeatedly interleaved in what can be shown in some cases (by symmetrical disposition of strata) to be isoclinal folds. In Glenelg and Morar-Knoydart these apparently face towards the east, contrary to the later Caledonian overfolding and thrusting, which is directed to the W or WNW. However, not every Lewisian inlier lies in the core of a D_1 fold and several, whatever their earlier history, are in cores of D_2 folds and thrust slices (Figure 17).

It has already been pointed out (p. 65) that the three Moine divisions established by Johnstone and others (1969) do not necessarily represent an upward stratigraphical succession, and that their mutual contacts are tectonically modified. Piasecki and van Breeman (1979a) and Piasecki and Wright (1981) interpret the radiometric ages and structural sequence of the south-western part of the Highlands to indicate that the Morar and Loch Eil divisions never underwent the Grenvillian metamorphism; however, they overlie a basement of Glenfinnan Division rocks which was affected by the Grenvillian episode. The interpretation of the Morar Division dates is somewhat at variance with the findings of Brook and others (1977) and Brewer and others (1979) but the inference concerning the Loch Eil Division is supported by the geochemical studies of Winchester and others (1981). If this basement/cover hypothesis were correct it would greatly extend the tectonic history of the rocks of part of the area. However, others hold that the Loch Eil Division/Glenfinnan Division boundary can be seen in places to be one of stratigraphical passage (BGS studies in Glen Cannich; Roberts and Harris, 1983). Roberts and Harris consider that, while both units have a common structural history, the more intensive deformation of the Glenfinnan Division is due to an early Palaeozoic crustal reworking which dies out eastwards in the Loch Eil Division.

Morar Division

The Morar Division is limited on the west by the Moine Thrust (Chapter 6) and on the east, as far as delineated at present (Figures 14,16) by the Sgurr Beag Slide or Slide Zone (see below). It forms a belt characterised by the presence of infolded or inthrust slices of Lewisian basement, which are best developed in the southernmost and northernmost parts of the outcrop.

In the south, the rocks are clearly folded by Caledonian events; a normal stratigraphic succession, based on abundant cross-bedding evidence, is found on the limbs of a large, open, late antiform (the Morar Anticline of Richey and Kennedy, 1939) between the Sound of Mull and Knoydart (Figure 16, 17). The rocks on the limbs of this simple structure show evidence of pre-antiform deformation and, between Loch Ailort and Loch Nevis, a culmination discloses a complex fold pattern at deeper levels. Within its core Lewisian rocks lie infolded (and possibly inthrust) in the Moines, with the folds having an easterly-facing aspect; this interleaving may be of pre-Caledonian age. The Lewisian is considered to be parautochthonous (see Chapter 2), representing infolds of basement, but that basement itself has probably been transported far on the underlying Moine Thrust. Further north, tight infolding of Lewisian and Morar Division rocks can be seen in the Glenelg–Attadale inlier (Chapter 2, Figures 3, 14) especially in the Glenelg–Arnisdale section.

Eastwards from the Morar Anticline, Moine rocks are isoclinally folded in early (or pre-) Caledonian structures, and segmented by early Caledonian slides, which themselves become more tightly folded as the limiting Sgurr Beag Slide is approached. The semi-diagrammatic section shown in Figure 17 represents structural interpretation of the area by Powell (1974). Powell has also produced 'three-dimensional' perspective drawings of the highly complex folding.

Eastwards from Glenelg–Attadale, numerous thin strips of Lewisian rocks (in some places only a few centimetres thick) appear as thrust inliers (possibly of F_2 age) usually accompanied by migmatisation of the adjacent (overlying) psammite, possibly a result of metasomatism or partial melting related to the thrusting (Figure 14). Platy zones and migmatisation in the enclosing psammites can be traced beyond the limits of the Lewisian outcrop. Larger areas of interleaved Moine and Lewisian rocks in the Coire nan Gall and Saddle inliers (Simony, 1973) may themselves be folded windows or 'klippen' of thrust sheets of deep-level structures of Morar type (Figures 3, 14).

Northwards from Kintail the Morar Division is mainly represented by what is taken to be the continuation of the Lower Morar Psammite, within which Lewisian strips occur only near the Moine Thrust. The succession appears little deformed, but between Attadale and Beinn Dronaig Langford (1980) has recognised zones of platy rock which probably represent the axial regions of the tight D_2 folds and slides. Near the south end of Loch Shin Peacock (1975) has also recorded thin Lewisian slivers and platy rocks which probably represent slides; they are possibly analogues to those found in the Kintail area. They lie in approximately the same position relative to the Sgurr Beag Slide (see below) as do the must larger Lewisian outcrops abutting the north coast of Scotland (Borgie, Tongue, ?Strathy). Mendum (1979) and Moorhouse and Moorhouse (1976) consider these to be slices of Lewisian basement emplaced in Moine rocks during F_1 folding and sliding. The slices were themselves folded and slid or thrust during the later F_2 phase; the tectonic history is therefore analogous to that of the Morar and Kintail areas.

The Lewisian and Moine rocks of the north coast (and, by inference, of the whole Northern Highlands area west of the Sgurr Beag Slide) may represent a zone of large-scale imbrication made up of relatively steeply inclined crustal segments. The crustal segments may, however, be far-travelled units overlying low-angle thrusts or listric surfaces. This matter is considered further in Chapter 5, which deals with the Moine Thrust Zone.

Sgurr Beag Slide

Independent evidence for this major structural break in the Northern Highlands Moines (Figures 3, 14) was obtained in the early 1960s by the Geological Survey in the Barrisdale area of Knoydart (GSGB Summaries of Progress, 1962–1964), by Tanner (1965) in the Kinloch Hourn area and by Simony (1963) in Glen Shiel. Its course and significance as a major feature was discussed by Tanner and others (1970), and by Tanner (1971).

As far south as Morvern (and probably Mull) (Figures 14, 16), recent studies by Rathbone and Harris (1979), Baird (1982), and Powell and others (1981), have shown that the Slide is a zone of high strain, separating rocks of the Morar and Glenfinnan Divisions. Traced northwards from Morvern, the slide becomes a progressively more important feature in terms of increasing stratigraphical excision or the size and importance of the Lewisian inliers which are associated with it (Figure 14).

In the area south of Loch Quoich its presence as a slide was not recognised by earlier workers and its course, shown in Tanner and others (1970), was largely interpretative. North of Loch Quoich, however, the presence of the slide is demonstrable by stratigraphical cut-outs and/or the presence of Lewisian inliers. Around the Fannich–Beinn Dronaig area a klippe of Glenfinnan Division rocks, underlain by the slide, lies surrounded by Morar Division rocks to the west of the main outcrop.

The slide's continuation north of the Dornoch Firth is less clear, but it is thought to be represented by the Navar Slide (Figure 3) of the north coast area (Moorhouse, *in* Soper and Barber, 1982).

The slide is probably an early Caledonian feature (e.g. Powell and others, 1981) and it has been folded during at least two later generations of deformation. There is some evidence in Glen Shiel that the slide there is not a single plane of movement, but rather a narrow zone with several planes of transport (BGS records). Along the slide, from at least Loch Eilt to Glen Affric, bands of psammitic rock adjacent to it are commonly gneissic (migmatitic psammitic gneisses). It is possible that, like the gneissic rocks overlying the minor thrust inliers of the Kintail area, these are due to the effects of partial melting during movements on the slide.

Glenfinnan Division

The Glenfinnan Division rocks show evidence of greater ductility during folding than the rocks of the Morar and Loch Eil divisions. The Morar Division, containing two major psammite formations, and the Loch Eil Division, essentially made up of variations of one massive psammite, were certainly highly deformed in several stages. However, the Glenfinnan rocks show a degree of polyphase isoclinal folding, the development of a strong penetrative schistosity and, in places, disruption and flowage, of much greater intensity than that seen in the adjacent divisions; this is due to their dominant pelitic and striped-schist lithology and their generally high degree of migmatisation (Plate 16). The evidence of radiometric dating shows that the earlier phases of folding and metamorphism were pre-Caledonian (van Breemen and others, 1974; Johnson and others, 1979; Tobisch and others, 1970). It has been mentioned earlier (p. 75) that there is current discussion whether the rocks of this division form a 'Grenvillian' basement to a cover of Morar and Loch Eil division strata (Piasecki and van Breemen, 1979a; Piasecki and Wright, 1981).

Plate 16   Refolded folds in striped semipelites and psammites of the Glenfinnan Division of the Moine Crop out at Loch Mullardoch   (D3115)

The inclination of strata within the division is generally steep (Figure 17); however, this stratification is composite banding, resulting in part from the repetition of beds in tight to isoclinal folds, and in part from the development of new schistosities parallel to the axial planes of folds of at least two Caledonian generations. The regional attitude of the bedding is almost entirely obscured, and the present steep dip is mainly the result of the Caledonian folding on steep axial surfaces which trend in a generally NNE–SSW direction.

The rapid alternation of psammite and pelite in the striped lithologies has given rise to extreme variations in fold style, even among folds of the same generation. Folds with strongly curvilinear axes, often varying in plunge by more than 90°, are typical. In extreme cases the rocks are so deformed that the striped banding can break up, with the production of disoriented blocks of psammite completely enclosed in pelite. The intricate nature of the outcrop pattern produced by the multiple phases of folding of the Glenfinnan Division is illustrated and described by Brown and others (1970) in the Morar–Loch Eil area and by Tobisch and others (1970) in the Glen Affric–Glen Strathfarrar area.

From Strath Orrin to Glen Affric the outcrop pattern within the Glenfinnan Division 'swirls' in large, closed or almost closed antiforms and synforms.

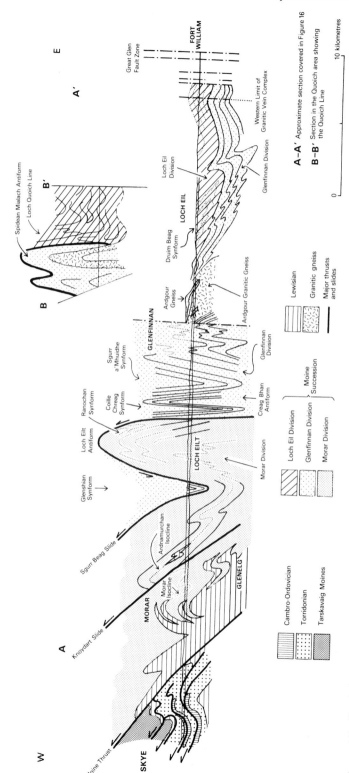

Figure 17 Semi-diagrammatic section across the southern part of the Northern Highlands, Skye to Loch Eil

The approximate lines of the mainland sections indicated as **A–A'** and **B–B'** are on Figure 16

Section courtesy of Dr D. Powell, following the work of Bailey, Clough, Cheeney and Matthews, Powell, Baird, and Ramsay; inset after Roberts and Harris, 1983

Southwards from Glen Affric the folding is tighter, and even compressed, with a very dominant NNE–SSW 'grain' of the D_2 and D_3 phases of Table 4. Within this compressed zone of tight upright folds, highly elongate closed structures can be detected (as around Glen Dessarry at the head of Loch Arkaig); they may represent the more open synforms and antiforms seen in the area further north.

Quoich Line

Originally named by T. N. Clifford (1957), the Quoich Line is a rather poorly defined zone (Figure 14) marking the change from 'steeply inclined' strata of the Glenfinnan Division south of Glen Moriston, to the 'Flat Belt' of the Loch Eil Division (see below). This change is probably due to the contrasts in ductility between the rocks of the two divisions; the rocks of the Glenfinnan Division are steep because they are affected characteristically by highly-compressive folding described above, and thus contrast with the beds of the massive Loch Eil Psammite which show more open folding.

The 'enveloping surface' or overall regional disposition of stratification in the Glenfinnan rocks could be 'flatter' than is immediately apparent. The view that the Loch Eil rocks represent post-Grenville cover has already been referred to as has the view of Roberts and Harris (1983) that the Quoich Line represents the easterly limit of strong early Palaeozoic deformation which dies out in the Loch Eil Division. In Glen Garry, Roberts and Harris suggest that the junction between the Loch Eil Psammites and adjacent pelitic and striped schists typical of the Glenfinnan Division was recumbently folded during an early folding episode, and that the interleaved sequence thus produced was itself folded on roughly N–S axes during the early Palaeozoic phase (Figure 17, inset). On the west (Glenfinnan) side of the zone which makes up the Quoich Line the interleaved folds are highly attenuated, on the east (Loch Eil) side deformation is less intense and the early folds can be made out as a series of arcuate tongues of pelitic rocks extending into the Loch Eil Psammite (Figure 14).

Around the head of Loch Eil, Strachan (1982) suggests that the Quoich Line is marked by a zone of early thrusting which displaces mappable subdivisions of the Loch Eil Psammite and the adjacent granite gneiss. This could account for the fact that some fairly conspicuous subdivisions recognised by Stoker (1983) further south in Ardgour are not represented at Loch Eil.

Northwards from Glen Moriston the junction of the Loch Eil Psammites and schists of the Glenfinnan Division is not as sharply defined as it is to the south.

Loch Eil Division

Over most of its outcrop the lithological banding of the Loch Eil Division appears to be undulating, but generally flat-lying (Figure 17 and Plate 12). This undulating aspect has given rise to the term 'Flat Belt' for the area covered by the rocks of the Division (Leedal, 1952) possibly occasioned by the fortuitous sections afforded by the main through road, but this is misleading to a considerable degree.

In western Ardgour, for instance, Stoker (1983) recognises an early phase of tight folding associated with the production of the regional schistosity (D_1: probably Precambrian) and a later D_2 phase of large folds which vary from open to tight along their axial surfaces, themselves affected by D_3 folds which trend NE–SW.

North from Loch Eil the pervasive flagginess of the rocks conceals at least one generation of isoclinal folds (Figure 17), and over much of the area this gently inclined flagginess is separated by narrower zones of steep rocks which may by an expression of the more open variants of the D_2 folds further south. In one upfold, near Clunes, striped migmatised rocks are possibly Glenfinnan Division strata appearing from under the Loch Eil Psammites.

REGIONAL METAMORPHIC GRADE

The grade of the Lewisian metamorphism (Scourian and Laxfordian) in the Foreland rocks is discussed in Chapter 2. Post-Lewisian metamorphism has affected foreland rocks in two main areas; firstly, along the Outer Isles Thrust, where hydrous retrogression (greenschist facies) was associated with movements along the thrust planes, and secondly, immediately below the Moine Thrust, where low-grade (weak to lower greenschist facies) recrystallisation is particularly noticeable in the Torridonian of southen Skye. Lewisian basement inliers within the Caledonides generally exhibit the same metamorphic grade as the surrounding Moine. In some localities, however, relic high-grade granulite-facies assemblages can be identified, for example, in the Borgie inlier of Sutherland (Moorhouse, 1976). High-grade relics can also be identified in Lewisian basement slices in the Moine Thrust Zone, for example in the Glenelg–Attadale inlier (Barber and May, 1976; Sanders, 1979).

In the Moine rocks the widespread development of aluminosilicate polymorphs has been largely inhibited by the unsuitable chemical composition of the rocks. As a result the metamorphic grade of the rocks is generally determined by using the mineral assemblages in the calc-silicate ribs and nodules (Kennedy, 1958; Soper and Brown, 1971; Winchester, 1974; Tanner, 1976; Powell and others, 1981). The most important boundaries are the first appearance, in order of increasing grade, of oligoclase, hornblende, bytownite/anorthite, and pyroxene. Increasing data on the distribution of index minerals in pelites show that the pelite-based isograds (garnet, kyanite, sillimanite), although broadly related to the calc-silicate-based isograds, do not parallel them in detail (Winchester, 1974; Powell and others, 1981). This necessitates certain generalisations in drawing facies boundaries.

The distribution of facies is shown in Figure 18, following the scheme proposed by Fettes and others (in press). This map shows the grade rising from west to east from greenschist facies to middle amphibolite facies (sillimanite + muscovite in pelites) and, locally, upper amphibolite facies (sillimanite + potash feldspar in pelites). In Inverness-shire the grade falls again eastwards to the lower amphibolite facies (kyanite + staurolite in pelites) which forms a broad belt across to the Great Glen. In general terms the high-grade areas coincide with areas of migmatisation (Winchester, 1974).

Whether this pattern reflects the effects of pre-Caledonian (M_1) or of Caledonian (M_2) metamorphic events is uncertain; and if both have left their mark, it is uncertain which was the more active. The problem is aggravated because there are no reliable correlations between local structural sequences, and consequently no regional framework nor widespread recognisable datum for the Caledonian event (see Powell and others, 1981).

In the extreme northern Moine of Sutherland the metamorphic grade appears to rise uniformly from west to east (Soper and Brown, 1971). The low grade of metamorphism (weakly metamorphosed to greenschist facies) in the west appears to post-date the development of the mylonites above the Moine Thrust and is

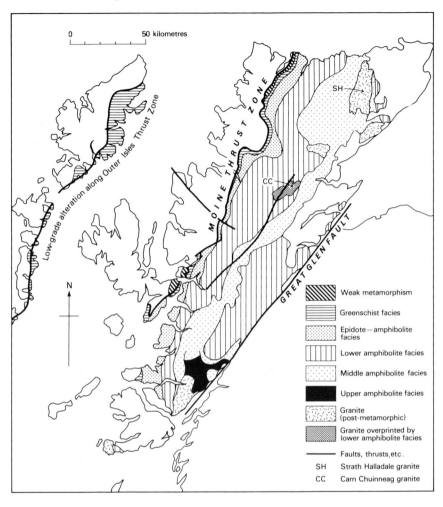

Figure 18   Map of metamorphic grade in the Northern Highlands produced by post-Lewisian events

therefore apparently of Caledonian age. In the east the Strath Halladale granite was intruded into high-grade (middle amphibolite-facies) rocks. This granite has given an age of 649 ± 32 Ma (Lintern and others, 1982) which would date the metamorphism as pre-Caledonian, although there is evidence of a late low-grade overprint affecting the granite. If the age for the granite is accepted, it follows that a considerable metamorphic break must exist somewhere between Strath Halladale and the Moine Thrust. It further follows that the Strath Halladale 'block' must have been sufficiently distant from the rocks now immediately east of the Moine Thrust to have been twice metamorphosed, the first metamorphism high grade, the second low grade, the pattern of metamorphism being distinct from that in the 'block' to the west. The two 'blocks' appear to have been juxtaposed with each other late in the Caledonian. The line of tectonic and metamorphic break could coincide with the Strath Naver slide (Moorhouse and Moorhouse, 1983) which forms the approximate westen boundary of the middle amphibolite-facies rocks.

The problem of the age of the metamorphism is further complicated south of Strath Halladale where the Carn Chuinneag granite (Figures 18,21) dated at 550 ± 10 Ma (Pidgeon and Johnson, 1974) was demonstrably emplaced before the peak of metamorphism (kyanite grade) was reached (Shepherd, 1973), thus defining the dominant grade as Caledonian. If the evidence is accepted, it follows that a discontinuity must exist between Strath Halladale and Carn Chuinneag similar to that between Strath Halladale and the Moine Thrust area. This discontinuity may be postulated as an extension of the Strath Naver slide along the western limit of high-grade rocks, although no direct field evidence is available to support such an extension.

In northern Ross-shire Winchester (1974) has suggested that the pre-Caledonian metamorphism increased in grade westwards from Carn Chuinneag and that the Caledonian metamorphism increased in grade eastwards.

In the south-western Moine of Inverness-shire, Powell and others (1981) suggested that the pre-Caledonian grade, dated at 1004 ± 28 Ma (Brook and others, 1976) rose from greenschist facies (garnet grade) in Skye to middle amphibolite-facies (sillimanite grade plus migmatites) in the east. This metamorphic pattern was foreshortened by ductile sliding which took place at the beginning of the Caledonian. The sliding coincided with the Caledonian overprint, the grade rising rapidly from lower greenschists facies in western Morar to lower amphibolite facies in eastern Morar; Brewer and others (1979) give a date of 467 ± 20 Ma as the minimum age for this event. The high grade of the Caledonian event is apparently confirmed by the fact that the pyroxene isograd (in calc-silicates) cuts folds of the early Caledonian slides (Powell and others, 1981). This view is also supported by Tanner's (1976) observation that high-grade metamorphism post-dated the sliding. To the east of Morar, Roberts and others (1984) have argued on textural and structural grounds that the Glendessary syenite, dated at 457 ± 5 Ma by van Breemen and others (1979b), is earlier than the Caledonian event, and this event here gave only a low-grade retrogressive overprint. This accords with textural work in the Glen Affric–Glen Urquhart area by BGS, which suggests that the peak metamorphism in that area was early in the deformational history, and therefore of possible pre-Caledonian age.

Brewer and others (1979) and Powell and others (1981) have suggested that the Caledonian recrystallisation probably spanned the period 470–400 Ma. This accords with the views of D. I. Smith (1979), who postulated the existence of regional thermal gradients affecting the recrystallisation of microdiorite dykes in the period 450–420 Ma.

Fettes and others (in press) suggest a marked contrast between the style and time of metamorphism in the Central Highlands and those in the Northern Highlands. The Central Highlands underwent recrystallisation in the period 520–440 Ma, following initial deformation and tectonic thickening of a nappe pile. The Northern Highlands were recrystallised in the period 470–400 Ma, an event possibly associated with initial deformation.

8 Early igneous activity within the Caledonides

Formerly all igneous and migmatitic rocks within the Caledonides (Figure 19) were considered to belong to a magmatic cycle related to the Caledonian Orogeny, and could be classed as Pre-, Syn- or Post-tectonic. It now appears that many of the 'Pre-tectonic' basic rocks are unrelated to the Caledonian cycle and that the migmatites, although having a Caledonian component, originated in a pre-Caledonian event.

The igneous activity within the Caledonides will therefore be discussed under the following headings.

Early basic rocks These comprise amphibolites and associated rocks which, though affected by Caledonian metamorphism, comprise members which may be pre-Morarian in age.

Migmatites These include rocks formed both in the pre-Caledonian and Caledonian events.

Early Caledonian igneous rocks These include intrusions of post-Morarian age involved in one or more periods of progressive regional metamorphism.

The Younger Caledonian Igneous rocks are discussed in Chapter 9.

Two major syntheses of Scottish igneous activity provide more detail than can be given in this Handbook. These are *Igneous Rocks of the British Isles* (Sutherland, editor, 1982) and the synopsis by Brown (in *The Geology of Scotland*, Craig, editor, 1983).

EARLY BASIC ROCKS

Apart from small masses of ultrabasic rocks, now serpentinites, which are found mainly in Sutherland (Read, 1931), the majority of the early basic rocks of the Northern Highlands were probably intruded into the Moine as sheets and dykes. These rocks, here referred to as metabasites, comprise metagabbros and metadolerites, epidiorites, hornblende schists and amphibolites which have been classed together by D. I. Smith (1979) as a pre- to syntectonic Amphibolite Suite.

The metabasites were first metamorphosed either prior to, or during, the early phases of Caledonian folding. They are cut by pegmatites dated at 450 Ma, which sets a younger age limit for their metamorphism. Their date of intrusion is not known. Although on the whole the rocks of the suite are concordant to the main regional foliation, transgressive relationships occur locally, showing that a few of the sheets cut the earliest foliation (probably parallel to bedding). Indeed some examples are thought to post-date both the first and the second phase of deformation of the country rocks. Smith points out that members of the suite cut the Carn Chuinneag Granite (c.560 Ma), but Moorhouse and Moorhouse (1979) consider that, in the northern part of the Northern Highlands, there are two suites of very similar rocks. One of these comprises hornblende schists, which appear to have been emplaced during the Caledonian Orogeny. Peacock (1977) argues that in Glen Moriston there is a suite of hornblende schists which is earlier than the period of emplacement of the main suite of metagabbros and metadolerites. Studies are currently in progress which may throw light on the discrimination of members of the suite.

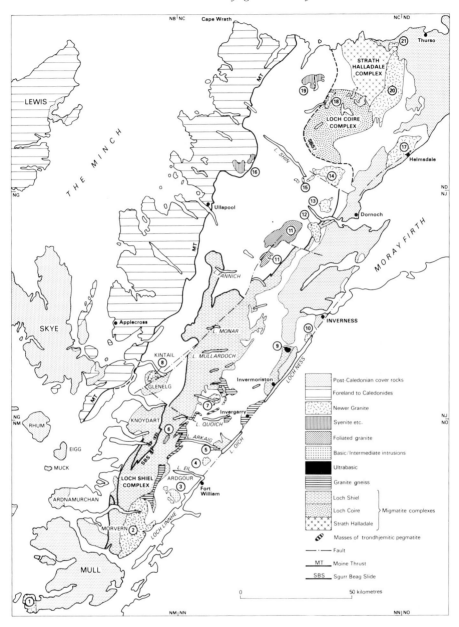

Figure 19   Major intrusions, granite gneiss and migmatites within the Caledonides of the Northern Highlands

Migmatites and granites   **1** Ross of Mull   **2** Strontian   **7** Cluanie   **8** Ratagain   **10** Abriachan   **12** Fearn   **13** Migdale   **14** Rogart   **15** Shin – Grudie   **17** Helmsdale   **18** Loch Coire   **20** Strath Halladale

Syenite   **6** Glendessary   **16** Borrolan and Loch Ailsh   **19** Ben Loyal

Foliated granite   **11** Inchbae and Carn Chuinneag

Basic and intermediate intrusions   **3** Glen Scaddle   **3** Glen Loy   **5** Clunes   **21** Reay

Ultrabasic intrusions   **9** Glen Urquhart

The only comprehensive description of the mineralogy and geochemistry of members of the suite is that given by Moorhouse and Moorhouse (1979). The most common types of metabasite are discussed below.

Hornblende schists

These are dark green to black rocks in which all traces of the original minerals and textures have been obliterated; they now show a strong schistosity and lineation of hornblendes. Their usual mineralogy is greenish-blue amphibole, andesine and quartz, with or without garnet, biotite and accessories. Bands of biotite-rich schist have, in places, been interpreted as being retrogressed hornblende schists.

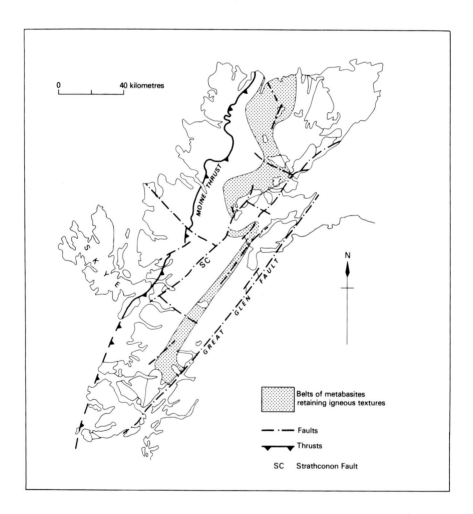

Figure 20　Metabasites of the Northern Highlands

The stippled belts contain metadolerites and metagabbros retaining igneous textures. To the west of the belts, the only metabasites are garnetiferous amphibolites in the Glenfinnan Division; to the east, hornblende schists and epidiorites are locally abundant in the Loch Eil Division (after Smith, 1979)

Metagabbros and metadolerites

These form bosses and thick sills of undoubted igneous origin. They contain cores in which the original igneous textures (although not necessarily the original minerals) can be made out (Peacock, 1977; Read, 1931). They commonly have schistose margins indistinguishable from the hornblende schists (Figure 20).

Epidiorites

These are sheet-like in some places, but are more often in the form of small hornblende bosses; typically, none of the original igneous minerals or textures are retained but they show no schistose foliation (although the hornblendes may show an irregular local alignment). They are usually medium- or coarse-grained rocks.

D. I. Smith (1979) has discussed the distribution of the metabasites in some detail. Metadolerites and metagabbros are found in two zones (Figure 20), one north and one south of the Strathconon Fault. In the western part of the southern zone, metabasites of any sort are restricted to the pelitic rocks of the Glenfinnan Division, where they occur as concordant boudins of coarse texture commonly rich in large garnets; Johnstone and others (1969) have shown that the field relations suggest that they may be of sedimentary origin. There are no metabasites within the rocks of the Morar Division in this area, but further north in Ross-shire, Winchester (1976) has found rare thin sheets of metabasite in the pelitic rocks of the Morar Division which he distinguishes as metamorphosed alkali-basalts; he differentiates them from those in the Glenfinnan Division, which he considers to be metamorphosed tholeiitic intrusions. Moorhouse and Moorhouse (1979) also consider the hornblende schists of 'normal' aspect of the northerly area to be tholeiitic intrusions.

To the east of the southern zone the rocks of the Loch Eil Division are cut by numerous sheets of fine-grained hornblende schist with subordinate bosses of epidiorite and metagabbro.

MIGMATITES

The term migmatite is applied to a rock comprising an intimate mixture of a schistose host (normally metasedimentary) referred to as the palaeosome (Menhert, 1971) and granitic (usually pegmatitic) material, the neosome, which has been derived from the host by a process of partial melting (anatexis) or by a process of segregation involving volatile components, some of which may have been introduced from an extraneous source. Migmatites are the products of high-grade metamorphism which required the rock to be at or about sillimanite grade (c. 700°C). The resulting rocks are lithologically very variable.

The typical rock of the migmatite complexes of the Northern Highlands Moines is a pelitic or semipelitic *lit-par-lit* gneiss, in which the palaeosome and neosome are intimately interbanded parallel to the foliation (Plate 17). As the migmatisation process preferentially concentrates quartz and feldspar in the neosome (leucosome) the relative increase in the biotite content of the palaeosome commonly renders it a matter of difficulty to decide whether the host rock was originally a pelitic or a semipelitic metasediment. The neosome commonly has a black selvedge (melanosome) or restite, of black biotite (Plate 18).

The body of the host rock is a much coarser grained than that of similar rocks outside the area of migmatisation, and there is a more distinct separation of mica and quartzofeldspathic material, the latter tending to aggregate into minute blebs or eyes (augen) rather than layers (Plate 20). (This more-or-less uniform material is sometimes referred to as 'permeation gneiss'; however, this term is best avoided because of certain genetic complications.) Within it, the quartzofeldspathic component aggregates gradually until it forms '*lits*' of coarse-grained granitic material (some of which are continuous along the foliation for several metres) giving a gneissic, banded (stromatic) appearance to the rock. Other concentrations are more distinctly lensoid, forming chains of small or large augen along the foliation. The spacing of the lits or augen chains is irregular.

The thickness of the neosome is variable, from barely discernable to several metres; it is evident that the thickest neosomes cannot be entirely of local origin. Possibly neosome material migrated from its source rock to aggregate in thicker bands. In places the neosome may make up large areas of country in which the host rock is only represented by relict streaks. The rock has become a nebulite. In the pelitic *lit-par-lit* gneisses the neosome (and the larger pegmatites probably derived from them) tend to be oligoclase-bearing (trondhjemitic) (Plate 19).

Lit-par-lit gneisses with a psammitic host are less common. As in the case of the pelite-hosted gneisses, the neosomes which have developed along the micaceous foliae commonly have biotite selvedges, but they are granitic rather then trondhjemitic in composition. The palaeosome may be much recrystallised to a coarse-grained rock; small porphyroblastic augen of potash feldspar are commonly found within it.

Within the migmatite complexes the host rocks themselves are commonly greatly altered. Coarse glassy quartzites result from the recrystallisation of siliceous granulites, and often resemble vein quartz. Calc-silicate bands acquire a vitreous lustre and contain basic plagioclase, indicative of high-grade metamorphism. Metadolerites and hornblende schists do not themselves readily form *lit-par-lit* gneisses but may be veined with pegmatitic material and streaked out to form poorly foliated hornblende gneiss (Read, 1931).

The migmatites of the Northern Highlands are all accompanied by pegmatite or granite vein stockworks whose members cross-cut the *lit-par-lit* neosomes; however, they may become indistinguishable from them in places. Like the neosomes, they are trondhjemitic. The pegmatites extend beyond the limits of the gneisses; they seem, however, to belong to two suites (see below), one of Precambrian and one of Caledonian age.

The migmatites lie in a belt extending from Morvern (and Mull) in the southwest to Sutherland and Caithness, a zone which is largely controlled by the availability of susceptible host rocks within the pelitic strata of the Glenfinnan Division. It must, however, be emphasised that the migmatites are not confined to rocks of that division in the south, and in the northern part of the Northern Highlands they appear in rock groups whose position within the Moine sequence is uncertain.

Plate 17   Migmatitic rocks: lit-par-lit gneiss. Loch Shiel Migmatite Complex, Coire nan Gall, Sgurr na Ciche area   (G. S. Johnstone)

Plate 18   Migmatitic rocks have developed in pelite in which feldspar is disseminated as micro-augen, producing pelitic gneiss with prominent pale neosome lits with black restite selvages. Moinian north side of Lochan nam Breac (Glen Garry – Carnoch River) watershed   (G. S. Johnstone)

Plate 19   Migmatitic rocks and pegmatites: lit-par-lit gneiss in an extreme form, with thick pegmatite bands showing a vague palimpsest banding. Loch Shiel Migmatite Complex, Coire nan Gall, Sgurr na Ciche area (G. S. Johnstone)

The following three 'migmatite complexes', each with somewhat different characteristics, have been identified. The limits of each complex are indefinite and probably gradational.

Loch Shiel Migmatite Complex

The rocks of this complex extend from the Sound of Mull to Ross-shire (Figure 19). They consist of *lit-par-lit* pelitic gneiss with associated pegmatites (Plates 17,18). The migmatisation is largely limited in the east by the unresponsive psammites of the Loch Eil Division but, well within that division, thin bands of pelitic rocks show some evidence of quartzofeldspathic segregation. The migmatisation diminishes more gradually westwards and crosses the Glenfinnan/Morar Division boundary (the Sgurr Beag Slide). Cross-cutting pegmatites and, eventually, quartz veins, extend well beyond the limits of *lit-par-lit* gneiss. There is no development of a granite specific to the complex, such as is found in the Loch Coire Complex to the north (Read, 1931; Brown, 1967, 1971), and no division of the Loch Shiel Complex into separate mappable subunits seems profitable at present. Within the Loch Shiel Complex lie several extensive masses of trondhjemitic pegmatite, notably at Beinn Odhar near Glenfinnan, Ile Choire at the head of Loch Morar and Coire nan Gall below Sgurr na Ciche. These large masses, which in the case of Ile Choire measures 3 × 2 km, are apparently a further development of those gneisses of pegmatitic aspect which shown relict metasedimentry structures.

Loch Coire and Strath Halladale Complexes

These two migmatite complexes of Sutherland differ in major respects both from each other and from the Loch Shiel Complex. There is a need for comparative studies of all three in order to quantify just what these differences amount to. The two northern complexes are not simple *lit-par-lit* migmatites of alternating pelite/semipelite host and pegmatite neosome, but contain in addition various granitic bodies. These are thought to be either the ultimate product of migmatisation or part of a metasomatic process which resulted in the development of both migmatite and granite, possibly with the larger granite masses being truly magmatic (Brown, 1967).

The *lit-par-lit* gneisses could be the products of isochemical anatexis (Stevenson, 1971; Butler, 1965), but Brown (1967) and Cheng (1944) have shown that their formation requires the metasomatic introduction of sodium. In the Loch Coire Complex, Brown has followed Read in identifying the sheet-like form of the migmatites with an upward transition (seen on Ben Klibreck) from unmigmatised metasediments to structurally overlying migmatised rocks. The progression is through a zone of veins and sills distinct from the transected rock into a zone in which the two are intimately mixed to form banded migmatites, which themselves are cut by other veins and sheets. These veins are of oligoclase granite or pegmatite. Masses of oligoclase-bearing granite lie within the complex, of which the Loch Coire granite is the largest. It is weakly foliated. The rocks of the complex are cut by seams of pink aplite, probably of separate, later generation.

Although the migmatitisation phenomena of the north coast of Scotland were reported by Horne and Greenly as long ago as 1898, little regional descriptive work has been published on the Strath Halladale migmatite complex. It appears that this comprises *lit-par-lit* migmatite of regional extent, with a more local migmatite associated with the early emplacement of a soda-rich granite found around the main outcrop of the Strath Halladale granite. This granite shows a foliation, and is considered by McCourt (1980) to be the same as that which forms the sheets and veins of the Loch Coire Complex. McCourt, however, cites evidence of feldspar zoning and quartz-plagioclase reaction, which he considers indicative of a magmatic origin for the rock. The migmatite and the sodic granites are folded, but the main mass of the Strath Halladale granite (previously classed with the migmatites) is of a later generation and is a true magmatic biotite granite. It is affected only by late-stage minor folding, and cannot be correlated with the migmatite complex.

Ardgour Granite Gneiss

Within the Loch Shiel migmatite belt and in the adjacent Loch Eil Psammite lie extensive outcrops of true granite gneiss (Figure 19). These outcrops, although disconnected, clearly form a related development from Ardgour to Glen Moriston.

The greater part of Ardgour Gneiss (possibly better referred to as the West Highland Granite Gneiss, as its outcrop in Ardgour is only a small part of the whole) consists of a coarse foliated microcline-oligoclase-quartz granite with subordinate biotite. The biotite defines a foliation along which pods of pegmatitic material, each margined by a biotite-restite selvedge, are commonly developed, giving a gneissose aspect to the rock. North of Sgurr Dhomhnuill, near Strontian, the rock has the appearance of a composite gneiss with augen of potash-feldspar and quartz developed both within the granite gneiss and in the surrounding pelitic migmatite. Elsewhere it is remarkably massive, and may even lose its biotite foliation, so that it strongly resembles a post-foliation granite.

The various granite-gneiss bodies are emplaced in widely separate parts of the Moine succession and some of the bodies appear themselves to transgress the lithostratigraphical divisions of the enclosing schists. In a few places the junction with the country rock is clearly cross-cutting, suggestive of local mobilisation. Overall, however, its contacts with the pelitic migmatites are quite gradational.

The granite gneiss has been interpreted in various ways. Harry (1953) considered it to be part of the regional migmatites, deriving it by potash metasomatism following the initial phase of soda-metasomatism responsible for the *lit-par-lit* gneisses. Dalziel (1963) considered it to have formed in-situ by anatexis from a host rock of suitable composition. This interpretation was based partly on the evidence of the gradational contacts of the granite gneiss with the metasedimentary gneiss, and partly on the habit of its contained zircons; these, he claimed, had never crystallised in a magma (a point later disputed by Pidgeon and Aftalion, 1978). Mercy (1963) considered that it had passed through a magmatic phase, either as an in-situ melt or as a true intrusion. Harris (*in* Winchester, 1974) suggested that it could represent a series of tectonic slices of basement. Whatever its origin, there is general agreement that it was emplaced or formed prior to the second deformation of the region; Brook and others (1976; 1977) suggest, from Rb-Sr isotope dates, that it has undergone the Grenville phase of metamorphism at c.1100 Ma.

The age of the migmatite complexes

The age of the migmatites and their accompanying pegmatites has been of vital importance in elucidating the history of deposition and metamorphism of the

Moine rocks of the Northen Highlands. In this respect the south-west part of the region, comprising the Loch Shiel Migmatite Complex, has been the most completely studied.

In that district, near Glenfinnan itself, the rocks were rendered schistose and were migmatitised prior to the folds of the second phase of deformation of the region (D_2 of Table 4). Lensoid pegmatites developed along the migmatite layers give an age of 730–740 Ma (Rb-Sr and U-Pb methods; van Breemen and others, 1974). These ages are similar to those from other pegmatites cutting the Moines of the west central Northern Highlands (Long and Lambert, 1963; Giletti and others, 1961). On this basis the first metamorphism and folding of the Moine rocks was Precambrian, and the age of deposition of the Moine sediments could be considerably older than 750 Ma. Lambert (1969) has proposed the name 'Morarian' for the tectonothermal episode which gave rise to the pegmatites.

The migmatites and concordant pegmatites are cut by a later suite of transgressive pegmatites. These span the period of development of the D_2 folds, and continue over the period of D_3 development. These pegmatites give radiometric ages which relate them to a Caledonian episode around 450 Ma, and during this period the earlier migmatites were reworked (van Breemen and others, 1974). Separate Precambrian and Caledonian tectonothermal episodes seem thus to be well established on the basis of the ages so far determined, and consistent results seem to extend over a wide area. The problem that these results pose to the interpretation of the structural and metamorphic history of the northern part of the Northern Highlands has already been alluded to.

However, the Ardgour Granite Gneiss adds still more complexity to the problem. From a Rb-Sr whole rock isochron this mass has a Grenvillian age of about 1020 Ma (Brook and others, 1976). If the gneiss is a migmatite developed in situ (see discussion above) this implies a Grenvillian episode of migmatitisation, earlier than the Morarian. If it is intrusive then the sediments into which it was emplaced are older. As has been pointed out above Brook and others (1977) have presented evidence for a Grenvillian episode of folding and metamorphism in the Morar area, while Piasecki and van Breemen (1979a) and Piasecki and Wright (1981) consider that the whole Glenfinnan Division represents a Grenvillian basement on which later Morar rocks were laid down. Like the *lit-par-lit* migmatites, the Ardgour Gneiss has been reworked in the Caledonian, and is cut by the later suite of pegmatites.

The relationship of the migmatite complexes of Loch Coire and Strath Halladale to this time sequence is not firmly established, as much depends on the interpretation of the fold history of the area. An age of c.650 Ma (M. Brook, personal communication) has been proposed for the intrusion of the Strath Halladale granite. On this basis, most or all of the migmatitisation and much of the folding of the area would be Precambrian, a proposal which does not fit with the current deductions about the history of the area (Soper and Brown, 1971; Soper and Wilkinson, 1975).

EARLY GRANITES

The Carn Chuinneag and Inchbae intrusions

The two adjacent masses of Carn Chuinneag and Inchbae (Figure 21) were formerly thought to be separate outcrops of the same sheet-like intrusion of foliated granite and associated rocks. More recent studies have suggested that

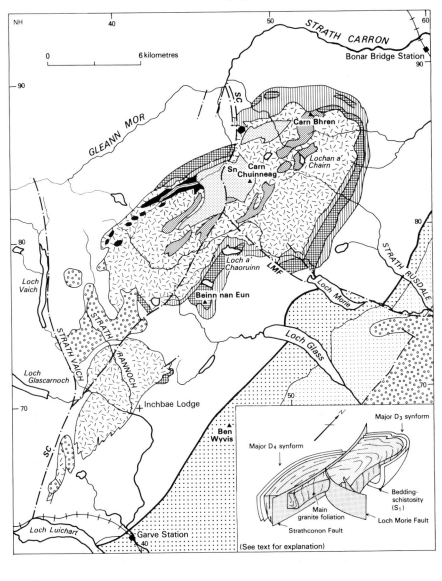

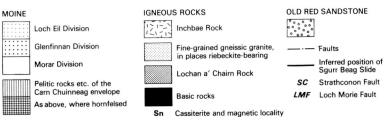

Figure 21   The Carn Chuinneag and Inchbae intrusions (inset after Wilson and Shepherd, 1979; Lochan a'Chairn Rock after Harker, 1962)

they represent two separate bodies emplaced at slightly different stratigraphic levels, but they are clearly magmatically linked. The intrusions were first described in detail by Peach and others (1912) and have subsequently been studied by several workers who have dealt with their structure or petrology, or both. During this time major changes of interpretation of the form and history of the bodies have take place (e.g. Harker, 1962; Wilson and Shepherd, 1979).

The earliest intrusions in the Carn Chuinneag mass were probably pyroxene gabbro and diorite (Flett, *in* Peach and others, 1912) now largely amphibolitised, veined and brecciated by the Inchbae Rock which forms the main bulk of both the Carn Chuinneag and Inchbae intrusions. This was originally a porphyritic granite with abundant orthoclase phenocrysts, but is now a coarse biotite-granite gneiss in which the phenocrysts are largely deformed to augen wrapped round by a streaked-out matrix of quartz, biotite, potash feldspar and plagioclase. The alignment of augen and matrix defines the main D_2 gneissic foliation. Garnet is common in the groundmass. A finer-grained, more acid augen gneiss—the Lochan a'Chairn Rock—intrudes and carries xenoliths of the Inchbae Rock. In the Carn Chuinneag intrusion there are small outcrops of riebeckite-bearing gneissic granite and, of more restricted occurrence, a garnetiferous albite gneiss with magnetite- and cassiterite-bearing bands which are found on the north-west flank of Carn Chuinneag (Figure 21). These latter rocks have been examined from time to time with a view to possible economic exploitation.

The intrusions (the structural history of which is best shown by the Carn Chuinneag mass) were emplaced subsequent to the first phase of deformation of the Moine country rock (D_1) and after these rocks had undergone regional greenschist-facies metamorphism (Shepherd, 1973). Neither deformation nor metamorphism of the host rocks had been sufficient to destroy the original sedimentary structures within it, and hornfelsing by the intrusions has protected these structures from effacement during subsequent tectonic and metamorphic events to a remarkable degree. The host rocks were originally laminated siliceous and argillaceous sediments, and within the contact aureole of the Carn Chuinneag intrusion sedimentary lamination, cross-bedding, mud-cracks and rain-pits are still preserved. The aureole is up to 1.5 km wide.

The rocks of the intrusions are unaffected by the D_1 deformation, but were strongly foliated during the second period of regional folding, when they were extensively recrystallised under amphibolite-grade conditions. The Carn Chuinneag intrusion was then refolded to form the core of a steep-sided (regional D_3) synform, the axis of which plunges moderately SW; it thus appears to occupy a D_3 basin structure similar to that around the Glendessary intrusion. This syncline was further affected by major NW–SE-trending folding (D_4), the combination of D_3 and D_4 folds giving the Carn Chuinneag outcrop its slightly arcuate form, convex to the north-west.

The structure at the south-west end of the Carn Chuinneag intrusion and of the Inchbae intrusion is less well known. Wilson and Shepherd (1979) suggest that the Inchbae granite lies on the continuation of the D_3 synclinal axis that affects Carn Chuinneag, but at a lower stratigraphic level. This implies that the banding of the country rock continues round the south-west end of the Carn Chuinneag mass. As only the base of the Carn Chuinneag intrusion is seen, the overall size and original form of the mass must remain uncertain.

The time of emplacement of the Carn Chuinneag and Inchbae masses (between the regional D_1 and D_2 events) makes them of particular importance in terms of the timing of structural events in the Northern Highlands. The age of emplacement of the Carn Chuinneag pluton has been found to be c.550 Ma (Rb-Sr whole rock; Long, 1964) and c.560 Ma (U-Pb zircon; Pidgeon and Johnson, 1974). If these ages are accepted then they provide a base line for the main penetrative deformation and metamorphism (D_2) of the Moine succession of the area.

The presence of the Carn Chuinneag aureole has provided an interesting opportunity to study the effects of three separate, but superimposed, metamorphic events; the early regional greenschist-facies metamorphism, the contact hornfelsing by the intrusion, and the later regional amphibolite-facies metamorphism. The contact hornfelsing has, in places, enhanced the D_1 fabric by mimetic growth of mica along it, but has more often destroyed it by random overgrowths. Andalusite and cordierite formed in the aureole during the contact metamorphism are now generally represented by pseudomorphs. Kyanite and biotite often define a new fabric parallel to the regional D_2 schistosity, but kyanite is specific to the aureole rocks, and in places, the aureole fabric is totally modified and indistinguishable from the surrounding regionally metamorphosed, garnetiferous, mica schists (Wilson and Shepherd, 1979).

SYENITES

The Glendessarry Intrusion

The Glendessarry Intrusion (Figure 22) comprises a complex of felsic and mafic syenitic rocks which was emplaced into Moine schists after the earliest (D_1) deformation and metamorphism, and possibly also after the D_2 deformation of the region. It has an elliptical outline, elongated NNE–SSW and measuring 4×2 km. The intrusion was largely recrystallised under amphibolite-facies conditions during the Caledonian Orogeny and now shows a well developed mineral lineation which is a function of D_3 strain and metamophism, and which is consistent with that developed in the surrounding schists.

First recognised by V. A. Eyles in 1938, it was described by Harry (1951) as an inlier of altered Lewisian rock. The complex was subsequently considered by the Geological Survey (Summary of Progress for 1961; Lambert and others, 1964) to be an igneous intrusion occupying the core of a steep-sided synform. Lambert and his colleagues obtained isotopic ages from the rocks which, while not precisely dating it, showed that the intrusion was unlikely to be Lewisian in age; and van Breemen and others (1979b) give a U-Pb zircon age of intrusion of c.456 Ma. The petrology of the intrusion has been described in detail by S. W. Richardson (1968). Van Breemen and his colleagues suggested that the intrusion was folded in both D_2 and D_3, and that the present form is the result of the combination of the two periods of folding. In this there are analogies with Carn Chuinneag, but recent research by Roberts and others (1984) interprets the structure of the Complex as a single conical fold. This fold is considered to be D_3 in the local sequence.

The intrusion consists of a mafic syenite and a felsic leucocratic syenite, both comprising alkali feldspar with variable amounts of pyroxene, hornblende and magnetite. The mafic syenite contains $50-70\%$ alkali feldspar, while the leucocratic syenite is more uniform with about 85% feldspar. The mafic rock forms the outer part of the complex, while the leucocratic rock has a main central outcrop and a long, thin outcrop near the western margin of the complex (thought by van Breemen and his colleagues to be a 'tail' to the main crop folded round in D_2). Both syenites have a strong mineral elongation plunging at $70°$ to the southwest. The less deformed parts of the leucocratic syenite may contain large $(1-5$ cm) phenocrysts of perthite, commonly showing oscillatory zoning and Carlsbad twinning; in places these are aggregated to produce a spectacular coarse-

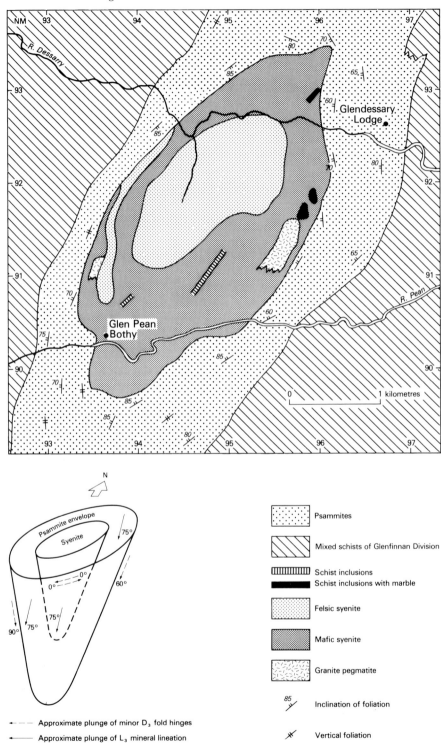

Figure 22   Glendessarry Intrusion, its psammite envelope and inclusions

grained rock. According to S. W. Richardson (1968) the intrusion of the mafic syenite preceded that of the felsic syenite. The only other component of the complex is granite pegmatite occurring in veins and irregular outcrops, the largest of which measures 0.6×0.2 km.

The psammitic rocks which form the immediate envelope comprise coarse-grained siliceous psammites and feldspathic, somewhat gneissic, psammites in which potash feldspar seems to have been generally redistributed. Apart from a strong linear fabric (quartz rodding) the rocks adjacent to the intrusion have a 'wispy' biotite foliation, which in places probably represents original cross-bedding or tight folds, deformed, and now flattened and streaked out. At the north-eastern end of the complex the fabric of the envelope has been completely disrupted to a pseudoconglomerate in which 'balls' or 'hooks' of hornblende and calc-silicate rock are set in reconstituted quartzofeldspathic matrix resembling coarse psammite; at the south-eastern end of the complex, related gneissic rock contains larger detached fragments of mafic syenite. This disruption may relate to internal shear planes, axial planar to the D_3 synform, which affect the syenite and give the north-east and south-west ends of the complex a stepped outcrop.

Within the complex are xenoliths of rocks not represented in the immediate envelope; these include small and large xenoliths of kyanite- and sillimanite-bearing metasediment, and marble. One narrow metasediment xenolith measures 0.6 km in length, while the marble forms several outcrops several tens of metres across. The presence of marble suggested to the earlier workers that they were dealing with a Lewisian inlier.

Although the Glendessarry intrusion and its psammitic envelope lie within the Glenfinnan Division of the Moines (Plate 15) it is thought that the enclosing psammites may represent an outlier of Loch Eil Psammite, such as is found elsewhere in the Glenfinnan Division (Johnstone and others, 1969; Dalziel, 1966; Roberts and Harris, 1974). The more pelitic xenoliths in the Glendessarry intrusion could, of course, be derived from mica schists of the Glenfinnan Division, but the marbles are uncharacterisic of the Moine Succession. Taken together, the pelitic inclusion, the marbles of the intrusion, and the feldspathic gneiss and calc-silicate-bearing rocks in the pseudoconglomerate of the envelope suggest that the intrusion has been emplaced as a sheet-like body in an unusual lithological group, possibly overlying the Loch Eil Psammite. This assemblage has strong similarities with that into which the Glen Scaddle Intrusion (see below) has been emplaced.

BASIC AND INTERMEDIATE ROCKS

The Glen Scaddle Intrusion

The Glen Scaddle mass and its associated intrusions (of which that of Coire nam Muic is the largest) was first described by J. S. Grant Wilson (*in* Bailey and others, revised edition, 1960). They were classed as epidiorite on the one-inch map (Sheet 53) but it was noted in the memoir that the rock was 'originally a diorite [which had] to a large extent escaped conspicuous alteration'. The Scaddle mass, and more particularly that in Coire nam Muic, was subsequently studied by Drever (1940) who stated that the rock was best called a gabbro-diorite of appinitic affinities. He noted that the rock was mainly massive in character, although in many places it was sheared and granulitised.

Drever considered that the intrusions were part of one sheet, emplaced more or less at the junction of Moine psammites (which would now be referred to as the

Loch Eil Psammite) and an overlying group of mixed schists, including feldspathic psammite, marble and calc-schist, which he likened to Dalradian rocks. To this list BGS surveyors have added a group of black schists, the whole assemblage resembling that of the Ballachulish Subgroup of the Spean Bridge/ Glen Roy area (see Chapter 7).

The Glen Scaddle and associated intrusions comprise a variable two-pyroxene gabbro-diorite which shows various degrees of amphibolitisation; it is possible that some of the hornblende is primary in places. Within the mass of relatively unaltered rock, however, lie narrow zones of intense shearing along which the rocks have a much reduced grain-size and have been converted to hornblende schist. These shear zones commonly contain lenticles of granulitised—even mylonitic—remnants of granite pegmatite which may in places be continuous with transgressive pegmatite veins outside the shear zone. Minor constituents of the intrusions include appinite and quartz-mica diorite, the latter probably being a reaction product between the appinite and surrounding schists; in places (as in the case of the Glen Loy Complex) the diorite grades into a sillimanite-bearing contact rock. Drever also describes small masses of serpentinite, a few tens of metres in length, which are contact-altered by the diorite. It seems likely that these are not part of the intrusion itself but are associated with the Dalradian-like rocks mentioned above.

The long axes of hornblendes in the gabbro-diorite are commonly aligned, and in the Coire nam Muic mass they lie parallel to the foliation of the folded schists round the margin, strongly suggesting that they share at least some of the regional fold history. Stoker (1983) has found evidence that the intrusions of Glen Scaddle and Coire nam Muic lie at two different structural levels, and has shown that the Glen Scaddle Intrusion has been folded during the regional D_2 and D_3 episodes. Its apparent small degree of reconstruction must therefore be due in part to its size, and possibly to the relatively resistant nature of the underlying Loch Eil Psammite. Like Drever, Stoker considers that the masses were originally sheet-like.

A 'feldspathised sedimentary gneiss' surrounds the Glen Scaddle/Coire nam Muic mass and its satellite intrusions. It is uncertain to what extent the characteristics of this rock are the result of contact effects adjacent to the gabbro-diorite, but Bailey (1960) and Drever both consider it to represent a distinct sedimentary unit 'that originally differed from the underlying more siliceous Moines' (Bailey, 1960, p.125). The rock is a massive, tough, pink psammite in which relict compositional variations can be made out; it is interbedded with siliceous psammitic material, itself coarsely recrystallised. Around Coire nam Muic, a strong lineation and mullion-structure have developed, related to tight SE-plunging minor folds. The fabric is defined by streaks of compositional variation (mainly more or less of biotite), disrupted hornblendic lenses and other 'xenolithic' material (including sillimanite gneiss) all flattened in the plane of foliation.

The Glen Scaddle intrusion is cut by late sheets of non-foliated granite pegmatite, whose relationship to the sheared pegmatites has not yet been established, and by members of the microdiorite suite (p.113) which have their own internal foliation.

The Glen Loy Complex

The basic complex of Glen Loy has been emplaced within the rocks of the Loch Eil Division, although certain rocks of unusual facies for that division occur

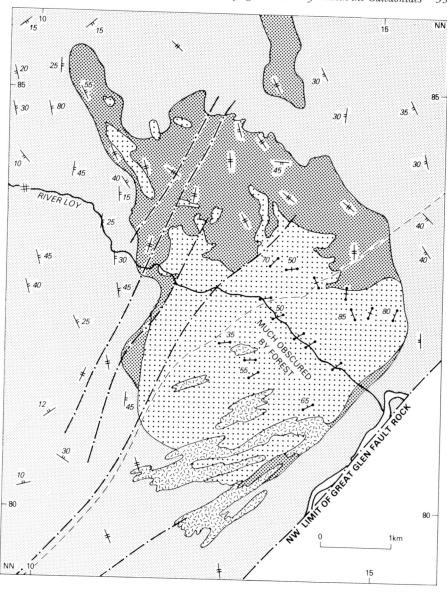

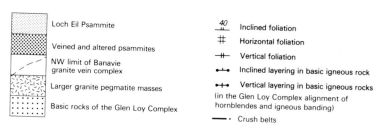

Figure 23 Glen Loy Complex and surrounding schists

around the margin of the complex in places and as xenoliths within it. It has strong petrological similarities to the Glen Scaddle–Coire nam Muic intrusions, and shows comparable features in the enclosing psammite envelope. Unlike the Glen Scaddle–Coire nam Muic intrusions, however, the rocks of the Glen Loy Complex show litte sign of alteration; they appear to have retained their primary igneous composition, although there is a strong suggestion that the mass has undergone at least one, and possibly two, periods of folding.

The outcrop of the complex is more or less circular, about 4 km in diameter and comprises hornblende gabbro, appinite and mica diorite (Figure 23). It is surrounded by a zone of altered rocks in which veins and minor masses of the types represented in the main complex have been emplaced, while the country rock itself is locally metasomatised, rheomorphosed or hornfelsed. This aureole is asymmetrically disposed, being narrow around the east and west sides of the outcrop of the complex but extending for 2.5 km to the north. The complex is cut by the late Caledonian dykes of the microdiorite suite (D. I. Smith, 1979) and by post-tectonic granite-pegmatite veins of the Banavie Vein Complex (see below).

The hornblende gabbro of the complex consists of labradorite feldspar and conspicuously prismatic hornblendes (a few millimetres to about 15 mm in length). Variations in the proportions of these minerals give rise to rhythmic banding, in places on a decimeter scale, but coarser banding is also inferred. The range in composition is from a feldspathic rock with sparse hornblendes to a hornblende-rich mafic end member. Individual layers commonly show grading, with a sharply defined base. This banding is interpreted as a primary igneous feature resulting from gravitational settlement of crystals in a residual melt. In the mafic layers, the long axes of the hornblendes lie within the plane of the banding but have no linear arrangement. In the more felsic parts of the layers the hornblendes are progressively less well orientated upwards from the mafic layers, suggesting that the mafic layers formed by crystal settlement. The rhythmic banding and alignment of hornblendes shows a semicircular disposition on the south-east half of the complex, parallel to the strike of the composite foliation of the surrounding schists. It is steep to vertical at the margin, decreasing towards the centre of the exposed mass. Grading indicates that progressively younger layers come towards the centre.

Although the rock has been described as a hornblende gabbro it is more basic than a typical gabbro and Dr N. Rock (personal communication) has termed it a 'mafraite' (Lacroix) and suggested that it is in fact a member of the appinite suite. The appinite of the complex occurs mainly, but not exclusively, on the north-west side of the outcrop and is characterised by the presence of hornblendes commonly about 5 mm in length. The feldspar content is variable, and some varieties of the appinite are almost ultramafic, including a black, ophimottled clinopyroxene-bearing variety. While spatially the appinite appears the be a late phase of the intrusion, the junctions between it and the hornblende gabbro are gradational.

A minor constituent found on the north-west side of the complex and in the surrounding schists is a biotite-diorite, interpreted as a hybrid of gabbro and country rock; various stages of assimilation are seen in xenoliths within the hornblende rocks.

Within the broad zone of veining and alteration surrounding the complex, the dominant igneous phase is the biotite diorite, although smaller outcrops of both appinite and hornblende gabbro are found. The country rock, however, is extensively feldspathised with the development of porphyroblasts of oligoclase, commonly forming nebulous vein-like concentrations which are very difficult to distinguish from intrusive biotite diorite and which, in places, appear to pass into true igneous veins. Locally the psammitic rocks show rheomorphic characteristics with disoriented blocks of psammite set in a mobilised and recrystallised matrix.

Within the complex there are sparse 'rafts' of garnet-cordierite-staurolite horn-fels, derived from a parent rock apparently more pelitic than any seen commonly in the adjoining Loch Eil Division. On the north-west margin lies an extensive area of sillimanite schist and hornfels in which sillimanite aggregates (up to 150 mm across) may make up to 30% of the rock.

The form of the complex is uncertain. If the igneous banding was originally horizontal (which would be expected if it formed by crystal settling as postulated above) then the south-east part of the complex lies in the closure of a steep-sided synform. No detailed structural mapping of the surrounding psammites was carried out during the original survey, but an examination of the strike and dip of foliation suggests that this synform has itself been bent by later folding. If the complex has been subjected to two episodes of deformation, then its lack of shear zones and metamorphic reconstruction (as seen in the case of Glen Scaddle) is difficult to account for. The only evidence of alteration noted comes from local examples of partial granulation of quartz and feldspar in the appinite, and from thermal clouding of plagioclase.

The Glen Urquhart Complex

The Glen Urquhart Complex is an ultrabasic body of serpentinite, approximately 3.5 km² in area, intruded into semipelites and psammites of the higher exposed units of the Loch Eil Division. However, around the complex unusual lithologies are developed, including kyanite schist and pink psammitic gneiss, and thick bands of limestone (marble). This whole assemblage, including the serpentinite, resembles that at Glen Scaddle – Coire nam Muic. Amphibolite bands, probably of the early basic suite (p. 84) are common.

The serpentinites and surrounding schists have previously been identified as an infold of Lewisian rock (Horne and Hinxman, 1914) but G. H. Francis (1958; 1964) took them to be Moine. Studies by Rock (1983) have not confirmed this conclusion, and their stratigraphic position is still under investigation. They may comprise a separate lithostratigraphic assemblage including serpentinites; they may in fact occupy a syncline, similar to the synclines of the Glen Scaddle and Glendessarry complexes.

The outcrop is characterised by a varied assemblage of calc-silicate rocks and 'skarns', the product of contact metasomatism related to the intrusion of the serpentinite. Rock (1983) has pointed out that the skarns and serpentinite comprise as assemblage of over 60 mineral species, and in this respect they are unique in the Highlands.

9 Younger Caledonian igneous rocks

The Caledonian igneous rocks so far described have all been involved in one or more episodes of regional folding, and some have also been modified by the effects of regional metamorphism. The Younger Caledonian igneous rocks on the other hand are all later than the main regional folding, though some have been emplaced during late thrust movements both within the Moine Thrust Zone and within the orogenic belt.

None of the major intrusions show significant recrystallisation attributable directly to regional metamorphism, but it is clear that many were intruded when the regional temperature was still relatively high. The schists surrounding the intrusions show little sign of contact metamorphism, though in several cases they show plastic deformation in response to the pressures of forceful intrusion. Moreover, many masses are cut by minor intrusions of the Microdiorite Suite, members of which show dynamothermal recrystallisation.

The available isotopic ages suggest that the major intrusions belong to the group of Late-Caledonian igneous rocks intruded in Ordovician and Silurian times. None of the 'permitted' Devonian intrusions (Read, 1961) found in the Grampian Highlands have been recognised north of the Great Glen Fault (however, see Chapter 11). The anomalous position of the little-deformed Strath Halladale Granite has been referred to earlier (Chapter 7).

The Younger Caledonian igneous rocks comprise the alkaline intrusions of Assynt and Ben Loyal, the Newer Granite intrusions, granitic and granodioritic vein networks and the Caledonian suite of minor intrusions (including appinites).

These groups do not represent a sequence of intrusions; in some places they are contemporaneous and in others they overlap; this makes logical description rather a problem.

ALKALINE INTRUSIONS OF ASSYNT AND BEN LOYAL

In Assynt, alkaline igneous rocks occur within and close to the Moine Thrust Zone and the intrusions cut rocks of the foreland, the autochtonous nappes and the Moine Nappe (Figure 19, 24). Around Loch Loyal they are emplaced within the Moine Nappe, well to the east of the Moine Thrust. Elliot and Johnson (1970) have argued for large displacements along the Moine Thrust Zone and, as certain of the intrusions of the Assynt Alkaline Suite are found both in individual nappes within the thrust zone and in the Foreland, it could be concluded that the suite was originally emplaced over a large area which is now much reduced. Parsons (1979) argues for a relatively local source and so envisages a limited thrust displacement. Possibly this anomaly can be resolved by suggesting that the rocks were emplaced at a time when most of the movements on the various thrust sheets had been accomplished.

The Assynt Alkaline Suite was first described by the Geological Survey (Peach and others, 1907; Read and others, 1926). The suite comprises two major intrusions centred respectively on Loch Borralan and Loch Ailsh, and a complex of dykes and sills.

Loch Borralan Complex*

The complex was first described in Geological Survey memoirs (Peach and others, 1907; Read and others, 1926), and its unusual petrology and position in the Thrust Belt has since made it the subject of several papers. It was considered by Shand (1909; 1910) to be a laccolith, differentiated in situ after assimilation of limestone, with the production of various saturated and undersaturated syenitic rocks whose varieties have been given local names, famous in petrological studies. It is now considered by Woolley (1970; 1973) to comprise an earlier rock suite of mafic to ultramafic syenites (ledmorite, assyntite, borolanite, nepheline syenite, cromaltite and other varieties) intruded as a sheeted complex. The roof and floor of the early intrusion were Durness Group limestones. A later plug-like body has intruded the early suite and it comprises a group of oversaturated and saturated syenites differentiated gravitationally in situ, with perthosites at lower levels and quartz syenites at upper levels. Various members of the earlier body show intrusive contacts, but all are thought to be derived from a common parent, differentiated gravitationally prior to emplacement.

Exposure of the complex is incomplete, and drilling for commercial purposes has shown several varieties of ultramafic rock not exposed at the surface; some of these are interpreted as metasomatic alteration products formed by contact with the enclosing limestone. According to Matthews and Woolley (1979) these ultramafic rocks have been squeezed from a possible subhorizontal position to form a steeply inclined sheet along the south-west margin of the complex.

The intrusion lies in the Thrust Belt between the Sole Thrust and the Assynt (or Ben More) Nappe, and the rocks of the earlier suite are commonly penetratively deformed by the movement along the Assynt (or Ben More) Thrust. It is inferred that the intrusion overlaps these movements, and a U-Pb age of the intrusion of c.430 Ma has been obtained by van Breemen and others (1979a). This sets the age for the main movement along that thrust. Undeformed nepheline syenite pegmatites of the later intrusion, however, cut the Assynt Thrust.

Loch Ailsh Complex

The Loch Ailsh intrusion lies within the Assynt (Ben More) Nappe and beneath the Moine Thrust; it is less diverse than that of Loch Borralan. It was first described by Phemister (*in* Read, 1926) and, like the Loch Borralan Complex, was though to be a stratified laccolith, gravity-differentiated to give an ultramafic base. Parsons (1965) has shown that the ultramific rocks, like those of Loch Borralan, form steep screens between syenites and the altered Durness Limestone country rock. The main rock types are rather sodic, saturated or slightly undersaturated, leucocratic syenites which Parsons has divided into three units, forming a regular chemical series emplaced at slightly different times. These units he designed S_1, S_2 and S_3. The combined unit, S_1-S_2, has a gently undulating upper surface overlain by S_3, which appears to be derived from a central plug-like body. A zone of xenoliths of pyroxene syenite at the junction between S_2 and S_3 is taken by Parsons to represent the remnants of a contact-altered limestone roof to S_1-S_2, prior to the emplacement of S_3.

---

*The Ordnance Survey has revised place-name spelling twice, and this has resulted in references in the literature to Loch Borrolan and Loch Borolan, and a well known rock from the complex is named Borolanite.

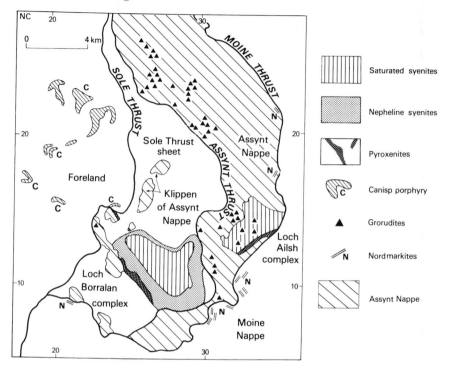

Figure 24 Geological sketch map of the alkaline complexes and minor intrusions of Assynt, showing the relationships of the outcrops to the thrust nappes within the Assynt Window (after Parsons (1979), compiled from various sources mentioned in the text)

The alkaline minor intrusions of Assynt

The rocks of the Foreland, Thrust Belt and Moine Nappe of Assynt are cut by a diverse, but petrographically linked suite of sills and dykes. Depending on their position, the rocks are either unaffected by the thrust movements or are variably altered. Sabine (1953) divided the suite into aegirine felsite (grorudite), Canisp porphyry (biotite-aegirine-albite-oligoclase porphyrite), hornblende porphyrite, nordmarkite, vogesite and ledmorite. The distribution of these rocks is shown in Figure 24; it indicates that, whereas the Canisp porphyry intrusions are confined to the Foreland and the grorudites to the Assynt Nappe, the nordmarkites occur in both the Assynt and Moine Nappes. It is believed that the minor intrusions were emplaced after most of the movement in the Moine Thrust Zone had been accomplished.

The Loch Loyal alkaline intrusions

Three syenitic masses similar to the larger intrusions of Assynt lie around Loch Loyal, well within the Moine Nappe. They comprise the Ben Loyal, Cnoc na Cuilean* and Beinn Stumanadh* intrusions respectively (Read, 1931; King, 1942; Robertson and Parsons, 1974).

*Current Ordnance Survey spelling (1986)

Plate 20   Granite-gneiss with neosome lits bounded by black biotite selvages. Loch Shiel Migmatite Complex, Forestry road to Loch Shiel, Callop area, near Glenfinnan   (D1585)

Plate 21   Ben Loyal, Sutherland: a pluton of quartz-syenite cuts Moine rocks (D1625)

The Ben Loyal Intrusion (Plate 21) consists of two quartz syenites of similar chemistry but slightly different mineralogy and habit. The outer syenite is a laminated two-feldspar rock in which the lamination is ascribed by Robertson and Parsons to flowage of a crystal mush. The lamination is roughly concordant with the foliation of the surrounding schists. The form of the intrusion is that of a sheet or laccolith, fed from the south-east, which distends and deflects the schist envelope on the north-west. The inner mass of coarse, non-laminated syenite makes up about half of the Ben Loyal intrusion. It has a gradational contact with the outer syenite and differs from it in that feldspar of the inner mass is mainly perthite. Aegirine-augite is the common mafic mineral of both rocks, with hornblende confined to the outer syenite.

The Cnoc na Cuilean intrusion is stock-like (Robertson and Parson, 1974) and of slightly different composition to Ben Loyal. Basic syenites of variable composition occupy a marginal zone to non-laminated, quartz-poor syenite. The Beinn Stumanadh intrusion is made up of sheets of dark brownish syenite, partly transgressing and partly concordant with the foliation of the Moine, the upper sheet being at least 400 m thick. Sodic and ultrasodic rocks are found round the Cnoc na Cuilean intrusion as metasomatic replacements of the enclosing schists and are probably related to the syenitic magma from which the main intrusion derives.

Similar small alkaline metasomatic patches have been noted in a few other places in the Northern Highlands, notably in the Loch Hourn–Glen Cannich area (Tanner and Tobisch, 1972; Peacock, 1973). These patches comprise albitites with sodic pyroxenes and amphiboles. No parent syenitic bodies are known to account for the presence of these rocks, and it is uncertain whether they are all coeval. (See also the description of fenitisation near the Great Glen, p.110.)

THE NEWER GRANITES

The Newer Granites of the Scottish Highlands (Figure 19) comprise a group of major plutons and some smaller masses, all intruded later than the main metamorphic recrystallisation and deformation of the surrounding schist, but earlier than the deposition of the Middle Old Red Sandstone. Most of the Northern Highland granites were emplaced during late Ordovician and Silurian times (c.440–400 Ma). Nearly all appear to belong to the class referred to by Read (1963) as 'Forceful Granites', which were emplaced by pushing aside their enclosing schists, although in some cases (e.g. the Ross of Mull Granite) this process may have been accompanied by magmatic stoping. Lack of metamorphic aureoles, the plastic deformation of their envelopes, and the metamorphosed state of the minor intrusions which cut them indicate that most of these masses were formed at a time when regional temperatures, although much declined from the metamorphic maximum, were still elevated (Watson, 1964; D. I. Smith, 1979). Although commonly referred to as 'granites' the rocks are usually mainly granodiorites, adamellites or even diorites, and comprise a calc-alkaline suite ranging from appinite through basic diorite to granite; several of the larger intrusions contain the complete range of these compositions.

The larger complexes show distension of the schist envelope and deformation of the outer, earlier, zones of the intrusion by continued growth of the inner components. The peripheral intrusion may show a foliation of its mineral constituents which parallels both the margin of the intrusion and the deflected strike of the surrounding schists. Where the rocks form intrusive complexes, the more basic intrusions are usually the older; however, the later rocks do not, in general, chill against earlier ones. Only the major Newer Granite masses will be discussed below.

Helmsdale Granite

This large intrusion (98 km²) is apparently a steep-sided or stock-like mass in which coarse porphyritic adamellite (with phenocrysts up to about 35 mm across) forms an outer zone, with a pink fine-grained non-porphyritic variety of adamellite making up the central area (Read and others, 1925). The body is in part unconformably overlain by rocks of Lower Old Red Sandstone age, and the rocks above the unconformity are enriched in uranium-bearing minerals in places; these have provided a target for economic investigations (Gallagher and others, 1971).

Rogart Intrusion

This intrusion (70 km²) has been described most recently by Soper (1963). It is a funnel-shaped granodioritic complex surrounded by a zone of contact migmatites, the generation of which is related to the formation of the complex itself. According to Soper's interpretation, a front of migmatitisation preceded the uprise of the granodiorite magma to a level where migmatite formation ceased, while the igneous magma continued to expand forcefully upwards, displacing its plastic envelope.

The granodiorite complex comprises three elements, an outer tonalite, a middle hornblende-biotite granodiorite and an inner adamellite and biotite granite. Foliation and lineation are prominent in the tonalite but decrease inward, although they are still sufficient to show the general concentric disposition of the intrusions and the funnel-shape of the complex. The last intrusion, the biotite granodiorite, cuts across the junctions of the earlier components. Large masses of appinite are found both in the granodiorite and the biotite granite, apparently as rafts of an earlier intrusion. These now form varying degrees of hybrid rocks similar to those of Ach'Uaine type (see p.114).

The migmatites of the complex (but not the granodiorite core) are unconformably overlain by sediments of Lower and Middle Old Red Sandstone age. The south-west margin of the complex is limited by the Strath Fleet Fault, which, as it cuts across the various components, renders the present outcrop asymmetrical.

Cluanie Intrusion

The Cluanie Intrusion (18 km²) also shows displacement of its envelope, with the strike and dip of the Moine rocks conforming to the attitude of the igneous contact (Leedlal, 1952). Only one rock type is present, a variably porphyritic hornblende-biotite granodiorite within which can be mapped several textural variants of the same rock type. The phenocrysts of oscillatory-zoned microcline-perthite are frequently megacrysts measuring up to 5 cm across and, by concentration of these, the rock in bulk can vary from tonalite to adamellite. In places, where the phenocrysts are abundant, their concentration defines a crude flow-structure.

The pluton is cut by many dykes of the Microdiorite Suite (p.113) while veins of Claunie granodiorite cut a suite of felsic porphyrites which, although similar in character to the main swarm, must have been emplaced earlier.

Ratagain Complex

The Ratagain Complex (18 km^2) is unusual for the Northern Highlands in several respects. Its rocks range from minor ultrabasics through major constituents of diorite, granodiorite and monzonite to adamellite. It is emplaced so near the out-crop of the Moine Thrust as to suggest that its base has been controlled by the Thrust; perhaps the intrusion was initiated along the thrust (Tuson *in* Beckinsale and Obradovich, 1973), or else it was transported *en masse* by the later movements along the thrust plane. In this respect it resembles the Ross of Mull granite (p. 110) and the syenitic intrusions of Assynt (p.102). It also lies in contact with Lewisian gneisses, which themselves overlie the Moine Thrust.

The sequence of intrusion differs from that commonly found in Caledonian plutons in that the rocks of the main complex, including the more basic diorites, cut an early intrusion of granodiorite (Nicholls, 1951). Berridge (BGS, unpublish-ed report) substantially confirmed Nicholls' work and noted granodiorite, diorite, monzonite and adamellite (emplaced in that order) showing a progressive migra-tion of the intrusive centre to the north-east. None of contacts is chilled, and all four major rock types are, at least in part, modified by hybridisation with the preceding members. From observations of internal foliations Berridge inferred that the intrusion is not a laccolith, as Nicholls thought, but, at this level of ex-posure, is steep-walled. (Note, however, the inference concerning the base of the intrusion referred to above.) Berridge also considered that the 'appinitic', basic and ultrabasic xenoliths in the mass are probably altered inclusions of melanic hornblendic rocks of Lewisian origin.

South of Loch Duich (and probably under it) the Ratagain Complex is trun-cated by the Strathconon Fault. A granitic body in Glen Lichd on the other (SE) side of the fault may be a displaced part of the mass. The complex is apparently the centre of an intrusive swarm of dykes (see p.116).

Strontian Complex

This intrusion (200 km^2) is the largest of the Newer Granites of the Northern Highlands (Figures 19, 25); it is truncated on its south-east margin by the Great Glen Fault. As its components resemble those of the Foyers Complex (100 km to the north-east on the other side of the Great Glen Fault), which is correspondingly truncated on its north-west side, it had seemed possible that the two complexes were displaced parts of the same intrusion (Kennedy, 1946). This correlation now seems to be less likely (see p.175).

Like the Rogart Complex, the Strontian pluton is a composite body (MacGregor and Kennedy, 1932; Sabine, 1963) with an outer foliated tonalite grading inwards to a non-foliated porphyritic granodiorite. During emplacement the magma of the pluton compressed and displaced its envelope of schists, the foliation of which now follows the periphery of the complex round its semicircular outcrop. As at Rogart, the schists were evidently at temperatures which permitted this plastic deformation. The foliation in the outer tonalite likewise follows the contact of schists and pluton, and has been attributed (Munro, 1965) to compres-sion of a partly crystalline outer intrusion during continued emplacement of an in-ner body. Both tonalite and granodiorite are cut by a later, passively intruded biotite granite (adamellite) which did not compress the earlier intrusions. The granite is apparently stock-like, but with a vein-complex in the north and east which penetrates both the earlier intrusions and the schist envelope.

Unlike the Rogart Complex, no extensive zone of contact migmatite is

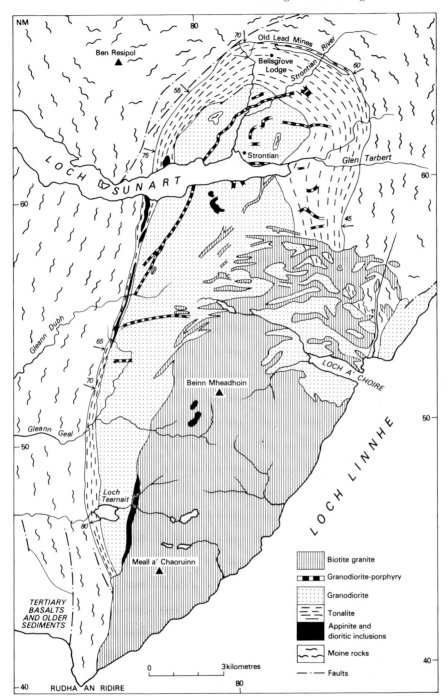

Figure 25   Map of the Strontian Complex (after Sabine, 1963)
The foliation in the Moine schists and the tonalite is indicated by the ornament

developed but, like it, the Strontian Complex has apparently expanded upwards into a rather hammer-headed shape, asymmetric by protrusion to the north (Munro, 1965). Because of this the present outcrop of the foliated tonalite is widest in the north and east.

Appinitic and dioritic rocks form large intrusions—up to 4 km long—within all components of the Strontian Complex, but they do not form hybrids to the same extent as at Rogart.

Ross of Mull Granite

The Ross of Mull intrusion ($52 km^2$) comprises a coarse-grained muscovite-biotite granite which contains small outcrops of an earlier quartz diorite in the south-western sector. The granite is a handsome pink-coloured rock, in which the jointing is quite widely spaced in places. It has been quarried and extensively used as a building stone. The intrusion is described in Bailey and Anderson (1925), largely following the work of Bosworth (1910).

The intrusion is wedge-shaped, thickening to the west (Tuson, *in* Beckinsale and Obradovich, 1973), with its base dipping eastwards at c.30° from the east shore of Iona. Beckinsale and Obradovich produced a K-Ar age of about 420 Ma for the intrusion, and pointed out that this implied both that the Moine Thrust was formed prior to that data and that it has not moved since. The granite may have been intruded along the plane of the Moine Thrust, which is generally taken as running between the island of Iona (Lewisian and Torridonian rocks) and the Ross of Mull (Moine rocks). Although the granite is never seen actually in contact with the Torridonian of Iona, Torridonian outcrop are seen in skerries only a few tens of metres offshore, and both Torridonian and Lewisian rocks show effects of contact alteration by the intrusion.

The Moine rocks (psammites of presumed Morar Division and mixed schists of the Glenfinnan Division) adjoining the upper surface of the granite have a thermal aureole (in part a contact migmatite) about 500 m wide. Within the granite, again mainly in the south-west part of the outcrop, there are small rafts and xenoliths of hornfelsed schists, apparently little displaced from their normal structural position. The thermal aureole has provided a classic site for the study of aluminosilicate polymorphs where kyanite-bearing regionally migmatised schists enter within the zone of contact metamorphism (MacKenzie, 1949).

The Ross of Mull intrusion cuts, and is itself cut by, members of the Microdiorite Suite (see below). It is also cut by Permo-Carboniferous dykes, for which Beckinsale and Obradovich obtained an age of c.275 Ma.

Other granites

The granites of Migdale (near Bonar Bridge) and Fearn (just south of the Kyle of Sutherland) are fairly uniform adamellitic or monzonitic masses rather than complexes. They consist of granite, pegmatite and microgranite, and have extensive areas of contact migmatite. The Fearn Granite shows extensive deep weathering in places.

The Grudie Granite to the south of Loch Shin is a small adamellitic mass with some associated veining. It appears to have been the locus of fairly widespread base-metal sulphide mineralisation, and molybdenite is unusually common (Gallagher and others, 1974). The small Abriachan Granite (on the north-west side of Loch Ness) is affected by fenite-type metasomatism which Deans and others (1971) relate to a possible carbonatite developed in depth along the line of the Great Glen Fault. Secondary 'abriachanite' (blue crocidolite), aegirine and hematite have been deposited along joints in this granite, and elsewhere in the region between Loch Ness and the Beauly Firth.

Reay Intrusion

The small intrusion at Reay in Caithness varies in composition from quartz diorite to granodiorite (McCourt, 1980). It has a strong foliation parallel to the margin along its north-west boundary, but this decreases away from the contact. It cuts the foliation of the schists and also the white granite phase of the Strath Halladale migmatite (p.90). A small separate stock is cross-cut by veins related to the main Strath Halladale granite.

GRANITIC VEIN COMPLEXES

Vein complexes or stockworks have been described in connection with the 'Regional Pegmatites' developed within the area of the migmatite complexes (pp.90–91). All of these are pegmatitic trondhjemite veins which were clearly derived from the migmatites which they traverse, although some of the later veins cut across the migmatite banding and the foliation of the host rock. In the south-west part of the Northern Highlands, mainly south of Glen Moriston and entirely within the Loch Eil Division, innumerable veins and sheets are found; these range from quartz diorite to leucogranite in composition, and from granitic to aplitic and pegmatitic in texture. They are clearly not directly related to the rocks which they cut, and appear to have been intruded from a remote magmatic source. Although widespread throughout the Northern Highlands (north of Glen Moriston their occurrence is not recorded in detail) there are areas where they form up to 30% or more of the total rock (Fettes and MacDonald, 1978) and the amount of igneous material they represent is enormous. The outer limits of these vein complexes are difficult to define and the mapped boundaries are highly subjective. The complexes so far delimited are shown on Figure 26, and described below.

The Loch Eil, Loch Arkaig and Mallie complexes

These consist of a suite of granite, aplite and the pegmatite veins. In all three rock-types the margins of the complexes are diffuse and the density of veining is very variable (ranging up to 30% of any one section). It is probable that the complexes are major concentrations within a more regionally developed belt of granite-pegmatites. The veins are individually sharply defined, but form a ramifying network without any obvious preferred orientation. Although large bodies do occur, the veins seldom exceed 2 m in width. There is no consistent cross-cutting relationship between the aplites, pegmatites and granites. Although the veins are massive and not recrystallised they are consistently cut by the foliated members of the Microdiorite Suite.

The Banavie Complex

These consist of a suite of potassic veins and subordinate amounts of pegmatite and aplopegmatite. The limit of the granite veins is fairly sharply defined (as shown on Figure 26) but the limit of pegmatites is more diffuse, and it is probable that they relate to the general pegmatite veining of the Loch Eil and Loch Arkaig complexes. This view is supported by the fact that the pegmatites are always cut by the microdiorites, whereas several microdiorite veins are cut by the granite. The term 'Banavie Complex' is therefore better restricted to the later granite veins; the earlier pegmatite veins should be regarded as part of the regional swarm. The granite veins are sharply defined, cutting across country rock; they generally range up to 1 m in width, although larger bodies are found. There is, in general, no preferred orientation, the veins forming ramifying networks. In places they form up to 50% of the total rock. Some of the large granite bodies cutting the Glen Loy Complex do, however, have a vague NE alignment. The Banavie Complex has been tentatively correlated with the late phase of the Strontian Granite (Sabine, 1963).

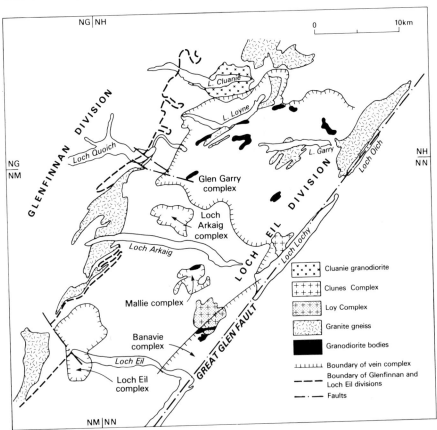

Figure 26   The vein complexes of the south-west part of the Northern Highlands (after Fettes and MacDonald (1978), based on BGS maps)

The Glen Garry Vein Complex

This complex differs from those described above in consisting largely of granodiorite. It appears to be younger than them in that it cuts most members of

the Microdiorite Suite, although some granite veins are cut by the late felsic porphyrites. The complex is about 300 km² in extent, the limit of veining being
relatively well defined. It is made up of veins and sheets ranging from a few
centimetres in width to bodies several hundred of metres in extent. The density of
veining is very variable, ranging up to intense ramifying networks which locally
make up 60% of the total rock. The composition of the veins ranges from quartz-
diorite to leucrogranite, the larger bodies tending to be tonalite or granodiorite.
Some of the granitic veins, cut by later granodiorite, may represent part of the diffuse granite veining of which the Loch Eil, Loch Arkaig and Mallie complexes are
concentrations. Members of the Glen Garry Complex cut foliated and non-
foliated members of the Microdiorite Suite.

Fettes and Macdonald (1978) consider that the variation in the composition of
the veins of the Glen Garry Vein Complex results from the fractionation of a
quartz diorite magma, but they point to chemical difficulties if it is assumed that
the vein complex derived from either a Moine or a Lewisian parent.

CALEDONIAN MINOR INTRUSIONS

Throughout the Northern Highlands there are minor intrusions (dykes, sheets
and small bosses). A few were affected by the last Caledonian folding; others were
sheared and recrystallised during late-stage minor movements when regional
temperatures were still elevated; others still are entirely post-tectonic. All,
however, are earlier than the deposition of the Old Red Sandstone cover. They
are sparsely distributed in the northern part of the area but are found in large
numbers south of the Glen Moriston–Glen Shiel through valley.

In early descriptions, such as those given in the one-inch Geological Survey
memoirs of the northern part of the district, they were thought to represent
members of one connected suite. Post-war mapping in the southern area, where
they are abundant, has shown that they belong to two suites, the entirely post-
tectonic Minette Suite (including the felsites), and the Microdiorite Suite, which
is late- to post-tectonic in age. D. I. Smith (1979) has described their distribution,
relationships to tectonism and varying metamorphism (see also Talbot, 1983).

The Microdiorite Suite

Rocks of the Microdiorite Suite show a continuous transition from leucocratic
felsic porphyrite though quartz microdiorite to microdiorite, and thence through
mafic microdiorite to a variable appinitic group consisting mainly of hornblende
diorite. The more felsic varieties of the suite cut the more mafic varieties, and
both felsic porphyrites and microdiorites show varying degrees of textural or
mineral reconstruction. The appinites do not appear to be affected in this manner.

Microdiorites and felsic porphyrites typically occupy joints dipping SE at 35°,
along which some degree of late-stage movement has taken place; D. I. Smith
(1979) discusses the mechanics of deformation which renders the rocks schistose.
In places the intrusion are numerous enough to impart a bedded appearance to
the slopes of a hillside when viewed from a distance.

Appinite

This name is now applied to members of the Microdiorite Suite which are coarse-grained, hornblende-rich (occasionally pyroxene-bearing) mafic diorites. They usually occur as thick sheets or small bosses, and the varieties found could all reasonably be derived from the differentiation of a potassium-rich basaltic magma. They commonly form masses of fairly homogeneous rock but, in Sutherland especially, they show gradation into patchy more acid and more basic material, and even into rock in which the basic fraction appears as xenoliths within the more acid fraction. These characteristics led Read and others (1925) and Read (1931) to regard the Sutherland rocks as the results of hybridisation of ultrabasic magma by granitic magma (the Ach'Uaine Hybrids). The appinites are absent from the central part of the Northern Highlands but show a notable concentration in the vicinity of the Rogart Complex (Ach'Uaine types) and the Strontian Granite, where they are cut by veins of the granite and form large inclusions in the main igneous body. These concentrations suggest a genetic relationship with the granite intrusions. In Glen Garry the appinites are cut by veins of the Glen Garry Vein Complex (p.112). A notable concentration of pyroxene-bearing appinite has been found in the area west of Invergarry.

Microdiorite

These rocks are the most numerous representatives of the Microdiorite Suite. They typically form thin sheets (average thickness about 1 m) cutting the foliation of the Moine country rock. They are abundant in the area south-west of Glen Moriston, and D. I. Smith (1979) has delimited the areas in which the intrusions are particularly concentrated. He defines a line north and west of which they are rare (Figure 27A).

Unmodified microdiorites contain zoned andesine and hornblende (both of which form phenocrysts) as well as biotite and subordinate interstitial quartz and potash feldspar. Many of the sheets, however, are schistose along their margin or throughout, but do not show cataclasis. The usual occurrence of the intrusions as swarms of parallel sheets along moderately inclined joints suggests that the schistosity is a feature of ductile deformation developed late in the tectonic history of the area. They appear to have been recrystallised during the process of deformation, and Johnson and Dalziel (1966), Dearnley (1967) and D. I. Smith (1979) note that this metamorphism took place under amphibolite- or greenschist-facies conditions in a manner which shows regular variation across the area (Figure 27A).

Though intrusions with igneous mineral assemblages are found throughout the area, there are some strongly metamorphosed microdiorites south of Glen Garry which seems to have involved in the regional (?D_3) folding of the Moine rocks. It thus appears that there may be more than one period of intrusion, and that the latest intrusions escaped the deformation and metamorphism which affected the earlier ones. As yet no clear evidence of sequential intrusion has been found.

Felsic porphyrite

The felsic porphyrites have a much more restricted occurrence than the microdiorites and are apparently confined to the central part of the area south-west of the Glen Moriston – Glen Shiel valley (Figure 27B) although it is possible that sparse representatives lie undetected outside that zone. The felsic porphyrites, where undeformed, are porphyritic microgranites with phenocrysts of oscillatory-zoned albite-oligoclase, biotite and, in places, hornblende, set in a

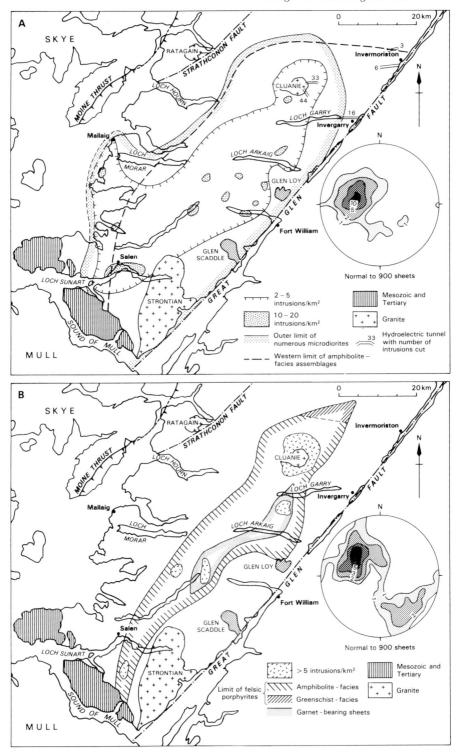

Figure 27 Distribution, orientation and metamorphic grade of intrusions of the Caledonian Microdiorite Suite (after Smith 1979); stereonet insets of poles normal to the sheets. Glen Scaddle and Glen Loy are mafic intrusions

A Microdiorite **B** Felsic porphyrite

granoblastic fine-grained groundmass of quartz, potash feldspar and acid plagioclase in equal proportions. Like the microdiorites, they are commonly schistose, having been deformed and recrystallised to produce amphibolite- or greenschist-facies mineral assemblages; amphibolite facies is dominant. Garnet-bearing varieties are found between Glenfinnan and the east end of Loch Garry.

Early representatives of the Microdiorite Suite

Rocks very similar to members of the suite, but earlier than the main phase of intrusion, are found in two areas. In a restricted area near the west end of Loch Garry microdiorites were apparently foliated during the last period of regional Caledonian folding. Around the Cluanie Granite a restricted swarm of acid dykes was emplaced earlier than the intrusion of the Cluanie Granite. Both these, and the Cluanie Granite itself, are cut by representatives of the main phase of intrusion of the Microdiorite Suite. They are distinguished from the younger felsic porphyrites by their greater abundance of phenocrysts of acid plagioclase, biotite and hornblende.

The Minette Suite and felsites

In contrast to rocks of the Microdiorite Suite, members of the Minette Suite are widely, if sparsely distributed throughout the Northern Highlands. They extend beyond the Caledonides across the Moine Thrust and cut Torridonian and Lewisian strata of the Foreland. They usually form vertical-sided dykes with sharp, chilled edges and have an average thickness of about 3 m (D. I. Smith, 1979). Many are traceable for several kilometres, commonly in an E–W direction. Most are typically minettes, lamprophyres rich in phenocrysts of biotite ± augite. A small number of hornblende lamprophyres (vogesites) are represented. The only place where these lamprophyres are sufficiently numerous to constitute a swarm is around the Ratagain Complex where they are displaced 6 km in a sinistral sense by late movement on the Strathconon Fault.

Thick dykes of felsite, mainly trending E–W for many kilometres, are also found in the Northern Highlands. Their relationship to the Minette Suite is uncertain, but around the Ratagain Complex smaller dykes of felsite are apparently represented in the same swarm as the Minettes. Minettes cut felsites and vice versa, but it is not certain if these localised dykes belong to the same phase of intrusion as the more extensive and thicker bodies.

Breccia-filled fissures

In the areas where intrusions of the Microdiorite Suite and the vein complexes are abundant there are a number of breccia-filled fissures, as well as some more extensive areas of broken and disoriented blocks. The main constituents of these breccias are blocks of country rock, mainly of local derivation, rotated but jammed together. They are set in a very minor matrix of more or less felsic microdiorite. In places even this minor igneous matrix seems to be lacking. The breccias are similar to explosion breccias described from Kentallen by Bowes and Wright (1967). J. D. Peacock (personal communication) considers that they may have formed by a filter-press mechanism following explosive activity, and were transported in a liquid rather than a gas. In the Cluanie area these breccias are veined by later felsic porphyrites and members of the vein complexes to form a second-generation agmatite.

North of Glen Garry, within the area of the Glen Garry Vein Complex, local areas of disoriented blocks of Moine psammite are found; they may measure several tens of metres across, but are not fissure-fillings. They may be similar in origin to the fissure breccias.

10   Old Red Sandstone

Old Red Sandstone strata form an almost continuous outcrop along the eastern side of the Northern Highlands from Loch Ness to the north coast of Caithness. West of the main outcrop there are a number of small outliers which suggest that rocks of this age formerly extended westwards along certain pre-Devonian topographic depressions. In the south of the region sediments of Old Red Sandstone age form only one small outlier, on the west shore of Loch Linnhe.

It has long been held that only Middle and Upper Old Red Sandstone rocks are present in the Northern Highlands. In recent years, however, the lower part of the previously accepted 'Middle Old Red Sandstone' has been tentatively assigned to the Lower Old Red Sandstone (Westoll, 1951; Armstrong, 1964) and this interpretation has been supported by miospore evidence (Richardson, 1967; Collins and Donovan, 1977). The rocks ascribed to the Lower Old Red Sandstone consist of coarse basal breccio-conglomerates and conglomerates overlain by, and interdigitated with, a sequence of generally fine-grained sandstones, siltstones and mudstones (Figure 30). In Easter Ross the fine sediments are olive-grey, dark grey or black; around Strathpeffer bituminous rocks form an important part of the sequence. These Lower Old Red Sandstone sediments were involved in localised folding and thrusting, and affected by a period of subaerial erosion prior to the deposition of the Middle Old Red Sandstone.

The Middle Old Red Sandstone sediments exhibit a marked change of facies from mainly lacustrine flags in Caithness to predominantly fluvial sandstones and conglomerates in Easter Ross and Inverness-shire. The Caithness flagstones were laid down in an extensive shallow lake which extended northwards across Orkney. They contain many fish-bearing beds, the best known of which is the Achanarras Limestone (p. 130). Easter Ross appears at that time to have been part of the flood plain of a large north-east flowing braided river bounded on its margins by alluvial fans. A few fish beds intercalated with the sandstone represent temporary transgressions of the Orcadian lake which lay to the north-east. The conglomerates on the west side of the Easter Ross outcrop contain pebbles of Torridonian and Cambrian rocks, which crop out in situ only west of the Moine Thrust.

Upper Old Red Sandstone crops out in the Tarbat Ness–Tain peninsula (Figure 29) and forms a narrow coastal strip north of Dornoch (Figure 28). Dunnet Head, Caithness, is part of a larger outcrop of Upper Old Red Sandstone which extends across the Pentland Firth to Hoy. In all these areas the sediment is a cross-bedded, locally pebbly, medium- to coarse-grained fluvial sandstone, probably laid down on large alluvial plains fed by rivers flowing from the west or south-west.

The terrain on which the Old Red Sandstone was deposited appears to have been mountainous in both Lower and Middle Old Red Sandstone times, with the relief being greatest in the west and south-west. The climate was tropical or subtropical; palaeomagnetic data suggest that in Devonian times Britain lay between 30°S and 10°S. Lower Old Red Sandstone sediments were laid down in isolated basins, the margins of which were, to some extent, controlled by faults which may have been active at the time of deposition. The Middle Old Red Sandstone basins were more extensive, and in parts of Caithness, around the Sutors of Cromarty,

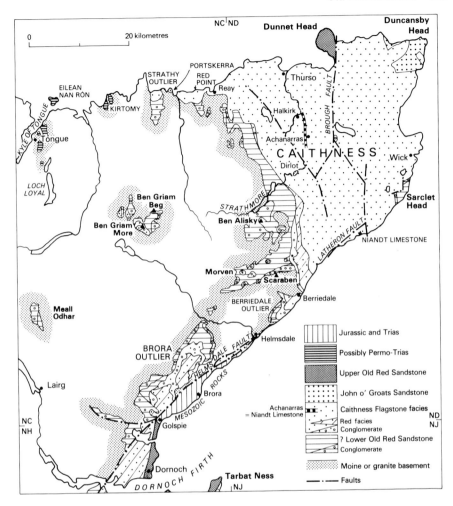

Figure 28   Old Red Sandstone of Caithness and Sutherland

and in some of the western outliers, Middle Old Red Sandstone rests directly on the crystalline basement. The base of both the Lower and Middle Old Red Sandstone is markedly diachronous. The basal Lower Old Red Sandstone appears to be oldest in the area south and south-west of Strathpeffer, becoming progressively younger north-eastward towards Ousdale in southern Caithness. The base of the Middle Old Red Sandstone, on the other hand, appears to be oldest at Sarclet on the east coast of Caithness, where there is a conformable upward passage from the Lower Old Red Sandstone, becoming younger in both a north-westward and a south-westward direction.

The most problematical rocks of possible Old Red Sandstone age in the Northern Highlands are those forming the outliers at Kirtomy, Eilean nan Ron and Tongue in northern Sutherland (Figure 28; see Peach *in* Crampton and Carruthers, 1914). These rocks consist of conglomerates, and bright red sandstones and siltstones with poorly developed incipient cornstone horizons. The finer sediments contrast strongly with the more compact dull purplish rocks of the outliers further east along the Sutherland coast. The Old Red Sandstone age of these western outliers has been questioned by MacIntyre and others (1956), who hinted at a possible Torridonian age, but the presence of pebbles of Durness Limestone, Cambrian Quartzite and Pipe Rock on the Ron Islands, and pebbles of Ben Loyal type syenite in the Tongue outcrops, rules out that possibility. Drill cores of similar red sandstones and conglomerates obtained by the Marine Geology Unit of BGS just offshore north of Sutherland have yielded poorly preserved spores of possible low Mesozoic age. Though Blackbourn (1981a; 1981b) and O'Reilly (1983) still regard the outcrops as Old Red Sandstone, they have produced no lithological or palaeontological evidence which would preclude a New Red Sandstone age (see p.148).

LOWER OLD RED SANDSTONE

Caithness and northern Sutherland

Beds ascribed to the Lower Old Red Sandstone crop out in a small anticlinal area around Sarclet Head in eastern Caithness, and in a larger outcrop extending along the western margin of the Caithness Old Red Sandstone outcrop, from Reay to Berriedale (Figure 28). The best documented section is that of the Sarclet Anticline, where the Sarclet Group (Figure 30) contains the following formations (Donovan, 1970):

Formations	Thickness (m)
4 Ulbster/Ires Geo Sandstone Formation	107
3 Ulbster/Riera Geo Mudstone Formation	172
2 Sarclet Sandstone Formation	85
1 Sarclet Conglomerate Formation	70

The Sarclet Conglomerate is made up of lenses of conglomerate and pebbly sandstone, with pebbles of granite, schist, quartzite, sandstone and basalt. The conglomerate and overlying Sarclet Sandstone appear to have been laid down by braided rivers and meandering rivers from the south-east. The Ulbster/Riera Geo Mudstone Formation is a rhythmic sequence, mainly of hard green mudstones with some thin calcareous marls, siltstones and sandstones. It appears to have been deposited in a shallow lake which periodically receded to give place to a deltaic alluvial plain. The Ulbster/Ires Geo Sandstone Formation consists of a thin lower sequence of red sandstone, lain down by small rivers and streams, overlain by grey mudstone of lacustrine origin, which, in turn, passes upward into fairly coarse red fluvial sandstone and grit. Miospores from a bed of grey-green mudstone 15 cm thick intercalated with the sandstone indicate an Upper Emsian age for the deposit (Collins and Donovan, 1977). The top of the formation is interdigitated with the Ellens Geo Conglomerate, which has been taken as the local base of the Middle Old Red Sandstone (Figure 30).

In the Berriedale Outlier (Figure 28) the Lower Old Red Sandstone rests on the Helmsdale Granite. Its basal member, locally termed the Ousdale Arkose, contains a conglomerate, but elsewhere consists of redeposited, unweathered granite debris which is difficult to distinguish from the underlying granite. The overlying Ousdale Mudstone (seen in road cuttings and in a quarry north of the Ord of

Caithness) consists of purple, pale green and red siltstones and mudstones alternating with thin beds of locally pebbly sandstone. The sandy siltstones have yielded unidentifiable plant remains. Miospores and a scale of *Porolepis* suggest a high Lower Devonian (Lower Emsian) age (Richardson, 1967; Collins and Donovan, 1977).

The Lower Old Red Sandstone was gently folded and eroded prior to the deposition of the Badbea Breccia, the basal member of Middle Old Red Sandstone in this area; the breccia oversteps on to the metamorphic basement.

North of Scaraben (Figure 28), Lower Old Red Sandstone forms an irregular outcrop along the western margin of the Caithness plain, with two westward-projecting tongues in the Morven and Ben Alisky districts. In this belt there are a number of lenticular outcrops of basal arkosic conglomerate and breccia, the pebbles of which can be closely matched with the lithology of the local basement. Over a large part of the outcrop, however, fine-grained purplish flaggy sandstones, mudstones and siltstones (the 'Braemore Mudstones') rest directly on the basement. The Lower Old Red Sandstone beds of this belt are steeply inclined in some places, but more generally they are concordant with the overlying Middle Old Red Sandstone. At its northern end, around Reay, the belt of Lower Old Red Sandstone beds is discontinuous, the isolated outcrops representing infilled N–S-trending pre-Old Red Sandstone valleys.

In the Strathy Outlier (Figure 28), conglomerates and arkoses of probable Lower Old Red Sandstone age occupy the southern part of the outcrop. The age of the three outliers around Ben Griam More and Ben Griam Beg is not certain. The sediments rest on a very uneven floor and the sequence, as seen in the largest outlier, is as follows, (Read, 1931, pp.205–207).

4   Arkose, red, cross-bedded with pebbly bands at base, but becoming yellow and massive at top
3   Conglomerate, with quartzite pebbles in arkosic matrix
2   Arkose, reddish, with conglomerate bands and some thin red mudstones with sun-cracks near top
1   Basal conglomerate and breccia-conglomerate, locally with huge boulders of local origin

No fossils have been obtained from these beds: on lithological grounds alone they could be ascribed to either the Lower or the Middle Old Red Sandstone. However, formations 1 and 2 show some similarities to the Lower Old Red Sandstone of western Caithness, and formations 3 and 4 may be fluviatile facies of Middle Old Red Sandstone age, broadly similar to the Middle Old Red Sandstone of the Brora Outlier (p.134). Further south-west, the outlier of Meall Odhar, 15 km north of Lairg, is probably entirely of Lower Old Red Sandstone age. It consists of red and chocolate micaceous sandstones with ripple marks and possible worm casts, passing upwards by interdigitation into coarse conglomerate (Read, 1931). Its probable Lower Old Red Sandstone age is, again, based largely on lithological comparison.

East Sutherland

The Old Red Sandstone of east Sutherland forms an irregular, partly fault-bounded outcrop extending from just south of the Strath of Kildonan to the Dornoch Firth. The part west of the Helmsdale Fault is known as the Brora Outlier, which forms a series of prominent hills. It has the structure of a basin elongated in a north-easterly direction. It contains two groups of strata separated by a marked angular unconformity (Figures 30, 31a). No fossils have been found, but the lower group is taken to be of Lower Old Red Sandstone age: it is lithologically similar to the spore-bearing Lower Old Red Sandstone of southern Caithness. The basal breccia and conglomerate (the Ben Lundie Formation) of the ?Lower Old Red Sandstone forms an almost continuous outcrop along the western and southern margins of the Brora Outlier and forms the hills north and west of Loch Fleet. It is thickest and coarsest in the south; in the craggy hills south-west and west of Golspie it contains angular boulders up to 60 cm in diameter set in a red gritty matrix and intercalated with impersistent sandstones. The boulders consist of schists and granite of the types which crop out immediately to the west; it is probable that the breccia was deposited as screes and torrential fan deposits at the foot of the fault-bounded hills lying to the west.

Above the basal conglomerates are pebbly sandstones which are in turn overlain by fine-grained, red and purple, ripple-marked sandstones, then locally by mudstones, and finally, by hard flaggy red sandstones (the Glen Loth Formation). The sandstones and mudstones have some sun-cracked surfaces, and there are several beds of desiccation-breccia. The mudstones are best developed at the north-eastern end of the outlier where they reach a thickness of 500 m. They are the probable equivalents of the Ousdale/Braemore Mudstones of southern Caithness and, like the latter, they were probably laid down in a shallow lake.

Ross and Cromarty

The Old Red Sandstone south of the Dornoch Firth forms an open syncline trending south-west, the axial trace of which extends south-westwards from Inver through the centre of the Black Isle to the vicinity of Beauly (Figure 29). Sediments of probable Lower Old Red Sandstone age, termed the Struie Group (Armstrong, 1977), form a continuous outcrop along the western margin of the syncline. Their contact with the underlying Moine is in part an unconformity and in part a fault; on Struie Hill, folded and faulted beds have been thrust over the Moine basement (Figure 31b). They consist of lenticular conglomerates intercalated with grey and black flaggy sandstones, siltstones and mudstones. The conglomerates thin out immediately south of Struie Hill, giving place to a fine-grained sequence of dark grey siltstones and calcareous mudstones, which have yielded no determinable fossils. South of the Loch Morie Fault (Figure 29) breccia and conglomerate are to be seen again, and south of Strathpeffer conglomerate gives rise to a series of prominent hills along the rivers Conon and Orrin. Still further south coarse breccio-conglomerate is exposed in the Aigas Gorge of the River Beauly, where some of the rugged, pre-Old Red topography can be seen (Smith, 1963).

Above the basal breccio-conglomerates the sequence comprises green and grey shales, flagstones, fetid dark shales and calcareous mudstones. In the Strathpeffer district the following succession has been recorded (Horne and Hinxman, 1914).

4   Red shales passing up into sandstone (200 m thick)
3   Olive shales with shaly, fetid limestones (85 m thick)
2   Spa Beds: fetid bituminous and calcareous shales with thin limestones (30 m thick)
1   Ord Beds: olive shales with fetid calcareous bands (250–300 m thick)

The fetid beds give off a smell of hyrogen sulphide when hammered and are the source of the 'sulphur waters' to which Strathpeffer owes its development as a spa during the 19th century.

Some of the shales and limestones of the Ord Beds contain structures which resemble stromatolites and may be of algal origin. The olive shales have yielded

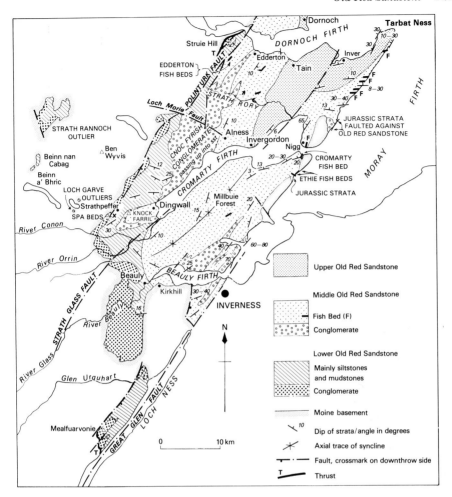

Figure 29   Old Red Sandstone of Easter Ross and Inverness-shire

spores of Lower Devonian aspect, which include *Emphanisporites* and pseudo-saccate spores (Richardson, 1967). These are comparable with the spore assemblages obtained from the Lower Old Red Sandstone of Strathmore in the Midland Valley of Scotland. The outcrop of the fetid calcareous shales can be traced southwards from Strathpeffer to Beauly and Kirkhill.

Beds of Lower Old Red Sandstone age have not been recorded on the east limb of the Inver–Black Isle Syncline, and the Moine inliers of Hill of Nigg and Cromarty are directly overlain by conglomerates of the Millbuie Sandstone Group, which is ascribed to the Middle Old Red Sandstone (p.136; Figures 30, 31c). In the south-east part of the syncline, Westoll (1977) has equated the Ord Hill conglomerate and overlying sediments with the Lower Old Red Sandstone Strathpeffer beds, but this correlation is not supported by either lithological or fossil evidence.

Western outliers of Ross-shire

The Strath Rannoch Outlier (Figure 29) is situated some 10 km north-west of Ben

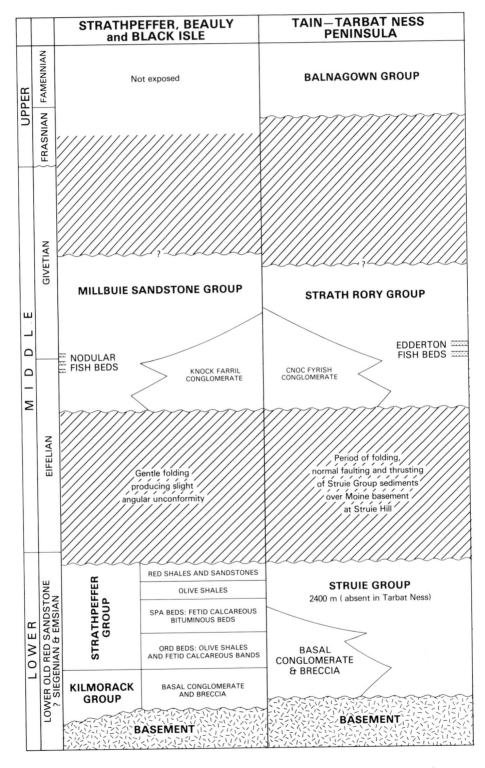

Figure 30   Correlation chart of the Old Red Sandstone of the Northern Highlands

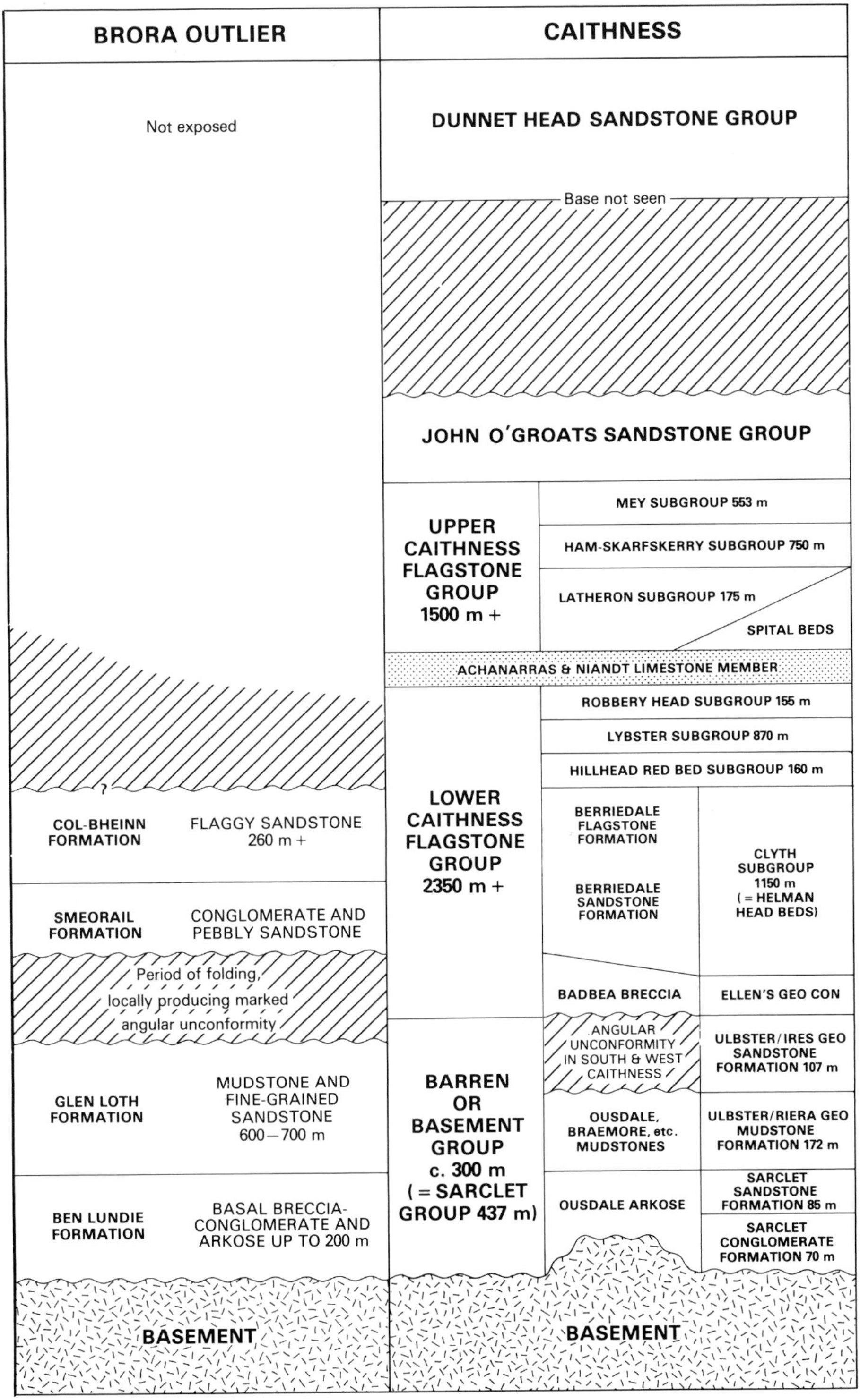

BRORA OUTLIER	CAITHNESS

Not exposed

DUNNET HEAD SANDSTONE GROUP

Base not seen

JOHN O'GROATS SANDSTONE GROUP

UPPER CAITHNESS FLAGSTONE GROUP 1500 m +	MEY SUBGROUP 553 m	
	HAM-SKARFSKERRY SUBGROUP 750 m	
	LATHERON SUBGROUP 175 m	
		SPITAL BEDS

ACHANARRAS & NIANDT LIMESTONE MEMBER

LOWER CAITHNESS FLAGSTONE GROUP 2350 m +	ROBBERY HEAD SUBGROUP 155 m	
	LYBSTER SUBGROUP 870 m	
	HILLHEAD RED BED SUBGROUP 160 m	
	BERRIEDALE FLAGSTONE FORMATION	CLYTH SUBGROUP 1150 m (= HELMAN HEAD BEDS)
	BERRIEDALE SANDSTONE FORMATION	

COL-BHEINN FORMATION — FLAGGY SANDSTONE 260 m +

SMEORAIL FORMATION — CONGLOMERATE AND PEBBLY SANDSTONE

Period of folding, locally producing marked angular unconformity

CAITHNESS	
BADBEA BRECCIA	ELLEN'S GEO CON
ANGULAR UNCONFORMITY IN SOUTH & WEST CAITHNESS	ULBSTER/IRES GEO SANDSTONE FORMATION 107 m
OUSDALE, BRAEMORE, etc. MUDSTONES	ULBSTER/RIERA GEO MUDSTONE FORMATION 172 m
OUSDALE ARKOSE	SARCLET SANDSTONE FORMATION 85 m
	SARCLET CONGLOMERATE FORMATION 70 m

GLEN LOTH FORMATION — MUDSTONE AND FINE-GRAINED SANDSTONE 600–700 m

BEN LUNDIE FORMATION — BASAL BRECCIA-CONGLOMERATE AND ARKOSE UP TO 200 m

BARREN OR BASEMENT GROUP c. 300 m (= SARCLET GROUP 437 m)

BASEMENT   **BASEMENT**

Wyvis and consists of sediments which fill a steep-sided valley within metamorphic basement. The sediments comprise coarse massive conglomerates, which give rise to prominent escarpments along the western margin of the outcrop, as well as red fine-grained sandstone and mudstone with thin calcareous bands. The finer-grained sediments crop out in the valley bottoms and along the east side of the outlier. No order of succession has as yet been established and it is likely that there are marked lateral facies changes, owing to the pronounced pre-Old Red Sandstone topography of the area. The coarse conglomerate capping the summit of Meall a' Ghrianan [NH 366 776], just north-west of the Strath Rannoch outlier, contains huge blocks of locally derived augen gneiss up to 6 m in diameter. In this area the Moine – Old Red Sandstone junction rises about 400 m over a horizontal distance of less than 2 km.

Smaller outliers of Old Red Sandstone breccia and conglomerate crop out on the summits of Beinn nan Cabag [NH 356 670] and Beinn a' Bhric [NH 345 652], some 5 km south of the Strath Rannoch Outlier (Figure 29). These sediments were also deposited on a mountainous topography; in one locality the junction with the basement is a steep cliff.

Inverness-shire

Mealfuarvonie

Along the north-west side of Loch Ness a fault-bounded outcrop of tightly folded, faulted and locally thrust sediments extends for 16 km south-west from Glen Urquhart (Mykura and Owens, 1983). This contains nine lenticular masses of breccio-conglomerate and pebbly arkosic grit which give rise to prominent craggy hills; they range in thickness from 50 m to 400 m. These are interbedded with a sequence of at least 1800 m of predominantly planar-bedded, reddish, fine-to medium-fine-grained sandstone. Mudstones and siltstones generally form only thin films and intraformational clasts within the sandstone but, near the north-east end of the outcrop, they are thicker. In the extreme north-east a number of pale green mudstones have yielded poorly preserved non-diagnostic plants as well as a rich microflora, which suggest an Emsian or possibly Eifelian age. In the extreme south-west of the outcrop the conglomerates and arkosic grits contain many clasts of granite which must have been derived from a nearby outcrop on the south-east side of the Great Glen Fault. The most likely source for the clasts is the small granite outcrops now exposed on the east side of the Great Glen between Loch Lochy and Loch Oich, suggesting a post-Lower Devonian dextral displacement of the order of 25 km along the Great Glen Fault.

Loch Linnhe

The small outcrop of Old Red Sandstone within the Great Glen Fault Zone at Rubha na h-Earba, 17 km south-west of Fort William, comprises a coarse basal scree-breccia, about 15 m thick, overstepped by an interdigitating sequence of conglomerate and sandstone (Stoker, 1982). The conglomerates represent sheet-flood deposits of an alluvial fan, while the sandstones were probably laid down by braided rivers on an alluvial plain. The beds have been faulted, folded and overthrust. Though formerly taken to be of Middle Old Red Sandstone age, Stoker now believes that they may be Lower Devonian. The evidence for this is, however, not conclusive.

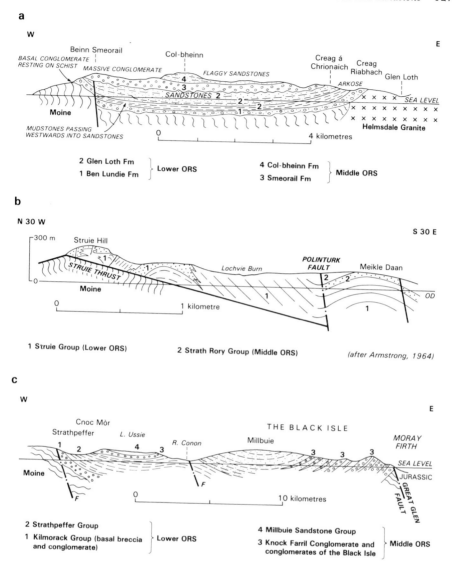

Figure 31   Sections across the Old Red Sandstone of Sutherland and Easter Ross
a Across northern part of Brora Outlier   **b** Across Struie Hill, near Edderton, to
illustrate Struie Thrust and associated folds   **c** Across the Inver – Black Isle Syncline
from Strathpeffer to Fortrose

Conditions of deposition

It is believed that the Lower Old Red Sandstone rocks were laid down in a
number of fault-bounded basins of relatively limited extent. The coarse breccio-
conglomerates originated as screes and terrestrial fan deposits laid down at the
foot of the emerging mountains. The absence of medium-grained fluvial sandstones and the preponderance of siltstones and mudstones among the finer-
grained sediments suggest that there were no large, swift-flowing rivers at that
time, possibly because rainfall was low. Some of the basins contained lakes, which

received only fine sediment. The organic content of the Strathpeffer lake must have been high, possibly containing abundant blue green algae and bacteria.

MIDDLE OLD RED SANDSTONE

Caithness and north Sutherland

The greater part of Caithness is underlain by grey, fissile, thinly bedded flagstones which may be up to 4 km thick. They have been extensively quarried in the past for use as paving slabs, roofing slates and building stones. The flagstone sequence is divided into the Lower and Upper Caithness Flagstone Groups (Donovan and others, 1974), the boundary between which is drawn at the horizon of the Achanarras Limestone (Figures 30, 34). The Achanarras Limestone is a distinctive, thinly laminated, calcareous bed with a characteristic fish assemblage similar to those found in the Niandt Limestone of east Caithness, the Sandwick Fish Bed of Orkney, the Melby Fish Beds of west Shetland, and the Cromarty and Edderton Fish Beds of Easter Ross.

The base of the Middle Old Red Sandstone of Caithness is diachronous, being oldest at Sarclet, where there is no stratigraphic break between Middle and Lower Old Red Sandstone. It becomes progressively younger along the western margin between Berriedale and Reay. In south-east Caithness there are nearly 2.5 km of sediment below the Achanarras horizon; at Reay the base of the Middle Old Red Sandstone is just below the Achanarras Limestone, and further west at Strathy it is just above this horizon.

Lithology and depositional environment of the flags

At first sight the Caithness Flags appear to consist of a monotonous sequence of laminated, carbonate-rich siltstones and shales with subordinate fine-grained, thinly bedded sandstones. Closer examination shows the sequence to be made up of well defined rhythmic units or cycles; these are generally 5 to 10 m thick, but reach 60 m in the Achanarras Limestone cycle. The flags were deposited in an extensive shallow lake (Figure 32) which extended from Caithness northwards, across and beyond Orkney and eastwards into the present North Sea. Every cycle represents a sequence of events caused by the very frequent, repeated fluctuations in the lake level (Fannin, 1970; Donovan, 1980). Five distinct lithological associations (Facies A to E) can be recognised in many cycles.

Facies A   The cycle commences with a bed of 'laminite', a dark grey or black, thinly laminated siltstone, generally carbonate- and bitumen-rich, which in many instances contains fish remains. Individual laminae are on avarage 0.5 mm thick and consist of triplets comprising micritic carbonate → organic carbon → fine silt. The laminite was laid down when the lake was at its deepest, when its waters were undisturbed by waves and when for most of the year little or no sediment entered the lake. The triplets have been interpreted as non-glacial varves formed by sequential deposition in a eutrophic lake whose waters were thermally stratified to some extent (Rayner, 1963). Seasonal algal bloom led to carbonate precipitation by increasing the pH of the lake water during photosynthesis. When the plankton died they fell to the (anaerobic) lake bottom to form a thin skin of organic carbon on top of the carbonate lamina. The final clastic lamina of the cycle is thought to represent a seasonal influx of fine sediment into the lake.

Facies B   The laminite is followed by a slightly more coarsely interlaminated (0.5 to 3 mm scale) facies of dark grey, carbon-rich shale, siltstone and carbonate. This has some very small-scale ripple lamination, and some laminae may be turbidites. Mound structures are common; they may have been formed by gas bubbles rising from decaying vegetation in the sediment (Donovan and Collins, 1978). Sub-

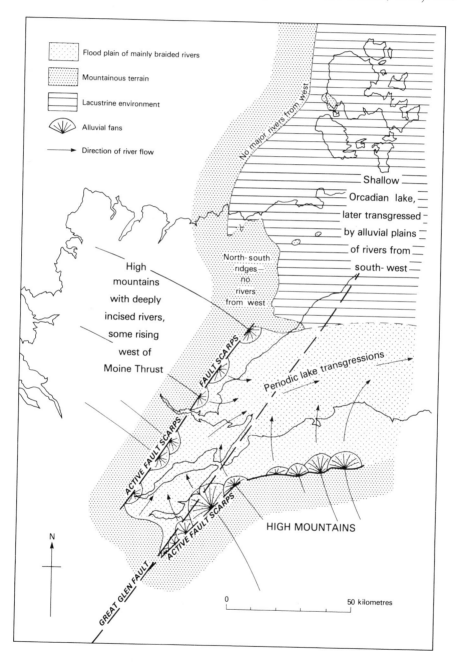

Figure 32   Middle Old Red Sandstone palaeogeography of northern Scotland (a post-Devonian dextral displacement of 27 km along the Great Glen Fault is assumed)

aqueous shrinkage cracks (syneresis cracks) also occur (Plate 22). These beds were formed below wave base in a quiescent lake which still received very little sediment.

Facies C   The succeeding facies consists of coarser alternations (up to 10 mm) of carbonaceous shale and coarse siltstone with ripple cross-bedding, indicating shallow water and some wave action. Syneresis cracks, which may be due to seasonal changes in salinity, are common (Donovan and Foster, 1972).

Facies D   This comprises successive beds of shale, siltstone and fine sandstone, and is up to 10 cm thick. Flaser bedding and surfaces with symmetrical ripple marks appear. Large subaerial shrinkage cracks are common; pseudonodules and convolute bedding are also found. At this stage the lake had become so shallow that its floor was periodically exposed, giving rise to extensive mud-flats.

In the Clyth Subgroup (Figure 30) and in the basin-marginal deposits of higher subgroups these shallow lake and mudflat deposits are interbedded with, and channelled by, thicker lenticular cross-bedded sandstones (*Facies E*), which represent the filled-in channels of either rivers crossing the mudflat or delta-distributaries in the shallow lake. The sandy phase is overlain by mudflat deposits of interbanded siltstones and mudstones with sun cracks and syneresis cracks (*Facies D and C*) followed by an abrupt change to the dark, laminated fish-bed facies (*A*) of the next cycle, representing the onset of the next period of quiescent, deeper water conditions (Figure 33).

The thickness of the various lithological components within the cycle varies according to their stratigraphical position in the Caithness Flagstone sequence (Figure 30) and their geographical position within the original lake. Thus the sandstone phases are relatively thick and laterally persistent in the Clyth Subgroup (the Helman Head beds of the original classification) but are thin and even absent in most areas within the succeeding subgroups. In the Mey Subgroup thick channel sandstones are again present. An even more characteristic feature of the Mey Subgroup is the common occurrence of slumped or foundered beds (with 'pseudonodules' or 'ball and pillow' structures) within the fluvial phase of the cylces. These beds were termed 'nodule-beds' by Crampton and Carruthers (1914). The quiet-water, 'fish-bed' facies are locally very carbonate-rich in the Clyth and Lybster subgroups, where some approach dolomitic limestone in composition. In the Achanarras cycle the fish-bed horizon is very thick and so finely laminated that it has been worked as a roofing slate. Other features of local significance are the presence of thick beds of pale grey, unlaminated mudstone and silty mudstone in the cycles overlying the Achanarras Limestone at Halkirk and Achanarras, the presence of thin, black, highly bituminous beds within the Ackergill Beds (lower part of Mey Subgroup) just west and south of Sinclair Bay, and the presence of thick beds of fine-grained, flaggy sandstone in the Field Beds (a local facies of the Latheron Subgroup exposed on the coast just north of Wick).

Disseminated carbonate forms an appreciable percentage of all flagstones and its composition determines the colour of the weathered rock faces. Thus the flags below the Achanarras horizon are usually dark grey or black when fresh but weather to drab or buff colour (calcite), and those above are lighter coloured when fresh and weather to an ochre and bluish colour (ferroan dolomite). Algal stromatolites, which are common in the Stromness and Rousay Flags of Orkney, are rare in the Caithness Flags.

The western margin of the Orcadian lake appears to coincide roughly with the western edge of the present-day outcrop of the Caithness Flags (Donovan, 1975). Within this area the lake floor was uneven and locally rocky. In some areas, such

Plate 22 Shrinkage (syneresis) cracks in Caithness Flags at Clairdon Head, east of Thurso   (C1556)

Plate 23 Stacks of Duncansby: sea stacks of John O'Groats Sandstone (Middle Old Red Sandstone)   (D1608)

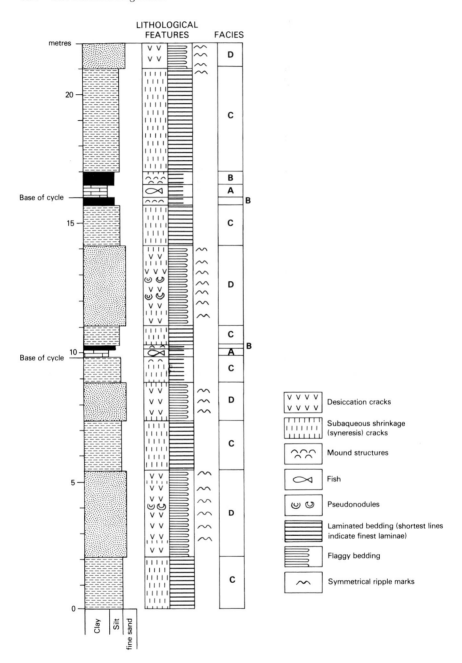

Figure 33   Lithological log of cyclic sequences in the Caithness Flags, Latheron Subgroup, on the shore NE of Dounreay (after Donovan, 1980, fig.1)

Lithological associations (facies): **A** 'Fish beds', laminite; originated as non-glacial varves   **B** Thinly-interlaminated siltstone and shale with mound structures   **C** Thicker laminae of shale and coarse siltstone, with abundant subaqueous shrinkage cracks   **D** Alternations of fine sandstone, siltstone and shale with symmetrical ripples, some pseudonodules and abundant desiccation cracks. Note: No fine-grained channel sandstones are present in this section

as Dirlot Castle [ND 127 488], Red Point [NC 930 660], Portskerra [NC 876 667] and Balligill [NC 856 663], the remains of rocky islets of Moine basement are preserved. These islets are surrounded by thin fossil scree fans of breccia and conglomerate and, at Dirlot, individual pebbles are coated with algal stromatolites (Donovan, 1973). At Cnoc nan Airidhe (5 km south-east of Reay, [NC 989 608]) and Red Point there are thin beds of limestone close to the unconformity (Donovan, 1975).

In the Berriedale Outlier and along the western margin of the main outcrop just north of Berriedale (Figure 28) the lowest member of the Middle Old Red Sandstone is a basal breccia or conglomerate, known as the Badbea Breccia at Ousdale. It is overlain by red arkosic sandstone (the 'Berriedale Sandstone') which is, in turn, succeeded by red and grey rhythmically bedded flags of Caithness Flagstone type (the 'Berriedale Flags'). The flags contain thick red channel-sandstone phases and well developed interbanded sandstone-siltstone ribs with syneresis and sun cracks. South of the Berriedale Outlier the only lacustrine flagstones of Caithness type are the clasts forming the 'Fallen Stack' and other boulders in the coastal strip of Kimmeridgian beds between Ord Point and Kilmote (p.158). Most of the Lower Caithness Flags succession appears to have passed southward via a lake marginal facies into fluvial sandstones.

Flora and fauna of the Caithness Flags (Figure 34 and Plate 24)

Fish remains have not as yet been found in the lower part of the Clyth Subgroup; they are rare and fragmentary in the upper part of the Clyth Subgroup and in the Hillhead Red Bed Subgroup, but are relatively abundant and, in places, well

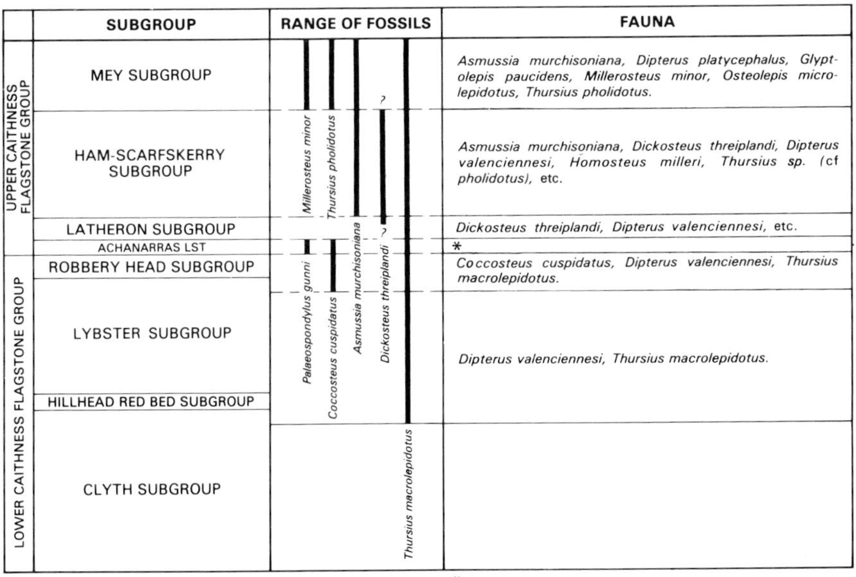

	SUBGROUP	RANGE OF FOSSILS	FAUNA
UPPER CAITHNESS FLAGSTONE GROUP	MEY SUBGROUP		Asmussia murchisoniana, Dipterus platycephalus, Glyptolepis paucidens, Millerosteus minor, Osteolepis microlepidotus, Thursius pholidotus.
	HAM-SCARFSKERRY SUBGROUP		Asmussia murchisoniana, Dickosteus threiplandi, Dipterus valenciennesi, Homosteus milleri, Thursius sp. (cf pholidotus), etc.
	LATHERON SUBGROUP		Dickosteus threiplandi, Dipterus valenciennesi, etc.
	ACHANARRAS LST		*
LOWER CAITHNESS FLAGSTONE GROUP	ROBBERY HEAD SUBGROUP		Coccosteus cuspidatus, Dipterus valenciennesi, Thursius macrolepidotus.
	LYBSTER SUBGROUP		
	HILLHEAD RED BED SUBGROUP		Dipterus valenciennesi, Thursius macrolepidotus.
	CLYTH SUBGROUP		

Range of fossils (columns, top to bottom): Millerosteus minor, Thursius pholidotus, Palaeospondylus gunni, Coccosteus cuspidatus, Asmussia murchisoniana, Dickosteus threiplandi, Thursius macrolepidotus

*The Achanarras-Niandt fauna: Cheiracanthus murchisonia, Cheirolepis trailli, Coccosteus cuspidatus, Dipterus valenciennesi, Glyptolepis paucidens, Homosteus milleri, Mesacanthus peachi, Osteolepis macrolepidotus, Palaeospondylus gunni, Pterichthyodes milleri, etc.

Figure 34 Faunal zones and ranges in the Caithness Flags

preserved in the 'laminites' (p.130) of the higher subgroups. The range of diagnostic fish fossils within the flagstone sequence is shown in Figure 34. This table shows that *Coccosteus cuspidatus* is confined to the Lower Caithness Flagstone Group and that the small, tadpole-like fish, *Palaeospondylus gunni*, has been recorded only at the horizon of the Achanarras and Niandt Limestones. *Dickosteus threiplandi* (a species easily confused with *C. cuspidatus*) occurs only in the Latheron and Ham-Scarfskerry subgroups; it has not been found below the Achanarras horizon. The two species confined to the Mey Subgroup are *Millerosteus minor* and *Thursius pholidotus*.

The only other fossil animal commonly recorded in the Caithness Flags is the conchostracan branchiopod, *Asmussia murchisoniana* (formerly *Estheria membranacea*), which occurs in the two highest subgroups only. Plant remains are scattered throughout the sequence, but these are not diagnostic for correlation. Miospores are present in many siltstones, but have not yet proved useful as detailed stratigraphic indicators.

John o'Groats Sandstone Group

The lacustrine flagstones of north-east Caithness are succeeded by a predominantly fluvial sequence which forms the John o'Groats Sandstone Group of Caithness and the Eday Beds of Orkney (Figure 30). Most of the John o'Groats Sandstone is composed of predominantly medium-grained, red sandstones with pebbly lenses, trough cross-bedding and some convolute bedding (Plate 23). Most of the sandstones appear to have been laid down by braided rivers; fining-upward cycles (with red overbank siltstones and mudstones) of the type formed on alluvial plains of meandering rivers are present near the base. Palaeocurrent indicators suggest deposition by rivers flowing mainly from south-west to north-east. The deepwater laminite of the cycles contains fish remains which include *Microbrachius dicki, Pentlandia macroptera, Tristichopterus alatus* and *Watsonosteus fletti*.

East Sutherland

In the Brora Outlier the basal conglomerate of the Middle Old Red Sandstone rests on the underlying Lower Old Red Sandstone sediments with a marked angular unconformity, best seen along the margins of the syncline (Figure 31a). The basal beds (Smeorail Formation) are of alternating lenses of conglomerate and pebbly sandstone, which pass upwards into massive conglomerate (Figure 30). The pebbles are of porphyritic granites and schists derived mainly from the north or north-west. The overlying sandstones of the Col-Bheinn Formation occupy the centre of the outlier; they are generally fine-grained, brick-red and predominantly flaggy. They have been correlated with the Berriedale Sandstone of the Lower Caithness Flagstone Group. No sediments with a lithology similar to the Berriedale Flagstone or Caithness Flagstones are found in the outlier; however, the presence of many boulders of Caithness Flagstone in the northern outcrops of the Kimmeridgian Helmsdale Boulder Bed (p.158) indicate that flags of Caithness type must originally have been present above the highest exposed strata seen today, in the northern part of the outlier.

A narrow strip of coarse conglomerate with rounded boulders forms an outcrop 6.5 km long along the south side of Strath Fleet. Sandstone and sandy marl, which rest directly on the igneous and metamorphic basement, have been recorded beneath the conglomerate.

Plate 24   Fossils from the Middle Old Red Sandstone

1 *Thursius* sp. Railway cutting, Scotscalder, Caithness   2 *Pterichthyodes milleri* ×0.5, Achanarras quarry (Royal Scottish Museum, 1897.55.3)   3 *Palaeospondylus gunni* ×2, Achanarras quarry
4 *Thursius pholidotus*, Kirk o'Taing, Caithness   5 *Coccosteus cuspidatus*, Edderton Fish Bed

South-west of Helmsdale, a narrow strip of Old Red Sandstone separates the Helmsdale Granite from the coastal strip of Mesozoic sediments; it is bounded by faults on both sides. It consists of white and yellow sandstone with bands of shale and 'limestone' which have yielded fragmentary fish remains. The age of these beds has not yet been determined.

Ross and Cromarty

The Middle Old Red Sandstone of Ross and Cromarty, termed the Strath Rory Group by Armstrong (1977), consists of fluvial sandstones with thick conglomerates, and subordinate calcareous fish-bearing shales. The lenticular basal conglomerates are up to 500 m thick and form conspicuous hills, including escarpments along the western limb of the Black Isle Syncline. On the east limb of the syncline conglomerates reappear at the base of the sequence. The Black Isle (Cnoc Fyrish) conglomerates contain pebbles of biotite granite and pink felsite in addition to Moine clasts. There are also some small quartzite pebbles which may have been derived from the Dalradian quartzites of Banffshire. The presence of Torridonian and Cambrian pebbles in the western conglomerates indicates that large rivers from both east and west entered the alluvial plain which occupied the site of Easter Ross and the inner Moray Firth (Figure 32).

The conglomerates throughout the area are interdigitated with, and overlain by, over 2.5 km of medium-grained yellow and red trough cross-bedded and locally convoluted fluvial sandstone; this is termed the Strath Rory Group north of the Cromarty Firth (Armstrong, 1977) and the Millbuie Sandstone Group in the Black Isle (Horne and Hinxman, 1914). In the Black Isle some sandstones contain pebbles of basic lavas. The sequence contains a number of grey calcareous, locally slightly bituminous shales and siltstones with concretionary nodules of limestone. The nodules contain fish remains, and well known fish beds are present at Black Park (the Edderton Fish Beds), along the east coast of the Tarbat Ness peninsula at and just north-east of Balintore, and in the Killen Burn within the Black Isle. Species recorded in the Black Park (or Edderton) Fish Bed include *Cheiracanthus murchisoni, Cheirolepis trailli, Diplacanthus striatus,* and *Osteolepis macrolepidotus.* A similar faunal assemblage has been recorded from the other fish beds. This assemblage has certain species in common with those of the Achanarras Limestone of Caithness (p.134), suggesting that the sandstones of Easter Ross can be roughly correlated with the middle part of the Caithness flagstone sequence.

The Middle Old Red Sandstone of Ross and Cromarty is primarily of fluvial origin, the sandstones and conglomerates having been deposited by swift-flowing, predominantly braided rivers which converged on the area now occupied by the Inver–Black Isle Syncline both from the west and the south-east and then flowed to the north-east (Figure 32). The fish-bearing calcareous siltstones represent temporary transgressions of a lake across the alluvial plain. This lake was probably a south-westward extension of the Orcadian lake. The Moine inliers along the Moray Firth shore appear to have been hills which projected through the alluvial plain.

UPPER OLD RED SANDSTONE

The only Caithness rocks classed as Upper Old Red Sandstone are the sandstones of the Dunnet Head Sandstone Group (Figure 30). The sandstones are lithologically similar to the Hoy Sandstone of Orkney; they are pink and yellow, cross-stratified, predominantly medium-grained with scattered pebbles and thin intercalations of red mudstone and shale. Trough cross-bedding is very common and many sections display slump-bedding, convolute bedding and miniature water-ejection structures. Sun cracks are common in the shaly beds and many sandstone sets contain chips of red and purple siltstone and shale. At certain horizons calcareous concretions are present, possibly marking the positions of incipient fossil soils. The sandstones have yielded scales of *Holoptychius sp.* (Halliday and others, 1977). The beds were probably laid down in a fluvial environment, possibly by braided rivers entering the area from the west.

In Easter Ross and east Sutherland (Figures 28, 29) sediments of Upper Old Red Sandstone age crop out in the axial region of the Inver–Black Isle Syncline within the Tarbat Ness peninsula where they have been termed the Balnagown Group (Armstrong, 1977). They also form a narrow coastal strip north of Dornoch (Figure 28). They consist of yellow and red, medium-grained, cross-bedded sandstone with scattered pebbles, and appear to be entirely of fluvial origin. No fish-bearing calcareous siltstones are present, but isolated fish-scales have been recorded at a number of localities. At Embo, north of Dornoch, *Holoptychius sp.* has been found, and Traquair (1896, p.260) identified *Psammosteus taylori* from a stream near Balnagown (6 km south of Tain).

There were two main episodes of post-Caledonian igneous activity in the Northern Highlands. In Permo-Carboniferous times the area was intruded by numerous dykes and several vents, but there are no outcrops of extrusive rocks of this age. In Tertiary times the area covering the Inner Hebrides, Ardnamurchan and Morvern was the site of intense volcanic activity associated with the fracturing of the north-west seaboard of Eurasia on the margins of the developing Atlantic Ocean. The Tertiary volcanic centres are described in *British Regional Geology: The Tertiary Volcanic Districts* and will not be discussed here. The Tertiary dyke swarms, however, extend well beyond the limits of the area covered in that book, into the Northern and Grampian Highlands and beyond.

LATE-CALEDONIAN

A small volcanic vent of unknown age cuts the basal Old Red Sandstone of Ben Griam More in Sutherland; the rocks comprise porphyrite and basic andesite. They could have been formed during the phase of late-Caledonian igneous activity which is well known in the Grampian Highlands.

PERMO-CARBONIFEROUS

Although dykes and vents of camptonite and monchiquite have long been known from the Northern Highlands and referred to briefly in several accounts, the overall importance of this suite was given curiously little recognition until the last three decades, when the rocks have received increasing attention. A review paper by Rock (1983a) helps to establish the significance of this major episode in the igneous history of the area.

The Permo-Carboniferous dykes and vents of the Northern Highlands belong to the same phase of igneous activity as that which produced the Permo-Carboniferous volcanic rocks of the Midland Valley of Scotland, the Midlands of England, the North Sea and Scandinavia (notably the Oslo region). The rocks comprise camptonites and monchiquites, grading to subordinate basalts, basanites and analcimites with rarer picritic, pyroxenitic and felsic varients. The camptonites were probably derived from a volatile-rich primary alkalic basalt-basanite magma, itself derived from mantle melting. The monchiquites may be varieties of this, or even of a more nephelinitic magma.

In the Northern Highlands over 3000 dykes (with a small number of vents) have been recorded; specific search has revealed many more previously unmapped. They are arranged in nine swarms comprising both types (Figure 35) of which that centred on Loch Eil and Loch Arkaig is the largest. The trends of the separate swarms define a roughly arcuate pattern from WNW–ESE (Outer Isles) through E–W (southern part of the Northern Highlands) to ENE–WSW in Orkney. The dykes are sparse, or absent, from the northern half of the Northern

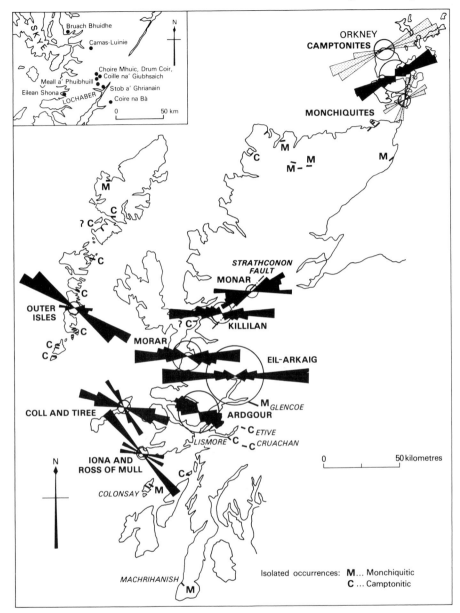

Figure 35 Camptonite-monchiquite dyke swarms of the Northern Highlands
Azimuth distributions are presented as total percentage of dykes in each swarm with a
particular orientation: thus long arms indicate swarms trending more uniformly than do
a series of shorter arms. The areas of the circles are proportional to the total number of
dykes in each swarm. (After Rock, 1983a)

Isolated occurrences: **M** monchiquitic **C** camptonitic
(N.B. In Orkney separate vectors are shown for comptonites and monchiquites. Only
one 'swarm' exists—the central figure)

Highlands but are abundant in south and central Orkney (Mykura, 1976). They average about 1 m in thickness, and rock dilation due to their intrusion varies from about 1% to 4%. The vents (Figure 35 inset) are composed of explosion breccias, commonly with a matrix of monchiquite. They are most abundant where the dykes (especially monchiquitic dykes) are also abundant.

Most of the dyke swarms lie beyond the limits of the Tertiary dyke intrusions, but in Ardgour and the Inner and Outer Hebrides not only do the swarms overlap, but the trends of dykes of different swarms differ little. The camptonite dykes (the dominant variety of the suite) can usually be distinguished from the Tertiary dykes by the presence within them of pinkish or white ocelli containing needles of mafic minerals (amphibole or biotite). Dykes of the swarm may contain megacrysts of apatite, anorthoclase and mafic minerals; many are xenolithic. The dykes are commonly carbonated, and their close association with lead-zinc mineralisation (as at Strontian (p. 177)) has led to speculation that the dykes and mineralisation may have a genetic connection. It seems that if any connection exists it is unlikely to be genetic, but more probably related to the fact that the dykes form pathways or barriers to later mineralising fluids.

Also thought to be of Permo-Carboniferous age are broad (up to 50 m wide) dykes and small elongate bosses of quartz dolerite, in places linearly arranged and trending between E–W and SE–NW. They are cut by the E–W camptonites. The bosses cause intense contact alteration of the schists at their margins, and Butler (1961) considers that in Ardnamurchan some of these may be of Tertiary age.

TERTIARY ACTIVITY

Basalt lavas forming a landward part of the lava plateaux of the Hebridean islands are found on the peninsula of Morvern, where they overlie Mesozoic sediments and locally rest directly on Moine basement. The western 17 km or so of the peninsula of Ardnamurchan, while including some lavas, is made up largely of the Ardnamurchan Plutonic Complex, the root zone of one of the volcanic centres of the Hebridean province. These basic plutonic igneous rocks form successive intersecting ring structures, with an intricate pattern of overlapping ring-dykes, cone-sheets, sills and dykes. This world-famous ring complex (and the other major centres on the islands) is described in *British Regional Geology: The Tertiary Volcanic Districts*. The dyke swarms of Tertiary age, however, extend well beyond the region of the lava fields and central volcanoes.

Tertiary dykes in the Northern Highlands (Figure 36) are confined to the area west of a line extending from Stornoway to the east end of Loch Sunart (and continuing in the Grampians towards Cowal). Two major concentrations are notable, passing through the central complexes of Skye and Mull respectively. The main trend of the dykes in each case is more or less NW–SE through the plutonic centre; some dykes deviate from the main trend (mainly to a more N–S direction).

It was formerly thought (Richey, 1939) that these concentrations defined two major swarms emanating (and to a slight extent radiating) from the plutonic centres, but recently more rigorous mathematical study of the orientation, numbers and dilation of the dykes (Speight and others, 1982) indicates that the swarms reflect a deep underlying pattern of elongate, magma-filled ridges arranged *en échelon* with cross-structures in the pattern more familiar as gash veins in sheared rock. These ridges developed by shearing stress during the fracturing of the crust, in response to stress occasioned by the opening of the Atlantic Ocean. The pattern of dykes developed over these ridges is thus linear, but intertwining. While the

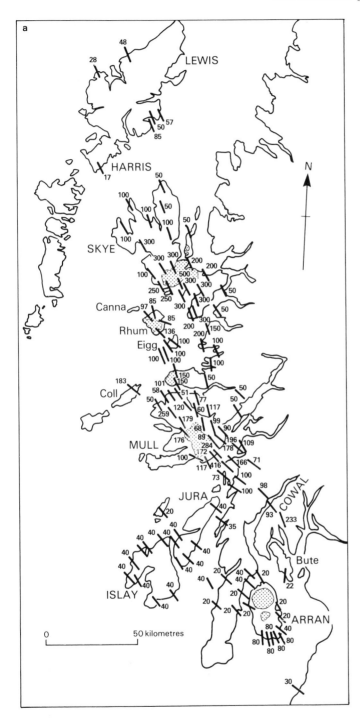

Figure 36 Tertiary dyke swarms of the Northern Highlands (after Speight and others, 1982)

a Arithmetic average trends of groups of dykes of the regional linear swarms of north-western Scotland (subswarms excluded). The number of observations is printed by each trend-bar

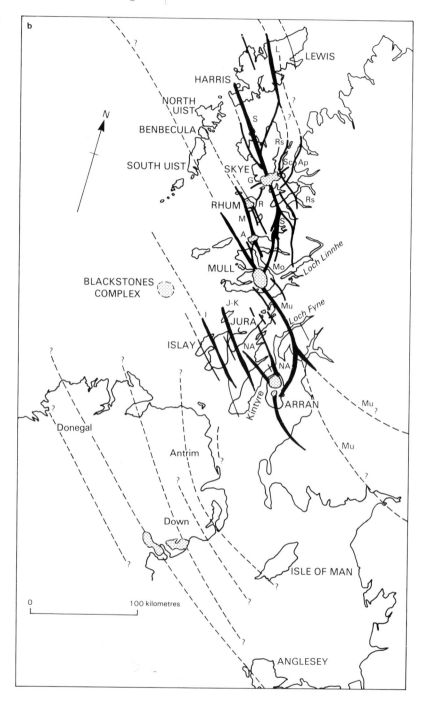

b Dilation axes of the Tertiary dyke swarms. Broader lines indicate the main axes of the regional swarms; broken lines indicate axes of uncertain definition. Central intrusive complexes shown stippled

L Lewis   S Skye   Rs Raasay   Sc Scalpay   Ap Applecross   G Glen Brittle
R Rhum   M Muck   Mu Mull   A Ardnamurchan   Mo Morvern   J-K Jura-Kintyre   I Islay   Na north-west Arran

plutonic centres lie within the swarms on the same ridges, they are not necessarily the prime centres of emanation.

The magma which supplied the intrusion of the Tertiary igneous province was a mantle-derived basic rock which varied in a complex manner by degrees of partial fusion of mantle material, by degrees of fractionation, and by contamination with crustal material from various levels. Several magma types thus became available. Rocks derived from the various varieties of magma are represented in both lavas and plutons, but the dykes themselves consist mainly of two contrasted suites: the alkali-olivine-basalt suite of the Mull Plateau Group or Skye Main Lava Series, and the tholeiitic suite of the Preshal Mhor type. Thomson (1982) has a major review article, with full bibliography, concerning this complex subject.

The intrusion of the dykes spanned the entire period of Tertiary igneous activity. Dykes both predate and post-date the effusion of the lavas and emplacement of the central complexes, but most were emplaced at a late stage in the volcanic history.

12   Carboniferous

Strata of Carboniferous age occur in the Northern Highlands only in the peninsula of Morvern; they crop out beneath Permo-Triassic sediments on the northeast shore of the Sound of Mull at Inninmore Bay, and probably also at the head of Loch Aline. This is one of only a small group of Carboniferous outcrops in the Highlands of Scotland, the other representatives of which are found to the south in the Pass of Brander near Loch Awe, at Glas Eilean near Jura, and at Machrihanish in Kintyre. These are described in *British Regional Geology: The Grampian Highlands*. It seems that these small outliers represent small basins of accumulation developed as the main basin of the Midland Valley Trough to the south intermittently extended into the bordering Highland massif (Francis, 1983).

The Inninmore sediments of the Northern Highlands are at least 100 m (and possibly as much as 160 m) thick, and dip gently to the north beneath the basal breccia of the Trias. The lower part of the sequence consists mainly of white, yellow and grey sandstones, grey and black sandy shales, and impure fireclay. Thin seams of coal occur but are of no economic value. The higher strata consist mainly of massive yellowish pebbly sandstone with some thin beds of lilac-coloured shale.

Various horizons in the sequence yield fossil plants but neither marine nor freshwater shells have been found. Though containing no diagnostic species, the flora* form an assemblage which suggests an early Coal Measures age; it includes the following species: *Asterophyllites charaeformis*, *A. equisetiformis*, *Calamites cisti*, *C. schutzeiformis*, *Mariopteris muricata*, *Neuropteris gigantea*, and *Samaropsis* sp.

*Revised names provided by P. J. Brand.

Since the discovery of North Sea Oil the small outcrops of Mesozoic rocks along the coast of Northern Scotland have taken on an importance quite disproportionate to the land area which they occupy. They, and the more extensive outcrops in the Inner Hebrides (Richey, 1961), are the only readily accessible representatives of the thick sedimentary sequences which occupy the large Mesozoic basins and grabens in the Moray Firth, the North Sea, the Hebridean seas, and parts of the eastern margin of the Atlantic west of Orkney and Shetland.

The most important Mesozoic outcrops on the Scottish mainland are the fault-bounded strips along the north-west and south-east coasts of the Moray Firth (Figure 37) which provide onshore sections of the thick (up to more than 5 km) sequence in the Moray Firth Basin (Chesher and Lawson, 1983). The coastal strip between Golspie and the Ord of Caithness is bounded on the north-west by the Helmsdale Fault, which was active as a normal fault with large downthrow to the south-east in both late- and post-Jurassic times. This strip contains a broken sequence ranging from Trias to topmost Kimmeridgian (or even basal Portlandian). The small foreshore outcrops further south at Balintore and Ethie lie along the Great Glen Fault and contain strata of respectively Bathonian to Oxfordian and Kimmeridgian age.

In the north-west of Scotland, by far the largest and most complete Mesozoic outcrops are in the Inner Hebrides, where they have been preserved by a cover of Tertiary lava (Richey, 1961). The only outcrops along the west coast of the mainland are small outliers of New Red Sandstone (and, more rarely, Lower Lias) between Gairloch and Applecross, and thin sequences, mainly preserved beneath Tertiary lavas, at Morvern and Ardnamurchan. The thin sequences include Triassic, Liassic and Upper Cretaceous sediments.

The small outcrops of conglomerate and bright red sandstone close to the north coast around Tongue and Kirtomy, which have in the past been regarded as Old Red Sandstone, may be of New Red Sandstone age. In the Outer Hebrides, the thick sequence of conglomerates and subordinate sandstones around Stornoway is now generally believed to be New Red Sandstone (Steel and Wilson, 1975).

NEW RED SANDSTONE

Wester Ross

The largest New Red Sandstone outcrop in this area (Figure 37) extends from Gruinard Bay to the Isle of Ewe. At Udrigle and Laide on Gruinard Bay the succession is over 250 m thick. It consists of a thin basal breccia overlain by c.100 m of thinly-interbedded, purple, pebbly sandstone and conglomerate; these deposits were derived from local uplands in the south-east and south-west, and laid down in alluvial fans. They are in turn succeeded by 135 m of fluvial sediments laid down on the floodplains of meandering rivers, whose source lay to the south-

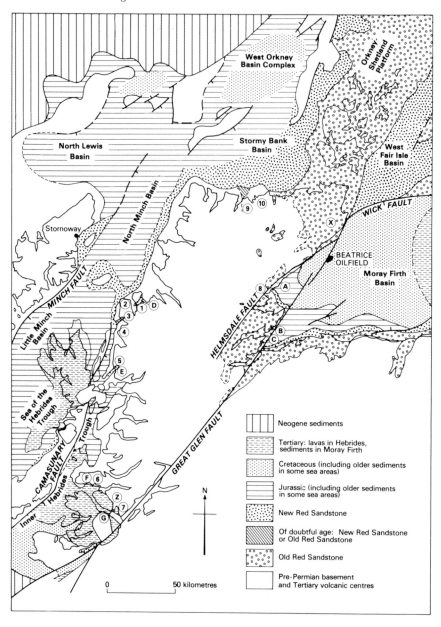

Figure 37   Mesozoic basins in the seas around Northern Scotland, and onshore outcrops (after Evans and others, 1982, fig.1)

New Red Sandstone outliers: **1** Gruinard Bay – Isle of Ewe   **2** Camas Mor, Rubha Reidh peninsula   **3** Big Sand, Gairloch   **4** Red Point   **5** Applecross   **6** Ardnamurchan   **7** Morvern   **8** Dunrobin, Golspie   **9** Outliers around Tongue   **10** Kirtomy Outliers

Jurassic outliers: **A** Golspie – Helmsdale   **B** Balintore   **C** Ethie   **D** Gruinard Bay   **E** Applecross   **F** Ardnamurchan   **G** Morvern

Cretaceous outliers: **Z** Loch Aline and Morvern   Cretaceous erratic: **X** Leavad (Caithness)

south-west; they show well defined fining-upward cycles, each containing the following units.

3 Fine sandstone with immature cornstones (overbank deposit with incipient fossil soil)
2 Bright orange sandstone (wind deposit)
1 Pebbly sandstone with conglomerate lenses (channel deposits)

Of the small outliers along the coast of Wester Ross which were thought to be of New Red Sandstone age (Phemister, 1960, fig.25), those at Achiltibuie, Little Loch Broom and near the Rubha Reidh lighthouse (10 km NW of Gairloch) have been shown to be Torridonian (Lowe, 1965). On the Rubha Reidh peninsula the only outcrop of New Red Sandstone age is at Camas Mor on the north coast, where coarse basal conglomerate is overlain by 15 m of pebbly sandstone with conglomerate lenses. Here many of the pebbles and cobbles are rounded and composed of Cambrian quartzite and limestone, and the sedimentary structure of the beds suggests that they were laid down in the channel of a NW-flowing braided river. Brick-red sandstone with conglomerate lenses crops out at Big Sand, Gairloch, and further south at Red Point there is a very small outlier of conglomerate and grit, with a cornstone at the base, which penetrates into the underlying Torridonian. At Applecross conglomerates and pebbly grits with well defined cornstone horizons containing chalcedony underlie marly beds with vertically aligned calcareous concretions.

Inverness-shire

Further south, in Ardnamurchan and Morvern, the New Red Sandstone consists of a thin basal breccio-conglomerate full of carbonate concretions (carbonate also penetrates as veins into the underlying Moine) overlain by a thin sequence of fluvial cycles of red sandstone and mudstone with well developed mature cornstone (caliche) profiles at the tops of some units (Steel, 1974a).

Lewis

A thick sequence of chocolate-red conglomerates with subordinate sandstones and rare siltstones forms extensive coastal exposures north and south of Stornoway, and on the Eye peninsula east of the town. The sediments are bounded by normal faults in the west and north, but they rest unconformably on the basement of Lewisian gneiss in the east. Though the apparent thickness of the formation is nearly 4 km, Steel and Wilson (1975) have shown that most of the succession was laid down in a number of overlapping alluvial fans formed along the foot of a retreating series of fault scarps located to the west and north, and that its true thickness at any one point may not exceed 1 km.

The conglomerates consist entirely of locally derived clasts of gneiss and 'flinty crush'; many are very coarse with boulders reaching 1 m and, exceptionally, 3 m in size. Steel and Wilson have recognised six distinct cyclic sequences, each representing a period of fan formation. The lower fans are thought to have formed at the foot of a NE-trending fault which lay just east of Stornoway, while the later fans are related to fault scarps which lay progressively further west and north. Four of the cyclic sequences are coarsening upwards, suggesting that the fault scarps were actively moving during deposition.

Thin purple sandstones and siltstones (with incipient cornstones) of fluvial origin are intercalated with the lower cyclic units. In contrast to the suggested palaeoslopes of the fans (from west and north), the fluvial sediments were laid down by streams flowing to the north-east, suggesting that the alluvial fans formed along the western margin of a major alluvial plain which drained to the north-east (Figure 38).

North Sutherland

Of the small outliers around Tongue (Figure 37), four consist entirely of conglomerate and basal breccia, with clasts of local Moine rocks and syenite from the eastern outcrops of the Bed Loyal intrusion. The fifth outcrop, at Coldbackie, has a basal breccia overlain by up to 120 m of bright red fluvial sandstone with fining-upward cycles and some incipient cornstones in the overbank deposits; these are overlain by up to 300 m of massive conglomerate, again with syenite clasts, suggesting a southerly derivation. By contrast, the Ron Islands north of Tongue are made almost entirely of up to 500 m of coarse, grey-brown conglomerate with clasts which include abundant Cambrian quartzites and Durness limestones. Clast composition and pebble imbrication in the Ron conglomerates suggest deposition by braided rivers from a west-north-westerly source.

The Kirtomy outliers occupy three fault-bounded N–S trenches and consist of red-brown pebbly arkose with conglomerate and breccia. They also appear to fill valleys with a northerly palaeoslope.

Though both Blackbourn (1981a;b) and O'Reilly (1983) still favour an Old Red Sandstone age for the North Sutherland sediments, a New Red Sandstone age is here preferred for the following reasons.

1   The fine sediments of the Watch Hill (Tongue) outcrops are very similar to sediments from offshore cores obtained along the southern margin of the Stormy Bank Basin and considered to be of Permo-Triassic or younger age by Evans and others (1982).
2   The bright red colours of the fine sediments match more closely with the red colours of the New Red Sandstone of Wester Ross, and contrast with the dull purple and drab colours of the Old Red Sandstone of Caithness.
3   The fluvial sediments contain incipient cornstones, similar in type to those found in Lewis and along Gruinard Bay. This contrasts with the absence of cornstones and incipient fossil soils in the Caithness Old Red Sandstone.

Palaeogeography of West Scotland

Steel (1978) has shown that the sediments of Hebridean outliers were laid down along the margins of major basins of deposition which accumulated in NNE- and NE-trending half-grabens, bounded by major normal faults on their north-western margins. Figure 38 shows the extent, thickness and major paleoslopes of these basins, and the probable direction of their drainage. The alluvial fan deposits had their palaeoslopes roughly normal to the axes of these basins, whereas the fluvial deposits were laid down by streams running subparallel to the basin axes.

East Sutherland

At Dunrobin (Figure 37) the New Red Sandstone (?Trias) consists of pale calcareous sandstone overlain by red and green marls with bands of cherty

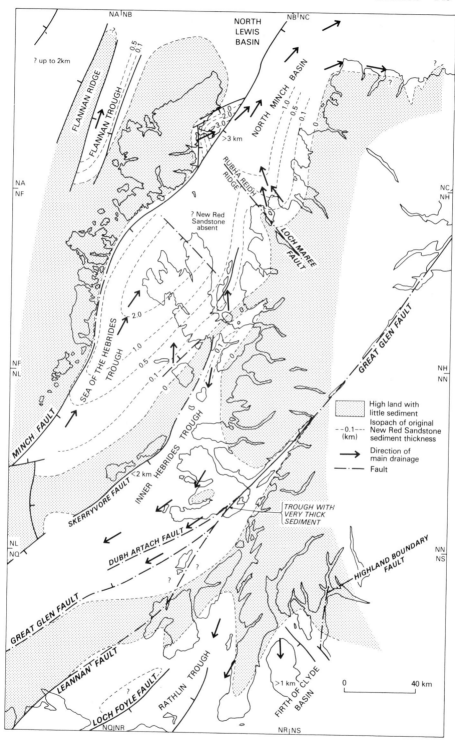

Figure 38 New Red Sandstone basins of north-west Scotland, showing possible original thickness of sediments and main directions of drainage (after Steel, 1978)

limestone. The cherty bands were correlated by Judd (1873) with the Stotfield Cherty Rock of Lossiemouth on the south shore of the Moray Firth. These are, in turn, overlain by intermittently exposed pebbly grits and conglomerates termed the Dunrobin Pier Conglomerate and commonly ascribed to the Rhaetic (though there is no direct evidence to support this). The conglomerate contains pebbles of chert and limestone derived from the underlying Trias.

JURASSIC

Lias

On the west coast at Applecross (Figure 37) about 58 m of Lower Liassic sediments are exposed in two stream sections and along the shore. They are equivalent in age to the lower Broadford Beds of Skye and range from Hettangian (*Alsatites liasicus* and *Schlotheimia angulata* zones) to Lower Sinemurian (*Arietites bucklandi* zone) (Figure 39). The lower part of the sequence contains several oolitic limestones and calcilutites, the upper is mainly sandstone and sandy shale with one prominent coral limestone. The abundant fauna includes the coral *Thecosmilia martini* as well as *Cardinia, Lima, Liostrea, Parallelodon* and *Schlotheimia* (Hallam, 1959). The sediments were laid down in a shallow sea which may from time to time have been brackish.

In the fault-bounded strip between Gruinard Bay and Loch Ewe, poorly exposed clayey limestone and blue clay overlie the Trias. Abundant loose lamellibranchs found on the shore of Loch Ewe suggest a Sinemurian age for these beds.

In the south of the region, Lower Lias (up to 90 m thick) is exposed in several fine sections in Morvern; strata ranging from Lower to Upper Lias occur in Ardnamurchan and are particularly well exposed on the shore east and west of Kilchoan. All these sediments are described in *British Regional Geology: The Tertiary Volcanic Districts* (Richey, 1961).

On the east coast of Sutherland, Lower Jurassic strata are intermittently exposed on the shore at Dunrobin Castle, Golspie (Figure 40). They form a condensed succession comprising a lower 72 m of argillaceous deltaic sediments with thin coal seams and rootlet beds, overlain by about 22 m of soft white quartzose sandstone with some shale partings, drifted plant remains and rootlet beds, succeeded in turn by over 18 m of dark micaceous, often marine, shales rich in ammonites and brachiopods. This sequence has been named the Dunrobin Bay Formation by Neves and Selley (1975) and its subdivisions are shown in Figure 41. Most zones of the Lower Lias may be present, although the only reliable zonal indicators are the ammonites in the Lady's Walk Shale which confirm the presence of the topmost Sinemurian *Echioceras raricostatum* zone and the basal Pliensbachian *Uptonia jamesoni* zone (Berridge and Ivimey-Cook, 1967).

Middle/Upper Jurassic

Sediments of this age crop around Brora (Figure 40) and on the foreshore south of Balintore (Figure 37).

At Brora the lowest Middle Jurassic rocks are probably of Bathonian age (Figure 41). They are termed the Brora Coal Formation and are exposed on the foreshore between 0.9 and 1.6 km south-west of the mouth of the Brora River. The lower member (termed the Doll Member) comprises soft white quartzose sandstone up to 20 m thick, overlain by grey mudstones with thin beds of sideritic

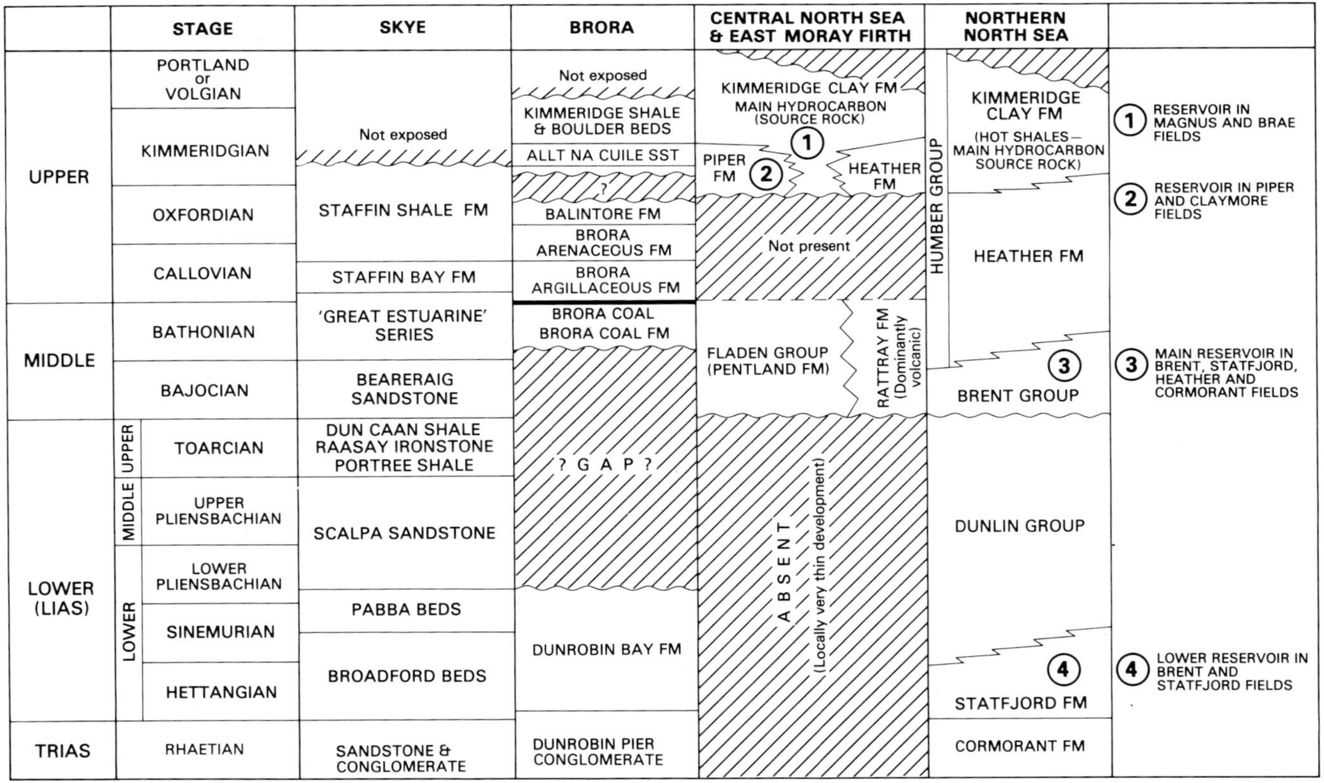

STAGE			SKYE	BRORA	CENTRAL NORTH SEA & EAST MORAY FIRTH	NORTHERN NORTH SEA	
UPPER		PORTLAND or VOLGIAN	Not exposed	Not exposed		KIMMERIDGE CLAY FM (HOT SHALES— MAIN HYDROCARBON SOURCE ROCK)	① RESERVOIR IN MAGNUS AND BRAE FIELDS
		KIMMERIDGIAN		KIMMERIDGE SHALE & BOULDER BEDS	KIMMERIDGE CLAY FM MAIN HYDROCARBON SOURCE ROCK) ①		
		OXFORDIAN	STAFFIN SHALE FM	ALLT NA CUILE SST BALINTORE FM	PIPER FM ②	HEATHER FM	② RESERVOIR IN PIPER AND CLAYMORE FIELDS
		CALLOVIAN	STAFFIN BAY FM	BRORA ARENACEOUS FM BRORA ARGILLACEOUS FM	HEATHER FM (Not present)		
MIDDLE		BATHONIAN	'GREAT ESTUARINE' SERIES	BRORA COAL BRORA COAL FM	RATTRAY FM (Dominantly volcanic)	③	③ MAIN RESERVOIR IN BRENT, STATFJORD, HEATHER AND CORMORANT FIELDS
		BAJOCIAN	BEARERAIG SANDSTONE		FLADEN GROUP (PENTLAND FM)	BRENT GROUP	
		TOARCIAN	DUN CAAN SHALE RAASAY IRONSTONE PORTREE SHALE	? GAP ?			
LOWER (LIAS)	UPPER	UPPER PLIENSBACHIAN	SCALPA SANDSTONE		ABSENT (Locally very thin development)	DUNLIN GROUP	
		LOWER PLIENSBACHIAN	PABBA BEDS	DUNROBIN BAY FM			
	LOWER	SINEMURIAN	BROADFORD BEDS			STATFJORD FM ④	④ LOWER RESERVOIR IN BRENT AND STATFJORD FIELDS
		HETTANGIAN					
TRIAS		RHAETIAN	SANDSTONE & CONGLOMERATE	DUNROBIN PIER CONGLOMERATE		CORMORANT FM	

HUMBER GROUP

Figure 39 Comparison of the Jurassic succession of east Sutherland with the successions in Skye and the North Sea

The main reservoir- and source-rock horizons of the North Sea oilfields are shown

cementstone. Comminuted plant debris is common and, near the top of the mudstone, well preserved plants and silicified logs have been found. The upper Inverbrora Member consists of black laminated bituminous shales (containing a poor oil shale) and grey shales, overlain by the Brora Coal, which averages 1 m in thickness. There are several shell beds packed with the freshwater bivalve *Neomiodon*, some horizons with the brackish-water branchiopod *Euestheria*, and others with the bivalve *Isognomon*, which may be marine. The Brora Coal has been mined intermittently since 1598. The early workings were near the shore but after 1810 mining was confined to the area west and north of Brora. Neves and Selley (1975) have suggested that the Brora Coal Formation was deposited in a deltaic/estuarine environment which culminated in the formation of delta-swamp coals at the top. Hurst (1981), however, believed that it was formed in a largely fluvial environment which later stagnated into a delta swamp.

The Callovian and Oxfordian sediments of Brora are mainly marine in origin. They have been reclassified by Sykes (1975) into the formations and members shown in Figure 41. The Brora Argillaceous Formation is 88 m thick and commences with a hard ferruginous bioturbated sandstone (the Brora Roof Bed) which marks the Callovian marine transgression and contains a diverse fauna dominated by *Corbula obscura*. The presence of the ammonites *Kepplerites gowerianus* and *Proplanulites koenigi* indicates a *Sigaloceras calloviense* zone (*P. koenigi* subzone) age for the bed. The remainder of the Brora Shale Member is a 30 m thick sequence, fining upward from silty sandstone to bituminous shale. There is much shell debris and some shell beds composed of ?*Protocardia*, *Meleagrinella* and *Trautscholdia*. Ammonites are fairly scattered but provide evidence for the presence of most subzones of the *S. calloviense* and *Kosmoceras jason* zones. The ammonites indicate an open-water marine environment.

The Glauconitic Sandstone Member is a muddy greenish glauconitic sandstone with bands of phosphatic nodules which contain *Rhaxella* spicules. Ammonites indicative of the *K. jason* and *Kosmoceras obductum* subzones are fairly common and other fossils include *Lingula*, *Meleagrinella* and *Cylindroteuthis*. The environment of deposition was a reworked marine bar sand. The overlying Brora Brick Clay Member consists of intercalated grey-green clay and bituminous sandy siltstone, and has a prominent row of doggers in the middle. It has an abundant fauna of bivalves and well scattered ammonites, indicative of the *Erymnoceras coronatum* and *Peltoceras athleta* zones. The Fascally Siltstone Member is a sequence of coarse siltstones grading upward into fine sandstone. Its fauna is sparser than that of the underlying beds, but ammonites are present throughout, indicating that most of the member belongs to the *P. athleta* zone.

The top few metres of the Fascally Siltstone mark the onset of a gradual shallowing of the sea, and during the Upper Callovian and Lower Oxfordian times there were extensive shallow marine (and latterly coastal) sand bars in the Brora area. The sequence is known as the Brora Arenaceous Formation. The lowest sandstone unit, the Fascally Sandstone Member, is a muddy sandstone intercalated with siltstone, and is characterised by intense bioturbation. However, ammonites and lucinoid bivalves are still abundant. All ammonites indicate a *Quenstedtoceras lamberti* zone age. The Clynelish Quarry Sandstone member is well exposed along the Brora River and was formerly worked in the Clynelish Quarries west of Brora. It is a fine, friable, poorly cemented, highly siliceous sandstone with layers of carbonaceous debris and several horizons of convolute bedding, some of which suggest water expulsion. Its fauna is patchily developed. There are lucinoid bivalves, large specimens of *Chlamys*, and scattered ammonites of *Quenstedtoceras lamberti* zone type indicate that the environment was still fully marine.

Plate 25 Fossils from the Cambrian, Ordovician and Jurassic

1 *Hormotoma antiqua*, Durness Limestone 2 *Olenellus sp.*, Fucoid Beds 3 *Olenellus reticulatus*, Fucoid Beds 4 *Ophileta complanata*, Durness Limestone 5 cf. *Lophospira borealis*, Durness Limestone 6 *Olenellus lapworthi*, Fucoid Beds 7 *Chlamys splendens*, Oxfordian, Brora 8 *Cardioceras (Subvertebriceras) densiplicatum*, Oxfordian, Brora 9 *Amoebites akantophorus*, Kimmeridgian, Ethie 10 *Echioceras tardecrescens?*, Sinemurian, Golspie 11 *Buchia concentrica*, Kimmeridgian, Helmsdale 12 *Prionodoceras* cf. *serratum*, Kimmeridgian, Balintore

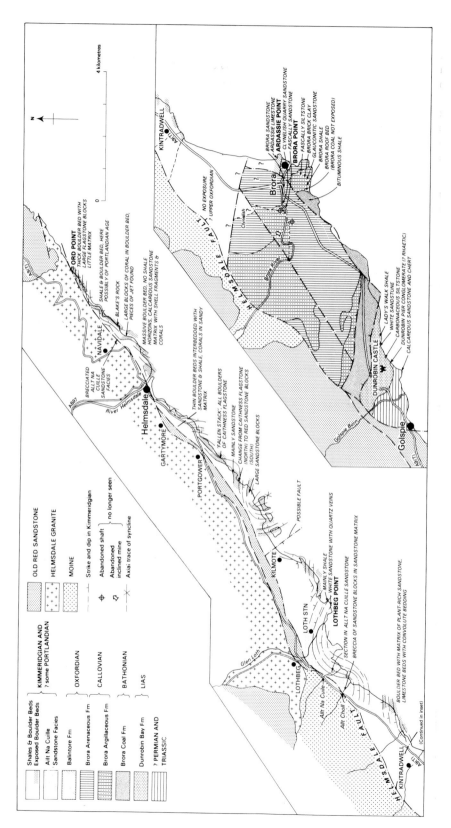

Figure 40 Map of Jurassic strata exposed on the coast between Golspie and Helmsdale

The Brora Sandstone Member forms prominent cliffs along the Brora River. Though mainly fine-grained and friable, it has some thin quartz conglomerates in the middle; trough cross-bedding indicates that the sediment was derived from the west. No ammonites have been recorded, but there are scattered marine bivalves, including *Gryphea dilatata*. The highest exposed part of the Oxfordian sequence at Brora, the Ardassie Limestone Member (Figures 40, 41), comprises alternate beds of muddy carbonaceous sandstone and 'limestone', 0.3 to 1.1 m thick. The 'limestones' consist largely of calcified *Rhaxella* spicules. There is also a rich fauna

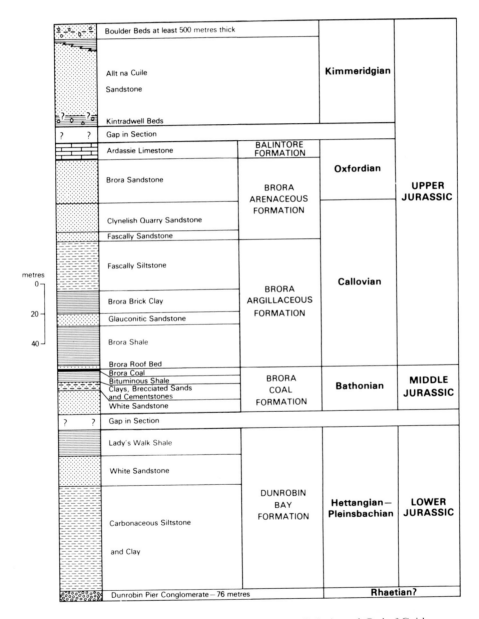

Figure 41   Mesozoic succession on the coast between Golspie and Ord of Caithness, East Sutherland (the distribution of strata in the area is shown in Figure 40)

of bivalves, with many *Cucullaea*, accompanied by *Gryphea and Pinna*. Ammonites, including several species of *Cardioceras*, indicate a *Cardioceras vertebrale* subzone age.

The foreshore section south of Balintore in Easter Ross (Plate 26) ranges in age from Bathonian to Middle Oxfordian, but the total thickness of the sequence is only 65 m, compared to 235 m of the roughly equivalent beds at Brora. The subdivisions, mainly established by Sykes (1975), are shown in Figure 42. The Brora Coal is only 20 cm thick here, and the overlying Brora Roof Bed only 50 cm. The latter has a similar lithology to the roof bed at Brora, but its upper surface is thickly covered with belemnites and wood fragments. The Cadh-an-Righ Shale is a condensed sequence which represents two ammonite zones; it is bituminous, with thin beds of glauconitic siltstone. Like the Glauconitic Sandstone of Brora it contains phosphatic nodules within a bed of limestone nodules. The overlying Shandwick Clay Member is a grey-green clay and siltstone with many burrows and rows of limestone nodules. Its main fossil is *Nuculoma*. Scattered ammonites indicate that it spans the *Peltoceras athleta* to the middle of *Cardioceras cordatum* zones.

The Brora Arenaceous Formation is represented by only 12 m of sandy siltstone interbedded with calcareous siltstone. It contains fairly abundant, poorly preserved fossils; the most prominent are *Pinna* and *Pleuromya*. The Middle Oxfordian Balintore Formation has at its base the prominent Port-an-Righ Ironstone, which is a red weathering, nodular, glauconitic limestone with abundant ammonites. It is overlain by 22 m of coarse, poorly fossiliferous, bituminous siltstone, comprising several coarsening-upward rhythmic units.

Sykes (1985) has suggested that the Brora sequence was laid down in a shallow near-shore environment with a subtidal and sand-bar complex developed in

	ZONE	SUBZONE		MEMBER	FORMATION
MIDDLE OXFORDIAN	Cardioceras tenuiserratum	C. tenuiserratum		Port-an-Righ Siltstone 22 m	BALINTORE
	Cardioceras denisplicatum	C. maltonense			
		C. vertebrale		Port-an-Righ Ironstone 2.2 m	
LOWER OXFORDIAN	Cardioceras cordatum	C. cordatum		Shandwick Siltstone 12 m	BRORA ARENACEOUS
		C. costicardia			
		C. bukowskii			
	Quenstedtoceras mariae	?		Shandwick Clay 27 m	BRORA ARGILLACEOUS
		C. scarburgense			
CALLOVIAN	Quenstedtoceras lamberti				⌐ 10 m
	Peltoceras athleta				
	Erymnoceras coronatum	K. grossouvrei		Cadh-an-Righ Shale 4.2 m	└ 0
	Kosmoceras jason	K. medea			
BATHONIAN				BRORA COAL 20 cm	BRORA COAL
				Sandstone & thin limestones 8 m	

Figure 42   Jurassic sequence from the foreshore south of Balintore (after Sykes, 1975)

Lower Oxfordian times. The condensed Balintore sequence, on the other hand, represents a deeper-water offshore facies.

The Bow Buoy Skerry south of Ethie consists of carbonaceous sandstone with lenticular limestone beds. These have yielded ammonites suggesting an Oxfordian age.

Kimmeridgian

Strata of this age crop out along the coast of East Sutherland between Kintradwell and the Ord of Caithness, and in a narrow strip at Ethie in the Black Isle (where they are visible only at low tide). The presence of Kimmeridgian strata below low water at Port-an-Righ (south of Balintore) is indicated by the occurrence of loose nodules on the beach which contain the Kimmeridgian ammonite *Pictonia baylei*.

At Ethie the succession consists of about 45 m of grey-green mudstone and shale with beds of sandstone and grit, some bituminous shales (oil shale) as well as some thin beds and septarian nodules of brittle blue limestone (Waterston, 1951). The sediments are cut by a number of prominent sandstone sills and dykes which were probably formed during earthquakes by the intrusion of liquified sand from below (Waterson, 1950). The Ethie sediments are very fossiliferous with many well preserved bivalves, ammonites, and belemnites. The oldest beds probably belong to the *Rasenia cymodoce* zone; the higher ones contain *Amoebites* and raseniids characteristic of the upper part of the *R. cymodoce* and basal *Aulacostephanoides mutabilis* zones.

East Sutherland

The Kimmeridgian sediments of this fault-bounded strip may be over 500 m thick. Their base is nowhere exposed and it is not certain if the lowest beds are the shales and boulder beds of Kintradwell or the Allt na Cuile Sandstone (Figure 41).

The Allt na Cuile Sandstone is best exposed (Figure 40) between Lothbeg Point and the railway bridge across the Loth River, and in the gorges of the Allt na Cuile and Allt Choll further south-west. It is up to 50 m thick, white to orange, medium-grained and generally well sorted, with thin beds of sandy carbonaceous shale. It contains a shelly, shallow-marine fauna and has a number of lenses of fine debris-flow conglomerate with predominantly sandstone clasts. Close to the Helmsdale Fault (e.g. in the Allt Choll gorge) the sandstone-breccias are very thick and contain some very large sandstone blocks. They were described as 'chasm breccias' by Bailey and Weir (1932), but Linsley (1972) considered them to have formed in submarine debris fans which accumulated along the relatively subdued submarine escarpment of the Helmsdale Fault. Farther from the Helmsdale Fault some of the graded sandstone units seen at Lothbeg Point have been described as grain-flow deposits (Neves and Selley, 1975).

The upper part of the Allt na Cuile Sandstone passes northward by interdigitation into a predominantly shaly sequence, termed the Lothbeg Shales. Though there has been considerable controversy about its age, the Allt na Cuile Sandstone is now thought to be Kimmeridgian and to range from the top part of the *Pictonia baylei* zone, via the *Rasenia cymodoce* and *Aulacostephanoides mutabilis* zones, possibly into the basal part of the *Aulacostephanus eudoxus* zone.

The greater part of the Kimmeridgian sequence of East Sutherland consists of thinly bedded bituminous shales, with ammonites and other fauna indicating deposition in a fairly deep sea. Interbedded with these shales are the boulder beds, which range in thickness from 1 m to nearly 10 m. These consist of mainly angular blocks and boulders varying in diameter from a few centimetres to the 'Fallen Stack' of Portgower which measures 34 m × 27 m × 9 m (Plate 27). The boulders are set in a sandy matrix which contains fossils of creatures that original- ly lived in a shallow-water or even a deltaic environment. The individual blocks have compressed and contorted the bedding of the underlying sediment, and some boulder beds display an upward fining. There are also some solitary blocks embedded directly in deep marine shales, which are contorted around them.

There is a marked variation in the composition of the boulder beds up the se- quence from south-west to north-east. At Kintradwell in the south-west (Figure 40) all the clasts are of sandstone, many of Old Red Sandstone type, with some Jurassic. Their matrix is a carbonaceous sandstone with the remains of tropical plants, probably derived from a deltaic environment. There are also some sandy and calcareous turbidites which are themselves slumped and contorted. At Loth and Kilmote all the clasts are red sandstone of Old Red Sandstone age, but be- tween Kilmote and Portgower blocks of Old Red Sandstone flagstone facies ap- pear and form all the blocks at Portgower and in the sections further north-east. From Kilmote northwards the matrix of the boulder beds changes to a gritty calcareous sandstone full of broken neritic and littoral fossils, including many brachiopods, echinoids and, particularly around Navidale, prominent blocks of reef coral (*Isastrea oblonga*). There are no boulders of Helmsdale Granite or Moine metasediment within any of the Boulder Beds.

The origin of the Boulder Beds has been the subject of much speculation. Early suggestions include crush-breccias (Murchison, 1829), ice-sheet deposits (Ram- say, 1865), violent flood deposits in an estuarine environment (Judd, 1873) and talus from cliffs, and the remains of fallen sea-stacks (M. Macgregor, 1916). Bailey was the first to postulate that they accumulated at the foot of a submarine escarpment along the line of the Helmsdale Fault (Bailey and others, 1928; Bailey and Weir, 1932). He suggested that the debris was swept down the fault scarp by tidal waves or 'tsunamis' generated by earthquakes. The submarine-fan concept has since been refined and amplified by the work of Crowell (1961) Linsley (1972), Neves and Selly (1975) and Pickering (1984). Crowell showed that the blocks slid relatively slowly down the submarine scarp, mainly along gulleys. Neves and Selley pointed out that the boulder beds consist of two facies: a south- western 'carbonaceous' facies of carbonaceous shales interbedded with turbiditic sandstones and boulder beds with Jurassic sandstone boulders set in a car- bonaceous matrix; and a north-eastern 'calcareous' facies which contains no tur- bidites or Jurassic sandstone clasts, but has a calcite-cemented matrix full of com- minuted shell material and corals. During the deposition of the southern facies the north-western (upthrown side) of the fault scarp was near sea level and covered by a vegetated delta; during the deposition of the northern facies, it was a shallow marine shelf with corals, neritic brachiopods and calcareous sands. Pickering has recognised a number of distinct facies within the Boulder Beds succession and has correlated these with the various physical environments along the fault scarp. The probable environment of deposition of the Helmsdale Boulder Beds is sum- marised graphically in Figure 43.

The age of the Boulder Bed succession has been obtained principally from the ammonites within the deep water shales, supplemented by the systematic study of palynomorphs (Lam and Porter, 1977). It is now believed that there is a virtually complete range of zones from the *Aulacostephanus eudoxus* zone in the south-west to the *Pavlovia pallasioides* zone at Navidale. Riley (1980) has suggested on palynological evidence (mainly dinocysts), that the youngest beds, exposed in Navidale Bay north of Helmsdale, may be of early Portlandian age.

Plate 26   Middle and Upper Jurassic sediments are exposed on wave-planed foreshore at Balintore, Easter Ross, with cliffs of Middle Old Red Sandstone behind (W. Mykura)

Plate 27   Helmsdale Boulder Bed (Kimmeridgian) at Portgower, with 'Fallen Stack' in background   (W. Mykura)

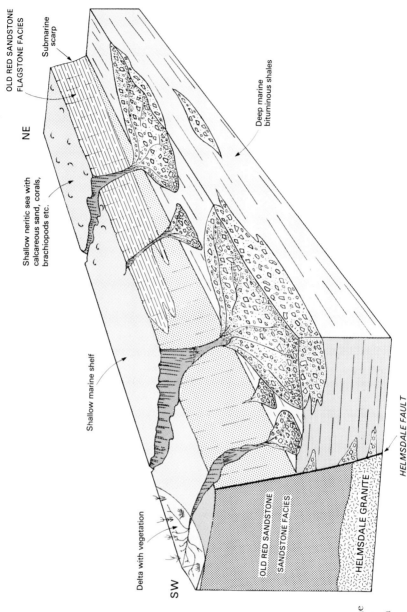

Figure 43   Possible model of the north-west margin of the Moray Firth Basin during the formation of the Helmsdale Boulder Beds

CRETACEOUS

The only Cretaceous sediments found in situ in the Northern Highlands occur in Morven (Figure 37), where they have been protected from erosion by overlying Tertiary lavas.

On the west side of Loch Aline the following succession underlies the Tertiary lavas (Figure 44; Humphries, 1961):

		Thickness (m)
Tertiary	Lava	
	Red Mudstone (Tertiary)	1.5
	White sandstone (locally discoloured)	1.2
Cenomanian White Sandstone	Rib of hard white sandstone	0.6
	Soft white, friable sandstone	6.0
	Rib of hard white sandstone	c.0.3
	Sandstone—generally slightly brown-stained	c.4
	Calcareous sandstone, with *Exogyra*	4.5
Greensand	Greensand with calcareous concretions full of *Exogyra*, *Pecten*, etc.	3.9
	Glauconitic sandstone, unfossiliferous	2

The Greensand is partly calcareous and characterised by the abundance of *Amphidonte obliqua* (formerly *Exogyra conica*), though other bivalves such as *Neithea quinquecostata* are also found. The overlying white sandstone, which has been extensively mined as a glass-sand, consists almost entirely of rounded, well sorted quartz grains ranging in diameter from 0.2 to 0.3 mm. Its silica content exceeds 99.7%, though a large suite of heavy minerals has been recognised. Only one fossil (a starfish) has so far been found in the sandstone.

Further north-west Cretaceous deposits form a number of outliers on hills which have a protective capping of Tertiary lava. On Beinn Iadain (10 km north of Loch Aline) the white sandstone is overlain by 0.3 m of clay, succeeded in turn by 0.4 m of silicified rubbly chalk which has yielded *Salenia geometrica*, suggesting a late Senonian age (Figure 44).

Bailey (1924) has argued that many of the sand grains of the White Sandstone have been rounded and polished by wind action, suggesting that the land adjoining the Chalk sea had a desert climate. Humphries (1961) has, however, shown that this hypothesis is not supported by the petrological evidence.

The only other Cretaceous sediment on the Scottish mainland is a large glacial erratic (230 m × 140 m) of sandstone at Leavad in Caithness (Figure 37). The sandstone has disintegrated into sand in which the hard concretions remain. It has yielded *Craspedites* and *Crioceras*. It is thought that this sandstone mass was carried inland by ice from an in-situ position in the North Sea near Lybster or Dunbeath.

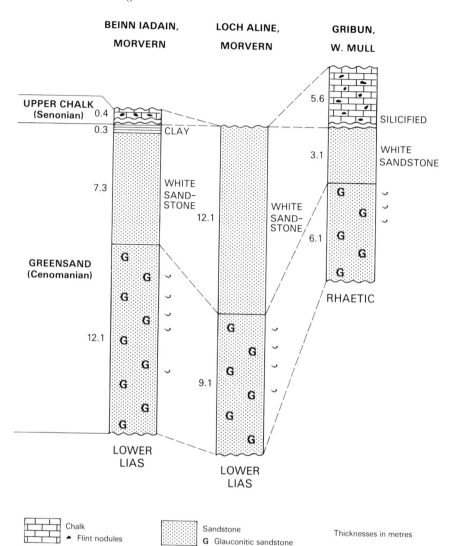

Figure 44   Cretaceous sediments of Morvern, compared with the Cretaceous sequence at Gribun, West Mull

The Northern Highlands, like other districts of Scotland and northern England, were glaciated during the Pleistocene epoch, and the pre-Pleistocene topography was modified by the widening, straightening and deepening of pre-existing river valleys. On the northern and eastern slopes in particular, freeze-thaw activity combined with glacial erosion produced spectacular corries, and the products of glacial deposition are found on the lower ground in the form of hummocky moraines (Plate 28) and extensive drift sheets. Some parts of the district, notably the western seaboard and the Outer Hebrides, are largely free of drift, and smoothed and striated rock knobs rise above the peat (Plate 29). So far, only three in-situ organic deposits are known which are older than the last glaciation, and criteria for the maximum extent of ice rest entirely on geomorphological considerations. Thus, though the area was certainly repeatedly glaciated, there is an element of doubt concerning the extent of the last (Late Devensian) glaciation.

EVIDENCE FOR EVENTS PERIPHERAL TO OR PREDATING THE LAST GLACIATION

In Lewis, an advance of ice (chiefly local but possibly with a tongue from the Scottish mainland) during what may have been the maximum of the Late Devensian glaciation failed to reach the extreme north of the island (von Weymarn, 1979; Peacock, 1984; Sutherland and Walker, 1984). Here, frost-shattering and extensive solifluction flows, perhaps originating during the very cold climate which accompanied the last glaciation, have been preserved, as has a pre-existing raised beach which rests on till deposited during an earlier glacial episode. Interstadial lacustrine deposits on Tolsta Head dated about 27 000 BP (radiocarbon years ago) are found below till of the last glaciation (von Weymarn and Edwards, 1973). A possible interglacial peat has been reported below the raised beach in north Lewis (Sutherland and Walker, 1984). Till older than Late Devensian has been described from St Kilda (D. G. Sutherland and others, 1982), together with interstadial deposits which may date to the same period as those on Tolsta Head. It is perhaps significant that a raised beach overlain by head has been reported from North Rona (Gailey, 1959), suggesting conditions similar to those in north Lewis. This island, likewise, may have been outside the limits of the Late Devensian glaciation. On the Scottish mainland, radiocarbon dating of the remains of reindeer from caves at Inchnadamph in Sutherland has yielded ages of up to 25 000 BP (Lawson, 1984).

Remains of rock terraces, cut by the sea and backed by fossil cliff lines, occur in Rhum, the Hebrides and parts of the west coast including the coastline of Ardnamurchan and Loch Linnhe. These, the 'pre-glacial' beaches of the Geological Survey Memoirs, occur mainly at heights between 6 and 45 m OD; some show clear evidence of glaciation in the form of striations and coverings of till. The raised platform and cliff in Rhum, which ranges in height between 20 and 37 m above local datum, is locally strongly glaciated; it has clearly been either faulted or tilted at some stage during the Pleistocene. On the other hand, the well marked platform backed by cliffs on Mull and on the shores of Loch Linnhe, which in the past has been thought to be pre-glacial and which is present even at localities well sheltered from marine action, is gently tilted westwards in a fashion which accords with that of Scottish late- and post-glacial beaches. It has been interpreted as having been formed during a short period of intense marine erosion under periglacial conditions of the Loch Lomond stade some time after the disappearance of the main Devensian ice-sheet (Sissons, 1974; Gray, 1978). Sissons (1982b) has suggested that the 'pre-glacial' rock platforms have also been isostatically tilted, and were formed during the last and previous glacial periods by wave and frost action.

Deeply decomposed igneous and metamorphic rocks are found below a cover of till at several localities, such as the Helmsdale area in the north-east, Ratagain and Glenelg in the south-west, and Lewis in the Outer Hebrides. The decomposition has been ascribed by some authors to tropical weathering in late Tertiary times, but the effects of faulting, hydrothermal activity and Pleistocene weathering have probably been responsible in some instances.

It was suggested at one time that interglacial marine beds existed on north Lewis, where shelly, till-like beds are separated by water-sorted deposits including laminated clay, sand and gravel. The mixed fauna and the broken molluscan shells, however, indicate reworking and transportation by the ice-sheet. Other features, such as the presence of numerous debris-flow deposits interbedded with glaciofluvial sands and gravels, support the theory of deposition chiefly peripheral to glacier ice.

LAST GLACIATION

The history of the last glaciation can be broadly considered under three headings. During the Devensian maximum, which coincided with an extremely cold climate (probably accompanied by high snowfall) an ice-sheet covered much of Scotand. During the following period of ice wastage, sheets of silt, sand and gravel were laid down; the movement of any active ice was controlled by the local topography. This was followed by the almost complete dissolution of the ice-sheet during the Windermere Interstadial, (13 000 – 11 000 BP) after which glaciers returned to the mountains of the Highlands and Islands between 11 000 and 10 000 BP. However, climatic considerations (considered briefly below) suggest that some glaciers may have reformed well before 11 000 BP, and a few in the highest corries may have survived throughout the Windermere Interstadial. The well documented readvance between 11 000 and 10 000 BP, termed the Loch Lomond Advance or Readvance, was marked by a brief return of arctic conditions before the rapid amelioration of climate about or somewhat before 10 000 BP.

Devensian maximum

From an ice-shed situated east of the present principal watershed of northern Scotland, ice flowed westwards into the Minch, eastwards into the Moray Firth and northwards into the Pentland Firth. Subsidary ice-sheds, or perhaps separate centres of dispersal, may have existed in parts of Sutherland (Figure 45). The Outer Hebrides appear to have supported their own ice-sheet during part if not all of the Devensian maximum (Peacock and Ross, 1978; Flinn, 1979; von Weymarn, 1979). It is likely that the combined mainland and Outer Isles ice occupied much of the Minch and the Sea of the Hebrides but failed to reach St

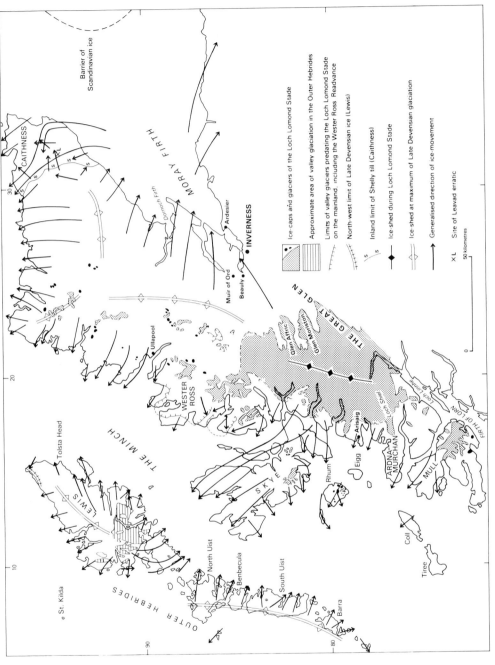

Figure 45

Ice movement directions and ice limits during the last (Late Devensian) glaciation

Kilda, which supported only a small valley glacier (D. G. Sutherland and others, 1982). Late-Devensian ice also failed to reach North Rona. In the central areas of the Highlands the ice seems to have been at least 1100 m thick. No sign of glaciation has been noted on the highest summits of mountains such as An Teallach (1061 m) and Ladhar Bheinn (1019 m) which lay west of the ice-shed. Such summits would have suffered minimal erosion and probably stood above the sheet for long periods, if not for the entire Late Devensian.

During the maximum glaciation, a great glacier extended into the Moray Firth where it came up against Scandinavian ice which occupied the North Sea. One arm of the Scottish ice was diverted across the Banffshire coast and the other across Caithness (Figure 45). The north-westerly flow in Caithness, which was both preceded and succeeded by an ice movement from the west, was responsible for the deposition of stiff, bluish to brownish grey, shelly till which contains, in addition to local rocks, gneisses from Ross-shire, Mesozoic rocks and shells from the bed of the Moray Firth, and fragmentary shells of Pleistocene marine molluscs (most of which are temperate species). The most remarkable erratic is the enormous mass of fossiliferous Lower Cretaceous sandstone and Tertiary clay which was at one time quarried at Leavad (Figures 37, 45). Some of the evidence suggests that parts of Caithness may have been subjected to a periglacial climate for much longer than adjoining ground (J. S. Smith, 1978) and were thus deglaciated early.

In the Outer Hebrides ice flowed outwards from ice centres in Lewis and South Harris (von Weymarn, 1979) and from an ice-shed which extended southwards near the west coast of Benbecula and the Uists to Barra (Figure 45; Flinn, 1979; Peacock, 1984). The eastward-flowing ice on Barra and South Uist reached a thickness of more than 400 m, the basal layers being diverted to the north and south around Beinn Mhor and Hecla. The erratics of Torridonian sandstone and Cambrian quartzite which occur along the west coasts of the more southerly Hebridean islands (Jehu and Craig, 1923–1934) suggest that Scottish mainland ice reached these districts at one time, probably during an earlier glaciation. A fragment of raised beach capped by till on the west coast of Barra may be the same age as the pre-Late Devensian beach of north Lewis.

Ice wastage

During retreat, the ice probably remained active for a time, and was only gradually constrained to the valleys as the mountain tops became ice-free. Readvances probably took place from time to time, either as a result of temporary climatic reversals or as a result of local glacier surges. Such a readvance has been identified in Wester Ross (Robinson and Ballantyne, 1979) on the basis of a terminal moraine (Figure 45). Other readvances have been suggested in the more central areas of the Northern Highlands (Sissons, 1982a) and in the Moray Firth (J. S. Smith, 1978; Synge, 1978) forming, for instance, the gravel and silt deposits at Chanonry Ness and Ardersier. On the east coast, outwash terraces are associated with the high sea levels of late-glacial times, and deltas formed in the sea by glacial meltwaters occur at Beauly and Muir of Ord. Similar features have been recorded elsewhere, including the delta on which Ullapool stands. The most widespread deposits left by the retreat on the wasting ice are the hummocky moraines (Plate 28) and gravels interspersed with sheets of boulder clay which cover large areas of the lower ground of central Sutherland and the valley bottoms in more mountainous areas.

Plate 28 Hummocky morainic drift: a fine example of the 'Ceud Cnoc' or 'Thousand Hills' topography found from place to place in the Highland glens. Near Lochan an Iasgair, Glen Torridon (D2737)

Plate 29 Glacially striated and polished rock surface: Middle Old Red Sandstone, on a hillside bordering Loch Ness. Forest road at Alltsigh, 8 km NE of Invermoriston (W. Mykura)

Plate 30   Raised beaches: '100 ft' beach and cliff, and platform of '25 ft' beach. Hilton of Cadboll, Ross-shire   (C1924)

Plate 31   Many hill slopes in the south-west part of the Northern Highlands within the area of the Loch Lomond Re-advance glaciation, especially those facing south (the 'sunny side'), show fissures associated with large-scale block movement or landslides. Movements took place mainly in late glacial times, although very rarely more recent slips can be detected. The fissures in this illustration are guided by WNW faults and joints. Sgurr na Ciste Dubh, the Five Sisters of Kintail   (G. S. Johnstone)

Loch Lomond Stade

In many valleys and corries in the western Highlands there is abundant evidence
for an advance or readvance of ice following the retreat from the glacial maximum
(Figure 45). Fresh-looking terminal moraines mark the readvance limit in many
Highland valleys (Sissons, 1979b), as for instance in Glen Moriston and Glen
Affric; at the west end of Loch Shiel the ice ploughed through late-glacial marine
deposits. In the area around Loch Quoich and Loch Arkaig, small ice-caps
developed with an ice-shed east of the present watershed, and the ice reached a
thickness of at least 600 m in the Great Glen. The readvance ice in the Glen
Moriston area dammed a subsidiary valley to form a glacial lake which is thought
to have drained catastrophically during glacier retreat (Sissons, 1977).

In the north, however, the glaciers of the Loch Lomond Readvance were scattered and small (Figure 45), but their location is marked, as in many localities farther south, by hummocky moraines and morainic features aligned in the direction
of ice movement (Sissons, 1979b). Similar landforms occur in south-west Lewis
and Harris, but the age of these is as yet uncertain (Peacock, 1984).

RAISED BEACHES

The eustatic lowering of sea level caused by the abstraction of water to form the
great continental ice-sheets was more than offset in Scotland by the isostatic
depression of the land caused by the weight of its ice-cap. In late- and post-glacial
times, isostatic recovery sometimes failed to keep pace with the eustatic rise in sea
level as the water was returned to the oceans. Consequently raised beaches and
associated marine deposits are now found well above Ordnance Datum around
much of the Northern Highlands. Isostatic uplift was greatest where the ice load
was at its maximum, as a result of which the beaches tend to be tilted towards the
coast, and beaches of the same height in different places are not necessarily of the
same age. The raised beaches are divisible into a late-glacial series formed
sometimes adjacent to retreating ice, and a lower post-glacial series, separated in
time by a period of relatively low sea level (Plate 30).

Late-glacial beaches

Because of the rapidly changing sea level caused by the disappearance of the ice
there are few erosional features in solid rock associated with the earlier late-glacial
beaches. Such beaches are usually accumulations of gravel which sometimes rest
on a platform cut in drift. They reach a height of nearly 45 m near Arisaig on the
west coast, and heights of 24 to 27 m are common both there and in the eastern
area around Beauly, Cromarty and Inverness. Perhaps the most spectacular
marine features to which a late-glacial age has been attributed are the raised rock
platform and cliff in the Firth of Lorn–Loch Linnhe area, mentioned earlier
(p. 163). Northwards, the marine limit is much lower, and there is disagreement
about whether late-glacial beaches occur on the north coast.

In the Dornoch Firth area, there is evidence that sea level was falling rapidly as
the ice retreated up the Firth, so that the later beach features near Bonar Bridge
are much lower than those in the Tain area. Though the late-glacial shorelines are
known to be tilted, there are few areas where records are as yet continuous enough
to define gradients. At Inverness, however, a gradient of 0.12 m per kilometre has
been reported (Synge, 1978).

Post-glacial beaches

Following a period of relatively low sea level, which is as yet little documented in the Northern Highlands, a marine transgression took place, reaching a culmination (by analogy with other parts of Scotland) about 6700 BP (Sissons, 1976). This highest post-glacial beach (the 25 ft beach of many older Geological Survey publications) is widespread and commonly takes the form of a gravel storm beach; in sheltered estuaries, silt and clay predominate. In places there is a rock platform and cliff, but this is usually a modification of one of the older marine benches mentioned earlier. Lower beaches occur below the main beach in places. Though few detailed and accurately surveyed measurements have been published, it has long been known that the highest post-glacial beach is tilted, reaching its greatest altitude within the Northern Highlands near Fort William (about 12 m OD), falling off to the north and west, to a metre or two above OD in Caithness. A gradient of 0.05 metres per kilometre has been calculated for the highest beach in the Firth of Lorne area. No raised beach of this age is known with certainty in the Outer Hebrides, though beach gravels slightly above the modern beach have been reported (Richie, 1971).

Near Beauly the deposits of the transgression are known to rest on peat, formed during the preceding period of low sea level (Haggart, 1982).

OTHER LATE-GLACIAL AND POST-GLACIAL EVENTS

Evidence from lake sediments shows that, as the ice wasted from its maximum position, the ice-free areas of the mainland were colonised by crowberry heath with juniper. Birch woodlands occurred locally in Skye. During the Loch Lomond Stade, however, the vegetation reverted to tundra. Work on the contemporaneous beetle faunas suggests that during the earliest part of the Windermere Interstadial July temperatures were at or above present-day levels in parts of England, but much lower to the north (Coope, 1977). Conditions were generally much colder after 12 000 BP. Marine beds in the inner Moray Firth probably dating from the interstadial show faunal assemblages comparable to those of the present day north of Lofoten in Norway (Peacock and others, 1980). It is likely that, given sufficient precipitation, a few corrie glaciers persisted through the interstadial (it would take only a small drop in temperature for glaciers to reappear in the Highlands at the present day) with a more general rejuvenation of glaciers from about 12 000 BP, and particularly from 11 000 BP onwards, when evidence from many sources suggests a very cold climate (Sissons, 1979b).

During the Loch Lomond Stade, the little-vegetated ground was subjected to intensive frost action; this gave rise to blockfields and stone lobes on the mountains, and to patterned ground and solifluction of till slopes at all levels. Extensive screes formed on suitable hillsides, and the rivers carried great quantities of sand and gravel. They also carried suspensions of silt and clay which were deposited as laminated sediments in the lakes. Of particular interest is the occurrence of isolated ice-wedge casts, such as those in the glaciofluvial gravels of the Oykell valley. The ice-wedge casts, which probably relate to the stadial, would today indicate permafrost and average annual temperatures several degrees below zero celsius.

Many of the numerous landslips in the Northern Highlands probably date from the periods of ice wastage (Plate 31). They would have been triggered by a combination of features, such as unloading of the rock faces as the ice melted, a high water table, the presence of suitably oriented joints and (in flat-lying Tertiary and

Mesozoic rocks) the presence of weak horizons such as shales and boles. There is increasing evidence that features resembling the protalus ramparts (ridge of debris formed at the base of a steep snowfield) and rock glaciers of present-day polar regions occur in parts of the Highlands (Sissons, 1979b). A fine example of a fossil protalus rampart has been reported from Baosbheinn, 10 km south of Gairloch in Wester Ross (Sissons, 1976). It is probable that, during the Loch Lomond Stade, interstitial ice also facilitated the renewed movement of some of the older landslips, such as those of Eigg and Skye.

After the final disappearance of the ice, heath was briefly re-established, soon to be replaced by birch and pine forests in many areas and mixed oak forest at more favourable localities in the south and south-west, including southern Skye (Birks, 1977). The windy Outer Hebrides may never have supported forests; however, pine, willow and birch stumps near the base of the peat at various localities show there were stands of trees at various times between 9000 and 4000 BP (Wilkins, 1984).

With the wetter and cooler climate initiated about 6000 years ago, part of the forest was destroyed by blanket peat (assisted to an increasing extent by the hand of man). Such peat still occupies extensive tracts, particularly in Sutherland and Lewis, though the area is being constantly reduced by erosion, exploitation and the demands of agriculture. The deposits left by the ice have been partly eroded and redeposited to form the alluvial haughs seen in many Highland valleys today, and it is probable that these processes were accentuated by the destruction of the forest.

Blown sand occurs at many coastal localities where there are sandy beaches. It is particularly important on the west coast of the Outer Hebrides, where flat 'machair', composed of shell sand blown inland, commonly forms almost the only agricultural land. The 'White Sands of Morar' are quartz-rich sands with occasional bands of pink garnet. There are extensive stretches of blown sand in the broader bays of Caithness and in north and west Sutherland in the form of dunes and flat links, the latter only slightly above sea level. Blown sand also occurs at the intakes of some of the inland lochs of Caithness.

15   Faults and seismicity

Numerous faults, major and minor, traverse the rocks of the Northern Highlands. Many affect only the older rocks, being unconformably overlain by younger formations or cut by unbroken intrusions and so can be related to specific episodes of crustal fracture, but it is also clear that many of ancient origin have been reactivated during later periods of movement.

FAULTS

Lines of Pre-Torridonian shear

The earliest fault-like features identified are planes of pre-Torridonian shear within the Lewisian gneiss of the Foreland (Peach and others, 1907). Properly speaking, these are not faults along which fracture has taken place at the level of crust now exposed. They are planes of ductile shear, trending NW–SE, in which rocks in narrow zones show grain-size reduction, mylonitisation and, in places, the development of flinty crush (pseudotachylite); they do not affect the overlying Torridonian strata. Certain of the shear planes may have acted as zones of weakness which guided the lines of the Caledonian faults (see below). Only two major structures are sufficiently defined to be shown separately on Figure 46. These are the Loch Seaforth Fault in Lewis and the Loch Maree Fault on the mainland.

Park (1961) and Peach and his colleagues noted less distinct areas of pseudotachylite development which are possibly of the same age as the more defined shear lines. Watson (1984) suggested that post-Caledonian faulting along the line of Loch Shin has been guided by a pre-Caledonian basement structure which, with others in the Scottish Highlands, she considered to be related to fundamental fractures in the lower crust.

Late-Caledonian faults

The main phases of Caledonian folding and igneous emplacement were followed by a period of crustal uplift and cooling during which ductile deformation gave place to block fracturing, with displacement either in a vertical or lateral sense (or both). Of the faults of this age the best-marked in the Scottish Highlands comprise two major groups whose trend are respectively NE–SW and NW–SE. In the Northern Highlands the NE–SW suite predominates. The NW–SE faults are less prominent, though in addition to those recognised by belts of crush and shift of strata, topographic lineaments suggest that there may be others (Auden, 1954; Watson, 1984).

Where relative sense of movement can be made out, it can be seen that there is an apparently straightforward arrangement of lateral sinistral slip on faults trend-

ing NE–SW and dextral slip on those trending NW–SE. The faults were formerly considered to represent a conjugate set resulting from the resolution of north-
south directed 'Proto-Armorican' stress (Anderson, 1942). Watson (1984),
however, came to a different conclusion. She pointed out that the NE–SW set is
dominant both in number of faults and amount of displacement and, in the Scottish Highlands as a whole, the faults of the suite seem to be the locus of emplacement of a group of Caledonian granites, which indicates a fundamental association with the Caledonian orogeny. Moreover, some of the NE–SW faults appear
to have existed before, or determined, the development of basins of Old Red
Sandstone deposition (Mykura, 1983a; 1983b). Watson accordingly suggested
that the NE–SW sinistral-slip faults were initiated as deep-seated crustal fractures
at the time of continental collision following the closure of the Iapetus Ocean in
late-Silurian times. These deep-seated structures gave rise to variations in local
strain which, in certain cases, facilitated the rise of late orogenic granites. The
NW–SE faults are not essentially conjugate to the NE–SW suite but represent
small-scale adjustments determined by pre-existing lines of pre-Caledonian (or
'pre-Torridonian') shear in the Lewisian basement. She speculated that the set of
E–W joints which are a prominent feature in the Northern Highlands could be
fractures conjugate to the NE–SW faults.

The main phase of movement on these transcurrent faults is thought to be pre-
Devonian or early Devonian (D. I. Smith and Watson, 1983; Watson, 1984), but

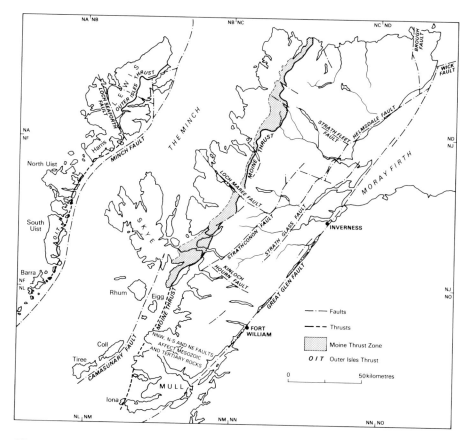

Figure 46   Major faults in the Northern Highlands and Hebrides

transcurrent movement continued to a lesser extent after the formation of the Old Red Sandstone basins. The NW – SE-trending faults show differential displacement of variously inclined strata of the Foreland and the Moine Thrust Belt, which indicates that vertical as well as horizontal movement has taken place (Coward, 1983) and this is probably also true of the faults of the NE – SW set (Mykura, 1983a;b).

By far the most important fault of the NE – SW group is the Great Glen Fault, which, once initiated as a fundamental fracture in Caledonian times, has been reactivated, with varied displacement, during subsequent periods of earth movement; and it is still active. Its net sinistral shift was considered by Watson (1984) to be about 100 km (see below). The other transcurrent faults, of both the NW – SE and NE – SW sets, show displacement of only a few kilometres at the most.

The larger faults have marked zones of cataclasis which have been eroded to form linear topographic features. As mentioned above, other linear features with no clear effect on the distribution of strata may mark the lines of concealed crushes or belts of broken rock. Several such zones (not clearly related to mappable faults) were encountered in hydroelectric tunnels in the Northern Highlands.

Post-Caledonian faults

A. G. MacGregor (1967) has analysed the fault systems of the south-west part of the Northern Highlands and finds evidence for an E – W suite of faults which he considers were initiated in Permo-Carboniferous times. However, they may represent activation as faults of the E – W joints referred to above.

The basins of Mesozoic rocks (including the Permo-Trias) of the Minch, Sea of the Hebrides and Malin Sea (see Chapter 13) are controlled by NNE – SSW-trending faults throwing down to the east, defining half-grabens in which deposits thicken to the west. The faults were probably initiated during the initial stage of the breakup of the large 'supercontinent' formed after the closure of the Iapetus Ocean (the breakup eventually resulting in the opening of the Atlantic). Of these faults, the Minch Fault (inferred from offshore studies) and the Camasunary Fault of south Skye are important members. Brewer and Smythe (1984) suggest that the location of the NNE – SSW faults of the Minch may be determined by pre-existing thrusts in the basement, while the age of the last movements on the Camasunary Fault seems to be established by the fact that its line, if continued northwards, does not cut the Tertiary Red Hills Complex of Skye.

The Mesozoic basin of the Moray Firth has been related to the widening of the North Sea Viking and Central grabens by rotation of the Northern Highlands block along the line of the Great Glen Fault with resultant dextral movement of 8 km (McQuillin and Donato, 1982). The Helmsdale Fault, limiting the Mesozoic rocks of the North Sea on their landward side, has a similar orientation to its counterparts on the western seaboard.

A. G. MacGregor (1967) recognised two sets of faults oriented N – S and NW – SE, to which he assigned a Tertiary date of movement.

The Great Glen Fault

The Great Glen Fault is such an important feature both geologically and topographically that it has attracted special attention and has an extensive literature. It consists of a zone of crushed rock (now represented mainly by indurated cataclasite) up to 0.5 km wide, flanked by zones of minor faulting and shattering. On the Northern Highlands side of the fault the zones of shattering extend up to about 1 km beyond the crush-zone. This broken rock has guided erosion to form the deep linear depression of the Great Glen, the floor of which rises to only c.40 m above OD but whose sides rise steeply up to 900 m; and the ground-level is even higher only a few kilometres away. Along this trench lie freshwater lochs, one of which (Loch Ness) is more than 200 m deep. The depression traverses the country from the Moray Firth to the Firth of Lorn, and a linear gravity anomaly indicates the south-westward continuation of the Great Glen Fault under the Mesozoic rocks of south-east Mull and thence offshore past the north end of Colonsay, possibly continuing across the Malin Sea to pass north of Ireland (Evans and others, 1979). North of Inverness the Great Glen Fault runs along the eastern shore of the Black Isle and the Tarbat Ness peninsula, and further north again the gravity anomaly indicates that it hugs the coast of Caithness. Just north of Wick, however, the course of the anomaly cannot be traced beyond the ENE-trending Wick Fault; the suggested continuation of the Great Glen Fault towards the Walls Boundary Fault of Shetland (Flinn, 1961; Mykura, 1975) has not been confirmed by offshore geophysical studies.

It was W. Q. Kennedy (1946) who first suggested that the Great Glen Fault is a major sinistral wrench fault. Using various criteria, including the shift of the metamorphic zones of the Scottish Highlands north and south of the Great Glen, and the possible former connection of the Strontian and Foyers Granites (apparently cut into two halves and displaced by the fault), he estimated a sinistral displacement of 104 km. However, though the two granite plutons contain similar rock types, the lack of a precise fit of their component members (Marston, 1971; Munro, 1973) and differences in their trace-element content (Pankhurst, 1979) and zircon distribution patterns (Pidgeon and Aftalion, 1978) suggest that they were never joined. The presence of two similar complexes adjoining a major fracture could be accounted for by the preferential location of plutons along the NE faults, as suggested by Watson (1984) and referred to earlier. Winchester (1972) suggests a large sinistral displacement of the metamorphic zones which he has refined and amplified from the initial studies of Kennedy. Piasecki and Wright (1981) likewise postulate a large pre-Mesozoic sinistral (c.160 km), based on analogous structural and stratigraphic features within the Northern Highlands. While much of the evidence for the amount of displacement along such a large fault must be open to more than one interpretation, the fact that a certain amount of sinistral slip has taken place can be shown by small-scale deflections of granite veins in the shattered rocks within the faulted zone. However, these never amount to more than a few decimetres.

Johnstone and Wright (1951) noted that the Permo-Carboniferous dykes cut the major crust rocks of the central fault zone but were themselves only broken, thus setting an upper age limit to the formation of the crush zone. Holgate (1969) postulated a considerable dextral shift of the Permo-Carboniferous dyke swarms across the fault, and Speight and Mitchell later (1979) suggested that this shift was of the order of 6–8 km. Presumably this displacement took place along lines within the earlier zone of crush and shattering. Some of the dextral displacement along the fault appears to have taken place during the Mesozoic, and Mc-Quillin and Donato (1982) have linked this with a 5–6 km distension of the Moray Firth Basin and the formation of the Viking and Central grabens of the North Sea. They estimate an 8 km dextral shift along the line of Great Glen.

Other opinions concerning the movement along the Great Glen Fault have been advanced by various authors. Garson and Plant (1972) proposed a major dextral shift. Their interpretation suggested that, before movement along the

Fault, the E–W-trending north coasts of the Northern Highlands and the Grampians were in line with one another. They supported this hypothesis by what they considered was displacement of a subduction-related zonal distribution of granite plutons, metamorphic zones and old suture lines. Van der Voo and and Scotese (1981) used dissimilarities in pole directions of the magnetism of Old Red Sandstone strata on either side of the Great Glen to suggest a sinistral shift of 2000 km. This view, however, is at considerable odds with the most likely interpretations of the crustal structures of Northern Britain (see among others Watson and Smith, 1983, and the review by Watson, 1984, referred to above). Storevedt (1987), using re-interpreted and new palaeomagnetic data, deduced that there was a 600 km late Caledonian sinistral displacement on the Great Glen Fault and a 300 km Hercynian dextral displacement.

If the magnitude of displacement suggested by Piasecki and his colleagues is accepted, then the Moine Thrust zone south of the Great Glen Fault would coincide with the line of the Great Glen from Fort Augustus southwards. The presence of a wide zone of early SE-dipping thrusts and mylonites in the area between Fort Augustus and Spean Bridge lends support to this concept.

SEISMICITY

The north of Scotland has a long recorded history of earthquake activity stretching back to 1597, when on 23 July an earthquake was reported to be felt over most of the area from Ross and Cromarty to Perth. Until recent years, however, the observed pattern of activity has been strongly influenced by population distribution, and it is likely that many events occurring in remote districts have gone unreported.

Using documentary sources to study past earthquakes in Scotland one can loosely discern two main areas of activity north of the Highland Boundary Fault. These are the west coast, from Inveraray and Lochgilphead north to Ullapool, and the Great Glen from Inverness to the vicinity of Invergarry. In addition, a few small events are known from other locations; for example, a major source of seismic activity near Comrie, very close to the Highland Boundary Fault itself, was responsible for many hundreds of earthquakes (most of them small) from 1788 to 1950. The eastern part of the area, the Grampians, and also the extreme north, are almost devoid of seismic activity.

Recent instrumental monitoring confirms the historical pattern, inasmuch as most seismic activity since 1967 has been concentrated on the west coast; relatively few events have been detected east of Spean Bridge or north of Kinlochewe. It is also notable that very little activity has been observed in the Inverness area, despite the occurrence in the past of damaging earthquakes that have affected that city, notably the events of 13 August 1816, and 18 September 1901.

Many of the earthquakes in the west of Scotland detected by BGS instruments are too small to be felt by people. In 1983 nine such events were detected in the north-west of Scotland, and only one felt. The last, which took place on 25 February, 1983, had a small Richter magnitude of 2.2 and was felt weakly at Spean Bridge.

16 Economic minerals

Minerals with an economic association are widespread in the Northern Highlands, but in only a few places are they found in sufficient concentration to warrant exploitation.

Most of the main prospects have been known since the 18th century, mainly as a result of specific prospecting surveys carried out on behalf of the large land-owners and, following the 1745 rising, the Commissioners for Forfeited Estates. It is evident that the old prospectors were well versed in the detection of vein ores and other concentrations of metallic minerals. Modern prospecting has been for bulk minerals, non-metallic minerals and low-grade ore deposits which, while not readily visible in outcrop, are still capable of abstraction by bulk handling and beneficiation.

A number of surveys were carried out on behalf of the Ministry of Supply during the 1939–45 war, and the Scottish Council (Development and Industry). Investigations that ranged more widely were subsequently undertaken by the Geological Survey as part of their Regional Geochemical Survey and their Mineral Reconnaissance Programme. The survey was sponsored by the Department of Industry, the programme in part by the Atomic Energy Authority. Additional investigations were undertaken by Robertson Research Ltd sponsored by the Highlands and Islands Development Board. The later investigations made use of all modern geophysical and geochemical techniques. While several prospects have been located, none in the Northern Highlands have so far warranted major economic exploitation. Reports are listed in the bibliography.

Several *Special Reports on the Mineral Reserves of Great Britain* cover specific aspects of the economic mineral potential of the Northern Highlands; they are out of print. However, a comprehensive survey of the actual and potential economic minerals of the Northern Highlands is given in IGS Report 69/5 *A summary of the mineral resources of the Crofter Counties of Scotland*. More detailed summaries of the availability of sand and gravel aggregate are given in IGS Reports 77/8 and 78/8, and in the series of mineral dossiers published by the Mineral Resources Consultative Committee. The following is a brief summary of the available information.

METALLIC ORES

In the Northern Highlands metallic ores (Figure 47) have been worked extensively only at Strontian, where veins containing galena associated with sphalerite were mined between 1722 and 1872. This region has since been the subject of several mineral surveys, including prospect-drilling. Between 1984 and early 1986 the Strontian Main Vein was worked for baryte, galena and sphalerite; subsequently small amounts of high grade calcite have been produced. Strontianite (strontium carbonate) from which the element strontium was first derived, is a collector's item and other rare minerals (such as brewsterite and harmotome) can also be found.

Lead and zinc vein ores were once worked on a small scale at Lurga in Morvern, at Struy in Strath Glass (IGS Mineral Reconnaissance Programme Report No.6) and at Achanarras near Halkirk in Caithness, the Achanarras area being one over which intensive investigations were carried out by IGS in the late 1960s.

Bands of magnetite are found in the Lewisian of Iona and Tiree, but extensive trials in Tiree did not lead to exploitation. No similar occurrences are known in the Lewisian gneiss of the Outer Isles or the mainland.

Ilmenite was found in concealed portions of the Borralan Complex (p.103) during boring intended to assess the apatite content of the rocks. No apatite has been exploited, but the area must be considered as having potential.

Small quantities of molybdenite were found around the Grudie Granite, Loch Shin. Although mainly concentrated in shear-zones in the schists the primary source of the molybdenite was probably in the granite itself (IGS Mineral Recon-

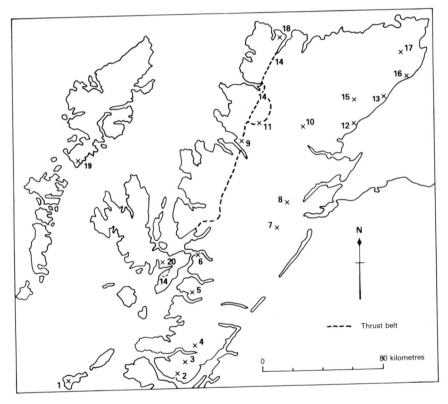

Figure 47   Main mineral localities in the Northern Highlands

Pb/Zn: 4 Strontian   **3** Lurga   **7** Struy   **17** Achanarras

Fe/Ti: 1 Tiree   **11** Borralan

Mo-U-Au: 10 Grudie (Mo)   **13** Ousdale (U)   **15** Strath of Kildonan (Au)

K-feldspar: 18 Ceannabeinne   **14** Potassic shales (generalised along the thrust belt)

Mica: 5 Knoydart   **8** Scatwell

Others: *Glass sand* **2** Loch Aline, **12** Brora; *Barytes* **4** Strontian, **16** Lybster; *Talc* **6** Ardintoul; *Dolomite limestone* **9** Ullapool, **20** Torrin; *Coal* **12** Brora; *Apatite* **11** Borralan; *Anorthosite* **19** Rodel; *Brick clay* **12** Brora

naissance Programme Report No.3).

Uranium-bearing minerals occur in certain shale bands in the Middle Old Red Sandstone Caithness Flags, and another notable uranium anomaly was found in the Lower Old Red Sandstone Ousdale Arkose, which overlies the Helmsdale Granite in southern Caithness. The occurrence in the Ousdale Arkose gives rise to the speculation that uranium-bearing deposits may lie concealed at the base of the Old Red Sandstone elsewhere in the area. On the whole, Caithness is still considered to be a minor uranium province, with a mining potential worth further study should economic and political circumstances justify it (Gallagher and others, 1971).

Alluvial gold was worked in the Strath of Kildonan in Sutherland between 1868 and 1870. At that time unofficial estimates of the value of metal abstracted were around £12 000, a considerable sum at that period. Gold is still found as a placer deposit in the streams of the area. It appears to be derived from the hydrothermally altered schists and granites of the hinterland of the Helmsdale River, in which the metal is sparsely disseminated. No main 'lode' has been found.

Other deposits of metallic minerals which have given rise to small-scale workings, trials, or investigations are copper ores at Rassal near Kishorn and at the Castle of Old Wick in Caithness; cassiterite in the aegirine gneiss found in the Carn Chuinneag intrusion (Figure 21); lead, silver and gold in the Loch Maree area; and hematite near Reay in Caithness, and near the head of Loch Kishorn.

NON-METALLIC MINERALS (Figure 47)

These can conveniently be considered in three categories, namely minerals which occur as concentrates or require concentration before use, those which can be used directly in bulk, and other non-metallic minerals.

Mineral concentrates

Potassic shales

In the early 1960s it was discovered that certain parts of the Fucoid Beds of the North-West Highlands (see p. 44) are abnormally rich in potash. It was recognised that the potash would be a useful fertiliser if an economic way of extraction could be devised. Although beneficiation from the silicate mineral was difficult, a satisfactory method was worked out resulting in a concentrate of potassium salts with the additional by-product of cement clinker. Estimated costs of extraction and transport were, however, too high for the product to compete economically with potash from the Yorkshire evaporite field. The shales are not only potassic, however, but also dolomitic and locally contain a small percentage of phosphates. The crushed material is being used in bulk, without treatment, as a raw fertiliser.

Ceramic feldspar

Granite pegmatites in South Harris (Northton and Roneval) were briefly worked during the last war as a source of ceramic feldspar. Other pegmatites, notably those near Beinn Ceannabeinne (near Durness) have since been investigated for this purpose and.many other potash-feldspar bearing pegmatites might also be considered. Alkali feldspar from the syenites of the Alkaline Suite (p.102), potentially a greater and more easily worked resource, has proved unsatisfactory because of the high proportion of iron-containing minerals present in these rocks.

Mica

Coarse book-mica (muscovite) was specifically sought during the Second World War as material for electrical insulation purposes, and the mica-bearing pegmatites of the migmatite belt of the Northern Highlands proved of major interest. Two important, if small, mines were operated, one in Knoydart in Wester Ross and one at Scatwell near Strathpeffer. It is unlikely that the Scottish mica could compete with imported material under normal conditions.

More recently the rocks of the Loch Shiel Migmatite Complex were investigated to assess their potential as a source of flake or ground muscovite mica, obtainable by working bulk mica-schist within the complex. While the quantity of material available was considerable in places, various commercial specifications which existed at the time (purity, colour) could not be met. If, as is possible, those specifications should change, or if other uses should be found for the material, then large reserves would exist.

Barytes

Barytes is a common gangue mineral in the lead-bearing veins which are found sporadically in the Northern Highlands. Only at Roy Geo, near Lybster in Caithness, has a vein (cutting Old Red Sandstone) been specifically worked for the mineral. Increase in demand for barytes as a constituent of heavy drilling muds in the North Sea oil industry has resulted in trial abstraction from the former lead-zinc vein workings at Strontian.

Apatite (calcium phosphate)

This occurs in concentrations in the layered complex of Loch Borralan (p. 103) but trial bores in the drift-covered parts of the complex have not yet been encouraging enough to promote exploitation.

Bulk Minerals

Coal, oil shale and oil

Coal and oil shale of Jurassic age are found in the Brora area of Sutherland, where the Brora Coal (p.150) was worked intermittently from 1598. This seam is on average 1 m thick. It has a high ash and sulphur content, but was used locally as a domestic fuel, in the local brickworks and as fuel in power stations. Although ample reserves still exist, production ceased in 1974. A thin bituminous shale underlying the coal contains subeconomic quantities of oil.

The nearest commercial offshore oil field to the Scottish Mainland, the Beatrice Field, lies 50 km east of Helmsdale (Figure 37). Its main reservoir rocks are of Middle Jurassic (Upper Callovian) age with lesser reservoirs in the Toarcian–Bajocian (Linsley and others, 1980). No oil or gas has been found in the onshore Jurassic rocks of Sutherland.

Limestone and dolomite

The Durness Limestone (p.47) consists of interbanded beds of dolomite and calcite rock (limestone) but, although the overall quantity is great, the economic potential of any area depends on whether either dolomite or calcite-limestone exists in workable quantities without dilution by the other. Several areas suitable for abstraction have been studied. At the present time the main workings are for dolomite for agricultural and general purposes near Ullapool, and for general purposes at Torrin, in Skye.

Hard-rock aggregate, etc.

Hard-rock for concrete and other aggregate is available within a short distance of any likely construction work almost anywhere in the Northern Highlands except, perhaps, in parts of Caithness. Limited demand, however, means that there are few large quarries, although the potential for coastal superquarries, whose product would be exported, is considerable. At the time of writing (1987) development work is being carried out on one such site in the Strontian granite, at Glensanda, close to the north-west shore of Loch Linnhe, facing the island of Lismore. Quartzite, some of high quality, is available if required from the extensive Cambrian outcrops in the north-west part of the region, and from Scaraben in Caithness.

Sand and gravel aggregate

Sand and gravel suitable for concrete aggregate is found in many of the major valleys of the Northern Highlands, mainly in the form of fluvioglacial outwash. Extensive deposits are found in the lower reaches of the major eastward-flowing valleys, but the material is less abundant in the westward-flowing valleys; it commonly occurs in terraces or deltas around the heads of the sea-lochs. A brief assessment of the extent, thickness and composition of the deposits is given in the following issues of the IGS Report Series: *The sand and gravel resources of the Strathclyde Region* (1977), and *The Sand and Gravel Resources of the Highland Region* (1978). These do not include assessments of the grade or the exact quantities available.

Glass-sand

A soft, white sandstone of Cretaceous age (p. 161) at Loch Aline, Morvern, has been worked for many years as a source of glass-sand. The deposit has extensive reserves and is extremely pure, containing $>99.7\%$ SiO_2 (Humphries, 1961). It has proved suitable for the manufacture of high-grade optical glass, but is at the present mainly worked as a glass sand for general purposes.

A soft white partly silicified Middle Jurassic Sandstone crops out in Clynelish Quarry, just west of Brora. It has been suggested that part of this deposit might be suitable for glass making.

Other non-metallic minerals

Talc rock of high purity was mined from the Lewisian gneiss at Ardintoul, near Glenelg. *Shell sand* is available for local purposes from various west-facing stretches of coastal sand or 'machair', and also in the northern and north-eastern bays from Durness to Wick. *Brick clay* is found in the Middle Jurassic Brora Argillaceous Series at Brora. *Anorthosite*, used to make white-rock powder, has been quarried at Rodel, Harris. *Peat* is extensively developed throughout the Northern Highlands and many bogs especially in the northern part of the mainland and in the Outer Isles have immense reserves (Second Report of the Scottish Peat Committee, 1962). Detailed studies of the peat deposits have been made by the Macaulay Institute for Soil Research, Craigiebuckler, Aberdeen.

ALDERMAN, A. R. 1936.   Eclogites from the neighbourhood of Glenelg, Inverness-shire.   *Q. J. Geol. Soc. London*, Vol.92, 488–533.

ANDERSON, E. M. 1942.   *The dynamics of faulting* (2nd Edition 1951). (Edinburgh: Scottish Academic Press.)

ANDO, C. J., COOK, F. A., OLIVER, J. E., BROWN, L. D., and KAUFMAN, S. 1983.   Crustal geometry of the Appalachian orogen from seismic reflection studies.   *Mem. Geol. Soc. Am.*, Vol.158, 83–101.

ANON. 1962.   Scottish Peat. Second Report on the Scottish Peat Committee, Department of Agriculture and Fisheries for Scotland. (Edinburgh: HMSO.)

ARMSTRONG, M. 1964.   The geology of the region between Alness River and the Dornoch Firth.   Unpublished PhD thesis, University of Newcastle upon Tyne.

— 1977.   The Old Red Sandstone of Easter Ross and the Black Isle   *In* GILL, G. (editor) *The Moray Firth area—geological studies.* Inverness Field Club.

AUDEN, J. B. 1954.   Drainage and fracture patterns in northwest Scotland.   *Geol. Mag.*, Vol.91, 379–394.

BAILEY, E. B. 1924.   The desert shores of the Chalk seas.   *Geol. Mag.*, Vol.61, 102–116.

— 1934.   The Glencoul Nappe and the Assynt Culmination.   *Geol. Mag.*, Vol.72, 151–165.

— 1951.   Scourie dykes and Laxfordian metamorphism.   *Geol. Mag.*, Vol.88, 153–165.

— 1955.   Moine tectonics and metamorphism in Skye.   *Trans. Edinburgh Geol. Soc.*, Vol.16, 93–166.

— 1960.   The Geology of Ben Nevis and Glencoe.   *Mem. Geol. Surv. UK.* (2nd Edition), Sheet 53.

— COLLET, L. W., and FIELD, R. M. 1928.   Palaeozoic submarine landslips near Quebec City.   *J. Geol.*, Vol.36, 577–614.

— and WEIR, J. 1932.   Submarine faulting in Kimmeridgian times: East Sutherland.   *Trans. R. Soc. Edinburgh*, Vol.47, 429–467.

BAIRD, A. W. 1982.   The Sgurr Slide within the Moine rocks at Loch Eilt, Inverness-shire.   *J. Geol. Soc. London*, Vol.139, 647–653.

BALLY, A. W., GORDY, P. L., and STEWART, G. A. 1966.   Structure, seismic data and orogenic evolution of Southern Canadian Rocky Mountains.   *Bull. Can. Pet. Geol.*, Vol.14, 337–381.

BAMFORD, D., NUNN, K., PRODEHL, C., and JACOB, B. 1978.   LISPB-IV. Crustal structure of northern Britain.   *Geophys. J. R. Astron. Soc.*, Vol.54, 43–60.

BARBER, A. J. 1965.   The history of the Moine Thrust Zone, Lochcarron and Lochalsh, Scotland.   *Proc. Geol. Assoc. London*, Vol.76, 215–242.

— BEACH, A., PARK, R. G., TARNEY, J., and STEWART, A. D. 1978. The Lewisian and Torridonian rocks of North-West Scotland. *Geol. Assoc. Guide,* No.21.

— and MAY, F. 1976. The history of the western Lewisian in the Glenelg Inlier, Lochalsh, Northern Highlands. *Scott. J. Geol.,* Vol.12, 35–50.

BEACH, A. 1973. The mineralogy of high temperature shear zones at Scourie, NW Scotland. *J. Petrol,* Vol.14, 231–248.

— COWARD, M. P., and GRAHAM, R. H. 1974. An interpretation of the structural evolution of the Laxford front. *Scott. J. Geol.,* Vol.9, 297–308.

— and FYFE, W. S. 1972. Fluid transport and shear zones at Scourie, Sutherland: evidence of over-thrusting? *Contr. Mineral. Petrol.,* Vol.36, 17–180.

— and TARNEY, J. 1978. Major and trace element patterns established during retrogressive metamorphism of granulite-facies gneisses, NW Scotland. *Precambrian Res.,* Vol.7, 325–348.

BECKINSALE, R. D., and OBRADOVICH, J. D. 1973. Potassium-argon ages for minerals from the Ross of Mull, Argyllshire, Scotland. *Scott. J. Geol.,* Vol.9, 147–115.

BERRIDGE, N. G., and IVIMEY-COOK, H. C. 1967. The geology of a borehole at Lossiemouth, Morayshire. *Bull. Geol. Surv.,* No.27, 155–169.

BICKERMAN, M., BOWES, D. R., and VAN BREEMAN, O. 1975. Rb-Sr whole rock isotopic studies of Lewisian metasediments and gneisses in the Loch Maree region, Ross-shire. *J. Geol. Soc. London,* Vol.131, 237–254.

BIRKS, H. J. B. 1977. The Flandrian forest history of Scotland: a preliminary synthesis. *In* SHOTTON, F. W. (editor), *British Quaternary Studies: Recent Advances,* 119–135. (Oxford: Clarendon Press.)

BLACKBOURN, G. A. 1981a. Probable Old Red Sandstone conglomerates around Tongue and adjacent areas, North Sutherland. *Scott. J. Geol.,* Vol.17, 103–118.

— 1981b. Correlation of Old Red Sandstone (Devonian) outliers in the Northern Highlands of Scotland. *Geol. Mag.,* Vol.111, 409–411.

BLAXLAND, A. B., AFTALION, M., and VAN BREEMAN, O. 1979. Pb isotopic composition of feldspars from Scottish Caledonian granites and the nature of the underlying crust. *Scott. J. Geol.,* Vol.15, 139–154.

BOTT, M. H. P., HOLLAND, J. G., STORRY, P. G., and WATTS, A. B. 1972. Geophysical evidence concerning the structure of the Lewisian of Sutherland, NW Scotland. *J. Geol. Soc. London,* Vol.128, 599–612.

BOWES, D. R. 1969. The Lewisian of Northwest Highlands of Scotland. *In* KAY, M. (editor), *North Atlantic geology and continental drift, a symposium. Mem. Am. Assoc. Pet. Geol.,* Vol.12, 575–594.

— 1972. Geochemistry of Precambrian crystalline basement rocks, North-West Highlands of Scotland. *24th Sess. Int. Geol. Congr., Canada 1972,* Sect.1, 97–103.

— 1975. Framework of the Precambrian crystalline complex of the Outer Hebrides. *Krystalinikum,* Vol.11, 7–23.

— 1978. Shield formation in early Precambrian times: the Lewisian complex. In: BOWES, D. R., and LEAKE, B. E. (editors), *Crustal evolution in northwestern Britain and adjacent regions, Spec. Issue Geol. J.,* No.10, 39–80. (Liverpool: Seel House Press.)

— DAROOAH, B. C., and KHOURY, S. G.   Original nature of Archaean rocks of North-West Scotland.   *Spec. Publ. Geol. Soc. Aust.* Vol. 3, 7–92.

— and GHALY, T. S. 1964.   Age relations of Lewisian basic rocks south of Gairloch, Ross-shire.   *Geol. Mag.*, Vol.101, 150–160.

—and HOPGOOD, A. M. 1969a.   The Lewisian gneiss complex of Mingulay, Outer Hebrides, Scotland.   *Mem. Geol. Soc. Am.*, No.115, 317–360.

— — 1969b.   Composition of a dolerite dyke, Mingulay, Outer Hebrides.   *Mineral. Mag.*, Vol.37, 427–428.

— — 1973.   Framework of Precambrian crystalline complex of north-western Scotland.   *In* PIDGEON, R. T., and others (editors), *Geochronology and isotope geology of Scotland, field guide and reference.*   3rd Europe Congr. of Geochronologists. (East Kilbride: Scottish Universities Research and Reactor Centre), A1–A14

— and KHOURY, S. G. 1965.   Successive periods of basic dyke emplacement in the Lewisian complex south of Scourie, Sutherland.   *Scott. J. Geol.*, Vol.1, 295–299.

— and WRIGHT, A. E. 1967.   The explosion breccia pipes near Kentallen, Scotland and their geological setting.   *Trans. R. Soc. Edinburgh*, Vol.67, 109–145.

— — and PARK, R. G. 1964.   Layered intrusive rocks in the Lewisian of the North-west Highlands of Scotland.   *Q. J. Geol. Soc. London*, Vol.120, 153–192.

BOWIE, S. H. 1963.   Report of the Atomic Energy Division.   *Geological Survey of Great Britain: Summary of progress for 1963*, 75–76. (London: Her Majesty's Stationery Office.)

— DAWSON, J., GALLAGHER, M. J., and OSTLE, D. 1966.   Potassium-rich sediments in the Cambrian of Northwest Scotland.   *Trans. Inst. Min. Metall.*, Vol.75, B125–145; and discussion, Vol.76, B62–68.

BRAND, P. J. 1965.   New Lower Cambrian fossil localities in North-west Scotland.   *Scott. J. Geol.*, Vol.1, 285–287.

BRASIER, M. D. 1977.   An early Cambrian chert biota and its implications.   *Nature, London*, Vol.268, 719–720.

BREWER, M. S., BROOK, M., and POWELL, D. 1977.   Grenville events in the Moine rocks of the Northern Highlands, Scotland.   *J. Geol. Soc. London*, Vol.133, 489–496.

— and SMYTHE, D. K. 1984.   MOIST and the continuity of crustal reflector geometry along the Caledonian–Appalachian orogen.   *J. Geol. Soc. London*, Vol.141, 105–120.

BRIDGWATER, D., KETO, L., McGREGOR, V. R., and MYERS, J. S. 1976.   Archaean gneiss complex of Greenland.   *In* ESCHER, A., and WATT, W. S. (editors), *Geology of Greenland*, 18–75. (Copenhagen: Grønlands Geologiske Undersøgelse.)

— WATSON, J., and WINDLEY, B. F. 1973.   The Archaean craton of the North Atlantic region.   *Philos. Trans. R. Soc.*, Ser.A., Vol.273, 493–512.

BROOK, M., BREWER, M. S., and POWELL, D. 1976.   Grenville age for the rocks in the Moine of northwestern Scotland.   *Nature, London*, Vol.260, 515–517.

— POWELL, D., and BREWER, M. S. 1977.   Grenville events in Moine rocks of the Northern Highlands.   *J. Geol. Soc. London*, Vol.133, 489–496.

— and ROCK, N. M. S. 1983.   Caledonian ages for pegmatites from the Glen Urquhart serpentinite-metamorphic complex, Inverness-shire.   *Scott. J. Geol.*, Vol.19, 327–332.

BROOKFIELD, M. E. 1976.   The age of the Allt na Cuile Sandstone (Upper Jurassic) Sutherland.   *Scott. J. Geol.*, Vol.12, 181–186.

BROWN, A. L., DALZIEL, I. W. D., and JOHNSON, M. R. W. 1970.   A review of the structure and stratigraphy of the Moinian at Ardgour, Moidart and Dunart–Argyll and Inverness-shire.   *Scott. J. Geol.*, Vol.6, 309–335.

BROWN, P. E. 1967.   Major element composition of the Loch Coire migmatite complex, Sutherland, Scotland.   *Contr. Mineral. Petrol.*, Vol.14, 1–26.

— 1971.   The origin of granitic sheets and veins of the Loch Coire migmatites, Scotland.   *Mineral. Mag.*, Vol.38, 446–450.

— 1983.   Caledonian and earlier magmatism.   *In* CRAIG, G. Y. (editor), *Geology of Scotland*, 2nd edition. (Edinburgh: Scottish Academic Press.)

— BURNS, D. J. 1966.   Chemical and mineralogical changes associated with the Laxfordian metamorphism of dolerite dykes in the Scourie–Loch Laxford area, Sutherland, Scotland.   *Geol. Mag.*, Vol.103, 19–35.

BUTLER, B. C. M. 1961.   Metamorphism and metasomatism of rocks of the Moine Series by a Dolerite plug in Glenmore, Ardnamurchan.   *Mineral. Mag.*, Vol.32, 866–897.

— 1962.   Biotite- and sphene-rich rocks in the Moine Series of Ardnamurchan, Argyllshire.   *Geol. Mag.*, Vol.99, 173–82.

— 1965.   A chemical study of some rocks of the Moine Series of Scotland.   *Q. J. Geol. Soc. London*, Vol.121, 163–208.

BUTLER, R. W. H. 1982a.   The terminology of structures in thrust belts.   *J. Struct. Geol.*, Vol.4, 239–245.

— 1982b.   A structural analysis of the Moine Thrust Zone between Loch Eriboll and Foinaven, NW Scotland.   *J. Struct. Geol.*, Vol.4, 19–29.

CADELL, H. M. 1889.   Experimental researches in mountain building.   *Trans. R. Soc. Edinburgh*, Vol.35, 337–357.

CHEENEY, R. F., and MATTHEWS, D. W. 1965.   The structural evolution of the Tarskavaig and Moine Nappes in Skye.   *Scott. J. Geol.*, Vol.1, 256–281.

CHENG, Y. C. 1944.   The migmatite area around Bettyhill, Sutherland.   *Q. J. Geol. Soc. London*, Vol.99, 107–54.

CHESHER, J. A., and LAWSON, D. 1983.   The geology of the Moray Firth.   *Rep. Inst. Geol. Sci.*, No.83/5.

— SMYTHE, D. K., and BISHOP, P. 1983.   The geology of the Minches, Inner Sound and Sound of Raasay.   *Rep. Inst. Geol. Sci.*, No.83/6.

CHRISTIE, J. M. 1963.   The Moine Thrust Zone in the Assynt region, Northwest Scotland.   *Univ. California Publ. Geol. Sci.*, Vol.49, 345–440.

CLIFF, R. A., GRAY, C. M., and HUHMA, H. 1983.   A Sm-Nd isotope study of the South Harris Igneous Complex, the Outer Hebrides.   *Contrib. Mineral. Petrol.*, Vol.82, 91–98.

CLIFFORD, P. 1960.   The geological structure of the Loch Luichart area, Ross-shire.   *Q. J. Geol. Soc. London*, Vol.115, 365–388.

CLIFFORD, T. N. 1957. The stratigraphy and structure of part of the Kintail district of southern Ross-shire—its relationship to the Northern Highlands. *Q. J. Geol. Soc. London*, Vol.113, 57–92.

CLOUD, P., and GERMS, A. 1971. New pre-Palaeozoic nannofossils from the Stoer Formation (Torridonian), northwest Scotland. *Bull. Geol. Soc. Am.*, Vol.82, 3469–3474.

CLOUGH, C. T. (in PEACH, B. N., and others). 1910. The geology of Glenelg, Lochalsh and south-east part of Skye. *Mem. Geol. Surv. Scotl.*

COLLINS, A. G., and DONOVAN, N. R. 1977. The age of two Old Red Sandstone sequences in southern Caithness. *Scott. J. Geol.*, Vol.13, 53–57.

COOK, F. A., ALBAUGH, D. S., BROWN, L. D., KAUFMAN, S., OLIVER, J. E., and HATCHER, R. D. 1979. Thin-skinned tectonics in the crystalline southern Appalachians. COCORP reflection profiling of the Blue Ridge and Piedmont. *Geology*, Vol.7, 563–567.

COOPE, G. R. 1977. Fossil coleopteran assemblages as sensitive indicators of climatic changes during the Devensian (last) cold stage. *Philos. Trans. R. Soc. London*, Vol.280B, 313–337.

COPE, J. C. W., GETTY, T. A., HOWARTH, M. K., MORTON, N., and TORRENS, H. S. 1980. A correlation of Jurassic rocks in the British Isles. Part One: Introduction and Lower Jurassic. *Spec. Rep. Geol. Soc. London*, No.14.

— DUFF, K. L., PARSONS, C. F., TORRENS, H. S., WIMBLEDON, W. A., and WRIGHT, J. K. 1980. A correlation of Jurassic rocks in the British Isles. Part Two: Middle and Upper Jurassic. *Spec. Rep. Geol. Soc. London*, No.15.

COWARD, M. P. 1969. The structural and metamorphic geology of South Uist, Outer Hebrides. Unpublished PhD thesis, University of London.

— 1972. The Eastern Gneisses of South Uist. *Scott. J. Geol.*, Vol.8, 1–12.

— 1973a. The structure and origin of areas of anomalously low-intensity finite deformation in the basement gneiss complex of the Outer Hebrides. *Tectonophysics*, Vol.16, 117–140.

— 1973b. Heterogeneous deformation in the development of the Laxfordian complex of South Uist, Outer Hebrides. *J. Geol. Soc. London*, Vol.129, 139–160.

— 1982. Surge zones in the Moine Thrust Zone of NW Scotland. *J. Struct. Geol.*, Vol.4, 247–256.

— 1983. The thrust and shear zones of the Moine Thrust Zone and the NW Scottish Caledonides. *J. Geol. Soc. London*, Vol.140, 795–811.

— FRANCIS, P. W., GRAHAM, R. H., MYERS, J. S., and WATSON, J. 1969. Remnants of an early metasedimentary assemblage in the Lewisian Complex of the Outer Hebrides. *Proc. Geol. Assoc.*, Vol.80, 387–408.

— FRANCIS, P. W., GRAHAM, R. H., and WATSON, J. V. 1970. Large-scale Laxfordian structures of the Outer Hebrides in relation to those of the Scottish mainland. *Tectonophysics*, Vol.10, 425–435.

—and KIM, J. H. 1981. Strain within thrust sheets. *In* McCLAY, K. R., and PRICE, N. J. (editors), *Thrust and Nappe Tectonics*, 275–292. *Spec. Rep. Geol. Soc. London*, No.9.

COWIE, J. W. 1974. The Cambrian of Spitsbergen and Scotland. *In* HOLLAND, C. H. (editor), *Cambrian of the British Isles, Norden and Spitsbergen*, 123–155. (London: Wiley.)

— and McNAMARA, K. J. 1978. *Olenellus* (Trilobita) from the Lower Cambrian strata of north-west Scotland. *Palaeontology*, Vol.21, 615–634.

— RUSHTON, A. W. A., and STUBBLEFIELD, C. J. 1972. A correlation of Cambrian rocks in the British Isles. *Spec. Rep. Geol. Soc. London*, No.2.

CRAIG, R. M. 1928. On the occurrence of flinty crust-rock in the Outer Hebrides. *Rep. Br. Assoc. Adv. Sci.* for 1928, 543.

CRAMPTON, C. B., and CARRUTHERS, R. G. 1914. The geology of Caithness. *Mem. Geol. Surv. G.B.*

CRANE, A. 1978. Correlation of metamorphic fabrics and the age of Lewisian metasediments near Loch Maree. *Scott. J. Geol.*, Vol.14, 225–246.

CRESSWELL, D. 1972. The structural development of the Lewisian rocks on the north shore of Loch Torridon, Ross-shire. *Scott. J. Geol.*, Vol.8, 293–308.

CROFTS, R., and MATHER, A. 1972. *The beaches of Wester Ross.* (Aberdeen: Aberdeen University Department of Geography.)

CROWELL, J. C. 1961. Depositional structures from Jurassic Boulder Beds, East Sutherland. *Trans. Edinburgh Geol. Soc.*, Vol.18, 202–220.

DAHLSTROM, C. D. A. 1969. Balanced cross-sections. *Can. J. Earth Sci.*, Vol.6, 743–757.

— 1970. Structural geology in the eastern margin of the Canadian Rocky Mountains. *Bull. Can. Pet. Geol.*, Vol.18, 332–406.

DALZIEL, I. W. D. 1963. Zircons from the granitic gneiss of Argyll; their bearing on its origin. *Trans. Edinburgh Geol. Soc.*, Vol.19, 349–362.

— 1966. A structural study of the granitic gneiss of western Ardgour and Inverness-shire. *Scott. J. Geol.*, Vol.2, 125–152.

DASH, B. 1967. The geology of the Lewisian rocks between Strath Dionard and Rhiconich, Sutherland. Unpublished PhD thesis, University of Glasgow.

DAVIDSON, C. F. 1943. The Archaean rocks of the Rodil District, South Harris, Outer Hebrides. *Trans. R. Soc. Edinburgh*, Vol.61, 71–112.

DAVIES, F. B. 1974. A layered basic complex in the Lewisian, South of Loch Laxford, Sutherland. *J. Geol. Soc. London*, Vol.130, 279–284.

— 1975. Origin and ancient history of gneiss older than 2800 Myr in Lewisian Complex. *Nature, London*, Vol.258, 589–591.

— LISLE, R. J., and WATSON, J. V. 1975. The tectonic evolution of the Lewisian Complex in Northern Lewis, Outer Hebrides. *Proc. Geol. Assoc.*, Vol.86, 45–61.

— and WATSON, J. V. 1977. Early basic bodies in the type Laxfordian complex, NW Scotland, and their bearing on its origin. *J. Geol. Soc. London*, Vol.133, 123–131.

DEANS, T., GARSON, M. S., and COATS, J. S. 1971. Fenite-type soda metasomatism in the Great Glen, Scotland. *Nature Phys. Sci.*, Vol.234, 145–147.

DEARNLEY, R. 1961. Humite and chondrodite in a Lewisian crystalline limestone from South Harris, Outer Hebrides. *Mineral. Mag.*, Vol.32, 910–911.

— 1962a. An outline of the Lewisian complex of the Outer Hebrides in relation to that of the Scottish Mainland. *Q. J. Geol. Soc. London*, Vol.118, 143–176.

— 1962b.   Diopside-orthoclase-hornblende rocks from the Lewisian paragneiss of South Harris, Outer Hebrides.   *Geol. Mag.*, Vol.99, 27 – 29.

— 1963.   The Lewisian complex of South Harris, with some observations on the metamorphosed basic intrusions of the Outer Hebrides, Scotland.   *Q. J. Geol. Soc. London*, Vol.119, 243 – 312.

— 1967.   Metamorphism of minor intrusions associated with the Newer Granites of the Western Highlands of Scotland.   *Scott. J. Geol.*, Vol.3, 449 – 457.

— and DUNNING, F. W. 1968.   Metamorphosed and deformed pegmatites and basic dykes in the Lewisian complex of the Outer Hebrides and their geological significance.   *Q. J. Geol. Soc. London*, Vol.123, 353 – 378.

DEEGAN, C. E., and SCULL, B. J. 1977.   A standard lithostratigraphic nomenclature for the Central and Northern North Sea.   *Rep. Inst. Geol. Sci.*, No.77/25.

DICKINSON, B. B. and WATSON, J. 1976.   Variations in crustal level and geothermal gradient during the evolution of the Lewisian complex of NW Scotland.   *Precambrian Res.*, Vol.3, 363 – 374.

DIVER, W. L., and PEAT, C. J. 1979.   On the interpretation and classification of Precambrian organic-walled microfossils.   *Geology*, Vol.7, 401 – 404.

DONOVAN, R. N. 1970.   The geology of the Coastal Tract near Wick, Caithness.   Unpublished PhD thesis, University of Newcastle upon Tyne.

— 1973.   Basin margin deposits of the Middle Old Red Sandstone at Dirlot, Caithness.   *Scott. J. Geol.*, Vol.9, 203 – 211.

— 1975.   Devonian lacustrine limestones at the margin of the Orcadian Basin, Scotland.   *J. Geol. Soc. London*, Vol.131, 489 – 510.

— 1980.   Lacustrine cycles, fish ecology and stratigraphic zonation in the Middle Devonian of Caithness.   *Scott. J. Geol.*, Vol.16, 35 – 50.

— and COLLINS, A. 1978.   Mound structures from the Caithness Flagstone (Middle Devonian) of northern Scotland.   *J. Sediment. Petrol.*, Vol.48, 171 – 174.

— and FOSTER, R. J. 1972.   Subaqueous shrinkage cracks from the Caithness Flagstone Series (Middle Devonian) of North-east Scotland.   *J. Sediment. Petrol.*, Vol.42, 309 – 317.

— FOSTER, R. J., and WESTOLL, T. S. 1974.   A stratigraphical revision of the Old Red Sandstone of North-eastern Caithness.   *Trans. R. Soc. Edinburgh*, Vol.69, 167 – 201.

— Dougal, J. W. 1928.   Observations on the geology of Lewis.   *Trans. Edinburgh Geol. Soc.*, Vol.12, 12 – 18.

DOWNIE, C. 1962.   So-called spores from the Torridonian.   *Proc. Geol. Soc. London*, Vol.1600, 127 – 128.

DREVER, H. 1940.   The geology of Ardgour, Argyllshire.   *Trans. R. Soc. Edinburgh*, Vol.60, 141 – 70.

DRURY, S. A. 1972.   The tectonic evolution of a Lewisian complex on Coll, Inner Hebrides.   *Scott. J. Geol.*, Vol.8, 309 – 333.

— 1974.   Chemical changes during retrogressive metamorphism of Lewisian granulite facies rocks from Coll and Tiree.   *Scott. J. Geol.*, Vol.19, 237 – 256.

ELLIOT, D., and JOHNSON, M. R. W. 1980.   Structural evolution in the northern part of the Moine thrust belt, NW Scotland.   *Trans. R. Soc. Edinburgh*, Vol.71, 69 – 96.

ESCHER, A., JACK, S., and WATTERSON, J. 1976. Tectonics of the North Atlantic Proterozoic dyke swarm. *Trans. R. Soc.*, Ser. A., Vol.280, 529–539.

EVANS, C. R. 1965. Geochronology of the Lewisian basement near Lochinver, Sutherland. *Nature, London*, Vol.207, 54–56.

— and LAMBERT, R. ST. J. 1974. The Lewisian of Lochinver, Sutherland; the type area for the Inverian metamorphism. *J. Geol. Soc. London*, Vol.1390, 125–150

— and TARNEY, J. 1964. Isotopic ages of Assynt dykes. *Nature, London*, Vol.204, 638–641.

EVANS, D., CHESHER, J. A., DEEGAN, C. E., and FANNIN, N. G. T. 1982. The offshore geology of Scotland in relation to the IGS shallow drilling programme. 1970–1978. *Rep. Inst. Geol. Sci.*, No.81/12.

— KENOLTY, N., DOBSON, M. R., and WHITTINGTON, R. J. 1979. The geology of the Malin Sea. *Rep. Inst. Geol. Sci.*, No.79/15.

EYLES, V. A., and MacGREGOR, A. G. 1952. The Great Glen Crush Belt. *Geol. Mag.*, Vol.89, 425.

FETTES, D. J., and MacDONALD, R. 1978. The Glen Garry vein complex. *Scott. J. Geol.*, Vol.14, 335–358.

— MENDUM, J. R., SMITH, D. I., and WATSON, J. V. *In press*. The geology of the Outer Hebrides. *Mem. Geol. Surv.*

FLETT, J. S. 1906. In *Mem. Geol. Surv. GB.* Summ. Prog. (for 1905), 155–167.

FLEUTY, M. J. 1961. The three fold-systems in the metamorphic rocks of upper Glen Orrin, Ross-shire and Inverness-shire. *Q. J. Soc. London*, Vol.117, 447–476.

FLINN, D. 1961. Continuation of the Great Glen Fault beyond the Moray Firth. *Nature, London*, Vol.191, 589–591.

— 1979. The Glaciation of the Outer Hebrides. *Geol. J.*, Vol.13, part 2, 195–199.

— 1981. A note on the Glacial and Late Glacial History of Caithness. *Geol. J.*, Vol.16, 175–179.

FOSTER, R. J. 1972. The solid geology of north-east Caithness. Unpublished PhD thesis, University of Newcastle upon Tyne.

FOSTER-COOPER, C. 1937. The Middle Devonian fish fauna of Achanarras. *Trans. R. Soc. Edinburgh*, Vol.59, 223–239.

FRANCIS, E. H. 1983. Carboniferous. *In* CRAIG, G. Y. (editor), *The geology of Scotland* (2nd edition). (Edinburgh: Scottish Academic Press.)

FRANCIS, G. H. 1958. Petrological studies in Glen Urquhart, Inverness-shire. *Bull. Br. Mus. (Nat. Hist.), Mineral.*, Vol. 1, part 5, 123–164.

— 1964. Further petrological studies in Glen Urquhart, Inverness-shire. *Bull. Brit. Mus (Nat. Hist.) Mineral.*, Vol.1, part 6, 165–199.

FRANCIS, P. W. 1973. Scourian–Laxfordian relationships in the Barra Isles. *J. Geol. Soc. London*, Vol.129, 161–189.

— MOORBATH, S., and WELKE, H. J. 1971. Isotopic age data from Scourian intrusive rocks on the Isle of Barra, Outer Hebrides, north-west Scotland. *Geol. Mag.*, Vol.108, 13–22.

— and SIBSON, R. H. 1973.   The Outer Hebrides Thrust.   *In* PARK, R. G., and TARNEY, J. (editors), *The early Precambrian of Scotland and related rocks of Greenland*, 95–104. (Keele: University of Keele.)

GAILEY, R. A. 1969.   Glasgow University Expedition to North Rona.   *Scott. Geogr. Mag.*, Vol.75, 48–50.

GALLAGHER, M. J., MICHIE, U. Mc.L., SMITH, R. T., and HAYNES, L. 1971. New evidence of uranium mineralisation in Scotland.   *Trans. Inst. Min. Metall.*, Vol.80, B150–173.

— SMITH, R. T., PEACOCK, J. D., and HAYNES, L. 1974.   Molybdenite mineralisation in Precambrian rocks near Lairg, Scotland.   *Trans. Inst. Min. Metall.*, B83, B99–134.

GARSON, M. S., and LIVINGSTONE, A. 1973.   Is the South Harris complex in north Scotland a Precambrian slice of oceanic crust and island arc?   *Nature, London*, Vol.243, 74–76.

— and PLANT, J. 1972.   Possible dextral movements on the Great Glen and Minch Faults in Scotland.*Nature Phys. Sci.*, Vol.240, 31–35.

— COATS, J. S., ROCK, N. M. S., and DEANS, T. 1984.   Fenites, breccia dykes, albitites and carbonatitic veins near the Great Glen Fault, Inverness, Scotland.   *J. Geol. Soc. London*, Vol.141, 711–732.

GEORGE, T. N. 1966.   Geomorphic evolution in Hebridean Scotland.   *Scott. J. Geol.*, Vol.2, 1–34.

GILETTI, B. J., MOORBATH, S., and LAMBERT, R. St.J. 1961.   A geochronological study of the metamorphic complexes of the Scottish Highlands.   *Q. J. Geol. Soc. London*, Vol.117, 233–272.

GODARD, A. 1965.   Recherches de géomorphologie en Écosse du nord-ouest. *Publ. Strasbourg Univ. Fac. Lett. Fond. Baulig.*, Vol.1.

GORDON, W. A. 1967.   Foraminifera from the Callovian (Middle Jurassic) of Brora, Scotland.   *Micropalaeontology*, Vol.13, 445–464.

GRAHAM, R. H. 1970.   A structural analysis of Lewisian rocks in parts of North Uist and the South of Harris, Outer Hebrides.   Unpublished PhD thesis, University of London.

— 1980.   The role of shear belts in the structural evolution of the South Harris igneous complex.   *In* CARRERAS, J., COBBOLD, P. R., RAMSAY, J. G., and WHITE, S. H. (editors), Shear zones in rocks, 29–37. *J. Struct. Geol.*, Vol.2.

— and COWARD, M. P. 1973.   The Laxfordian of the Outer Hebrides.   *In* PARK, R. G., and TARNEY, J. (editors), *The early Precambrian of Scotland and related rocks of Greenland*, 85–93. (Keele: University of Keele.)

GRAY, J. M. 1978.   Low-level shore platforms in the Highlands: altitude, age and correlation.   *Trans. Inst. Br. Geogr.*, Vol.3, 151–164.

HAGGART, B. A. 1982.   Flandrian sea-level changes in the Moray Firth area. Unpublished PhD thesis, University of Durham.

HALLAM, A. 1959.   The stratigraphy of the Broadford Beds of Skye, Raasay and Applecross.   *Proc. Yorkshire Geol. Soc.*, Vol.32, 165–184.

— and SWETT, K. 1966.   Trace fossils from the Lower Cambrian Pipe Rock of the northwest Highlands.   *Scott. J. Geol.*, Vol.2, 101–106.

HALLIDAY, A. N., McALPINE, A., and MITCHELL, J. G. 1977.   The age of the Hoy Lavas, Orkney.   *Scott. J. Geol.*, Vol.13, 43–52.

HAMILTON, P. J., EVENSEN, N. M., O'NIONS, R. K., and TARNEY, J. 1979. Sm-Nd systematics of Lewisian gneisses: implications for the origin of granulites. *Nature, London*, Vol.277, 25–28.

HARKER, R. I. 1962. The older ortho-gneisses of Carn Chuinneag and Inchbae. *J. Petrol.*, Vol.3, 215–237.

HARRIS, A. L., BALDWIN, C. T., BRADBURY, H. J., JOHNSON, H. D., and SMITH, R. A. 1978. Ensialic basin sedimentation: the Dalradian Supergroup. In *Spec. Issue Geol. J.*, No.10 *Crustal evolution in northwestern Britain*, 115–138.

HARRIS, T. M., and REST, J. A. 1968. The flora of the Brora coal. *Geol. Mag.*, Vol.103, 101–109.

HARRISON, V. E., and MOORHOUSE, S. J. 1976. A possibly early Scourian supracrustal assemblage within the Moine. *J. Geol. Soc. London*, Vol.132, 461–466.

HARRY, W. T. 1952. The migmatites and feldspar porphyroblast-rock of Glen Dessary, Inverness-shire. *Q. J. Geol. Soc. London*, Vol.107, 137–156.

— 1954. The composite granite gneiss of Western Ardgour, Argyll. *Q. J. Geol. Soc. London*, Vol.109, 285–309.

HIGGINS, A. C. 1967. The age of the Durine Member of the Durness Limestone Formation at Durness. *Scott. J. Geol.*, Vol.3, 382–388.

HOLDSWORTH, R. E., and ROBERTS, A. M. 1984. Early curvilinear fold structures and strain in the Moine of the Glen Garry region, Inverness-shire. *J. Geol. Soc. London*, Vol.141, 327–338.

HOLGATE, N. 1969. Palaeozoic and Tertiary transcurrent movements on the Great Glen Fault. *Scott. J. Geol.*, Vol.5, 97–139.

HOLLAND, J. G., and LAMBERT, R. ST.J. 1973. Comparative major element geochemistry of the Lewisian of the mainland of Scotland. *In* PARK, R. G., and TARNEY, J. (editors), *The early Precambrian of Scotland and related rocks of Greenland*, 51–62 (Keele: University of Keele.)

— 1975. The chemistry and origin of the Lewisian gneisses of the Scottish mainland: the Scourie and Inver assemblages and sub-crustal accretion. *Precambrian Res.*, Vol.2, 161–188.

HOPGOOD, A. M. 1965. Theoretical consideration of the mechanics of tectonic reorientation of dykes. *Tectonophysics*, Vol.3, 17–28.

— 1971. Structure and tectonic history of Lewisian gneiss, Isle of Barra, Scotland. *Krystalinikum*, No.7, 27–59.

— and BOWES, D. R. 1972. Application of structural sequence to the correlation of Precambrian gneisses, Outer Hebrides, Scotland. *Bull. Geol. Soc. Am.*, Vol.83, 107–128.

HORNE, J. 1923. The geology of the Lower Findhorn and Lower Strath Nairn. *Mem. Geol. Surv. GB.*, Sheets 84, part 94.

— and GREENLY, E. 1898. On foliated granites and their relations to the crystalline schists in eastern Sutherland. *Q. J. Geol. Soc. London*, Vol.52, 633–648.

— and HINXMAN, L. W. 1914. The geology of the area around Beuly and Inverness. *Mem. Geol. Surv. GB.*

HUMPHRIES, D. W. 1961. The Upper Cretaceous White Sandstone of Loch Aline, Argyll, Scotland. *Proc. Yorkshire Geol. Soc.*, Vol.33, 47–76.

HURST, A. 1981.   Mid Jurassic stratigraphy and facies at Brora, Sutherland. *Scott. J. Geol.*, Vol.17, 169 – 177.

HUTTON, V. R. S., INGHAM, M. R., and MBIPOM, E. W. 1980.   An electrical model of the crust and upper mantle in Scotland.   *Nature, London*, Vol.287, 30 – 33.

IRVING, E., and RUNCORN, S. K. 1957.   Analysis of the palaeomagnetism of the Torridonian Sandstone Series of northwest Scotland.   *Philos. Trans. R. Soc. London, Ser.A.*, Vol.250, 83 – 99.

JEHU, T. J. 1922.   The Archaean and Torridonian formations and the later intrusive rocks of Iona.   *Trans. R. Soc. Edinburgh*, Vol.53, 166 – 187.

— and CRAIG, R. M. 1923.   Geology of the Outer Hebrides.   Part I — The Barra Isles.   *Trans. R. Soc. Edinburgh*, Vol.53, 419 – 441.

— 1925.   Geology of the Outer Hebrides.   Part II — South Uist and Eriskay.   *Trans. R. Soc. Edinburgh*, Vol.53, 615 – 641.

— 1926.   Geology of the Outer Hebrides. Part III — North Uist and Benbecula.   *Trans. R. Soc. Edinburgh*, Vol.54, 467 – 489.

— 1927.   Geology of the Outer Hebrides. Part IV — South Harris.   *Trans. R. Soc. Edinburgh*, Vol.55, 457 – 488.

— 1934.   Geology of the Outer Hebrides. Part V — North Harris and Lewis.   *Trans. R. Soc. Edinburgh*, Vol.57, 839 – 874.

JOHNSON, M. R. W. 1960.   The structural history of the Moine Thrust Zone at Loch Carron, Wester Ross.   *Trans. R. Soc. Edinburgh*, Vol.64, 139 – 168.

— and DALZIEL, I. W. D. 1966.   Metamorphosed lamprophyres and the late thermal history of the Moines.   *Geol. Mag.*, Vol.103, 240 – 249.

— SANDERSON, D. J., and SOPER, N. J. 1979.   Deformation in the Caledonides of England, Ireland and Scotland.   *In* HARRIS, A. L., HOLLAND, C., and LEAKE, B. E. (editors), *The Caledonides of the British Isles — reviewed. Spec. Publ. Geol. Soc. London*, No.8, 165 – 186.

JOHNSTONE, G. S. 1975.   The Moine Succession.   *In* HARRIS, A. L., and others (editors), *A correlation of Precambrian rocks in the British Isles*, 30 – 42. *Spec. Rep. Geol. Soc. London*, No.6.

— SMITH, D. I., and HARRIS, A. L. 1969.   The Moinian assemblage of Scotland.   *In* KAY, M. (editor), *Northern Atlantic — geology and continental drift, a symposium. Mem. Am. Assoc. Pet. Geol.*, Vol.12, 159 – 180.

— and WRIGHT, J. E. 1951.   The camptonite-monchiquite suite of Loch Eil.   *Geol. Mag.*, Vol.88, 148.

JUDD, J. W. 1873.   The secondary rocks of the Scotland: First paper (including Introduction *and* North-East Scotland).   *Q.J. Geol. Soc. London*, Vol.29, 97 – 197.

KENNEDY, W. Q. 1946.   The Great Glen Fault.   *Q. J. Geol. Soc. London*, Vol.102, 41 – 76.

— 1955.   The tectonics of the Morar Anticline and the problem of north-west Caledonian front.   *Q. J. Geol. Soc. London*, Vol.110, 357 – 390.

— 1958.   On the significance of thermal structure in the Scottish Highlands.   *Geol. Mag.*, Vol. 85, 229 – 234.

KING, B. C. 1942.   The Cnoc na Cuilean area of the Ben Loyal igneous complex.   *Q. J. Geol. Soc. London*, Vol.98, 147 – 185.

KNORRING, O. VON 1959. Niobium-zirconium-thorium-uranium and rare-earth minerals from the pegmatites of South Harris, Outer Hebrides. *Nature, London*, Vol.183, 255–256.

— and DEARNLEY, R. 1960. The Lewisian pegmatites of South Harris, Outer Hebrides. *Mineral. Mag.*, Vol.32, 366–378.

KURSTEN, M. 1957. The metamorphic and tectonic history of parts of the Outer Hebrides. *Trans. Edinburgh Geol. Soc.*, Vol.17, 1–31.

LAM, K., and PORTER, R. 1977. The distribution of palynomorphs in the Jurassic rocks of the Brora Outlier, NE Scotland. *J. Geol. Soc. London*, Vol.134, 45–55.

LAMBERT, R. ST J. 1969. Isotopic studies relating to the Precambrian history of the Moinian in Scotland. *Proc. Geol. Soc. London*, No.1652, 243–245.

— EVANS, C. R., and DEARNLEY, R. 1970. Isotopic ages of dykes and pegmatitic gneiss from the southern Islands of the Outer Hebrides. *Scott. J. Geol.*, Vol.6, 208–213.

— and HOLLAND, J. G. 1972. A geochronological study of the Lewisian from Loch Laxford to Durness, Sutherland, NW Scotland. *Q. J. Geol. Soc. London*, Vol.128, 3–19.

— MYERS, J. S., and WATSON, J. 1970. An apparent age for a member of the Scourie dyke suite in Lewis, Outer Hebrides. *Scott. J. Geol.*, Vol.6, 214–220.

— POOLE, A. B., RICHARDSON, S. W., JOHNSTONE, G. S., and SMITH, D. I. 1964. The Glen Dessarry Syenite, Inverness-shire. *Nature, London*, Vol.202, 370–372.

LANGFORD, R. L. 1980. Deformation in the Moine south-east of Glen Carron, Highland region, Scotland. Unpublished PhD thesis, Council for Natural Academic Awards, Kingston Polytechnic, Surrey.

LAPWORTH, C. 1885. The highland controversy in British geology. *Nature, London*, Vol.32, 558–559.

LAWSON, D. E. 1972. Torridonian volcanic sediments. *Scott. J. Geol.*, Vol.8, 345–362.

LAWSON, T. J. 1984 Reindeer in the Scottish Quaternary. *Quat. Newsl.*, No.42, 1–7.

LEE, G. W. 1920. The Mesozoic rocks of Applecross, Raasay and north-east Skye. *Mem. Geol. Surv. GB.*

— and BAILEY, E. B. 1925. The pre-Tertiary geology of Mull, Loch Aline and Oban. *Mem. Geol. Surv. GB.*

— and PRINGLE, J. 1932. A synopsis of the Mesozoic rocks of Scotland. *Trans. Geol. Soc. Glasgow*, Vol.19, 158–224.

LEEDAL, G. P. 1952. The Cluanie igneous intrusion, Inverness-shire and Ross-shire. *Q. J. Geol. Soc. London*, Vol.108, 35–63.

LINSLEY, P. N. 1972. The stratigraphy and sedimentology of the Kimmeridgian deposits of Sutherland, Scotland. Unpublished PhD thesis, University of London.

— POTTER, H. C., McNAB, G., and RACHER, D. 1980. The Beatrice Field, Inner Moray Firth, UK North Sea. *In* HALBOUTY, M. T. (editor). *Giant oil and gas fields of the decade 1968–1978.* (American Association of Petroleum Geologists, Mem. 30, 117–129.)

LINTERN, B. C., McCOURT, W. J., STOREY, B. C., and BROOK, M. 1982. Pre-Caledonian granitic rocks in the Strath Halladale complex of Sutherland and Caithness. *Newsl. Geol. Soc. London*, Vol.ii, No.1, 12 – 13.

LISLE, R. J. 1974. The application of methods of structural analysis to the study of the basement complex in NW Lewis. Unpublished PhD thesis, University of London.

— 1976. The evaluation of Laxfordian deformation in the Carloway area, Isle of Lewis, Scotland. *Tectonophysics*, Vol.42, 183 – 208.

LIVINGSTONE, A. 1965. An olivine-bearing sagvandite from Berneray, Outer Hebrides. *Geol. Mag.*, Vol.102, 227 – 230.

— 1967. A garnet peridotite and a garnet-amphibole pyroxenite from South Harris, Outer Hebrides, and their bearing on the South Harris eclogite facies status. *Mineral. Mag.*, Vol.36, 380 – 388.

— 1976a. A metamorphosed, layered alpine-type peridotite in the Langavat valley, South Harris, Outer Hebrides. *Mineral. Mag.*, Vol.40, 493 – 499.

— 1967b. The paragenesis of spinel- and garnet-amphibole lherzolite in the Rodel area, South Harris. *Scott. J. Geol.*, Vol.12, 293 – 300.

LONG, L. E. 1964. Rb/Sr chronology of the Carn Chuinneag Intrusion, Ross-shire, Scotland. *J. Geophys. Res.*, Vol.69, 1589 – 1597.

— and LAMBERT, R. ST J. 1963. Rb-Sr isotope ages from the Moine Series. *In* JOHNSON, M. R. W., and STEWART, F. H. (editors), *The British Caledonides.* (Edinburgh: Oliver and Boyd.)

LOWE, M. J. B. 1965. Some aspects of the stratigraphy and sedimentation of the Triassic rocks of the Hebrides. Unpublished PhD thesis, University of St Andrews.

LYON, T. D. B., PIDGEON, R. T., BOWES, D. R., and HOPGOOD, A. M. 1973. Geochronological investigation of the quartz-feldspathic rocks of the Lewisian of Rona, Inner Hebrides. *J. Geol. Soc. London*, Vol.129, 389 – 404.

McCOURT, W. J. 1980. The geology of the Strath Halladale – Altnabreac district. *Env. Prot. Unit Inst. Geol. Sci.*, No. ENPU 80-1.

MacCULLOCH, J. 1819. *A description of the Western Islands of Scotland.* (Edinburgh: Constable.)

MacGREGOR, A. G. 1967. Faults and fractures in Ardnamurchan, Moidart, Sunart and Morvern. *Bull. Geol. Surv. GB.*, No.27, 1 – 15.

— and KENNEDY, W. Q. 1932. The Morvern-Strontian Granite. *Summ. Prog. Geol. Surv. for 1931*, part II, 105 – 119.

MacGREGOR, M. 1916. A Jurassic shore line. *Trans. Geol. Soc. Glasgow*, Vol.16, 75 – 85.

— and MANSON, W. 1934. The Carboniferous rocks of Inninmore, Morvern. *Summ. Prog. Geol. Surv. for 1935*, part II, 74 – 84.

McCLAY, K. R., and COWARD, M. P. 1981. The Moine Thrust Zone: an overview. *In* McCLAY, K. R., and PRICE. N. J. (editors), *Thrust and Nappe Tectonics*, 241 – 260. *Spec. Rep. Geol. Soc. London*, No.9.

McINTYRE, D. B., BROWN, W. J., CLARKE, W. J., and MacKENZIE, D. H. 1956. On the conglomerates of supposed Old Red Sandstone age near Tongue, Sutherland. *Trans. Geol. Soc. Glasgow*, Vol.22, 35 – 47.

McLEISH, A. J. 1971. Strain analysis of deformed pipe rock in the Moine Thrust Zone, northwest Scotland. *Tectonophysics*, Vol.12, 469 – 503.

MaClennan, R. M. 1949. A starfish from the glass sand of Loch Aline. *Geol. Mag.*, Vol.86, 94–96.

— 1953. The Liassic sequence in Morvern. *Trans. Geol. Soc. Glasgow*, Vol.21, 447–455.

MacQueen, J. A., and Powell, D. 1977. Relationship between deformation and garnet growth in Moine (Precambrian) rocks of western Scotland. *Geol. Soc. Am. Bull.*, Vol.88, 235–240.

McQuillin, R., and Donato, J. A. 1982. Development of basins in the Inner Moray Firth and the North Sea by crustal extension and dextral displacement of the Great Glen Fault. *Earth Planet Sci. Lett.*, Vol.60, 127–139.

— and Watson, J. V. 1973. Large-scale basement structures of the Outer Hebrides in the light of geophysical evidence. *Nature, London*, Vol.245, 1–3.

Marston, R. J. 1971. The Foyers granitic complex, Inverness-shire, Scotland. *Q. J. Geol. Soc. London*, Vol.126, 331–368.

Mather, R. A., and Crofts, R. 1972. *The beaches of west Inverness-shire and North Argyll.* (Aberdeen: Aberdeen University Department of Geography.)

Matthews, D. W., and Woolley, A. R. 1977. Layered ultramafic rocks within the Borralan complex, Scotland. *Scott. J. Geol.*, Vol.13, 223–236.

Mendum, J. R. 1976. A strain study of the Strathan Conglomerte, North Scotland. *Scott. J. Geol.*, Vol.12, 135–146.

— 1979. Caledonian thrusting in NW Scotland. *In* Harris, A. L., Holland, C., and Leake, B. E. (editors), *The Caledonides of the British Isles—reviewed. Spec. Publ. Geol. Soc. London*, No.8, 291–297.

Menhert, K. R. 1971. *Migmatites and the origin of granitic rocks* (2nd impression). (Amsterdam: Elsevier.)

Mercy, E. L. P. 1963. The geochemistry of some Caledonian granitic and metasedimentary rocks. *In* Johnson, M. R. W., and Stewart, F. H. (editors). *The British Caledonides*, 189–215. (Edinburgh: Oliver and Boyd.)

Miles, R. S., and Westoll, T. S. 1963. Two new genera of Coccosteid Arthrodira from the Middle Red Sandstone of Scotland and their stratigraphic distribution. *Trans. R. Soc. Edinburgh*, Vol.66, 179–210.

Mitchell, G. F., Penny, L. F., Shotton, F. W., and West, R. G. 1973. A correlation of Quaternary deposits in the British Isles. *Spec. Rep. Geol. Soc. London*, No.4.

Moorbath, S. 1969. Evidence for the age of deposition of the Torridonian sediments of north-west Scotland. *Scott. J. Geol.*, Vol.5, 154–170.

— 1975. Evolution of Precambrian crust from strontium isotopic evidence. *Nature, London*, Vol.. 54, 395–398.

— and Park, R. G. 1972. The Lewisian chronology of the southern region of the Scottish mainland. *Scott. J. Geol.*, Vol.8, 51–74.

— Powell, J. L., and Taylor, P. N. 1975. Isotopic evidence for the age and origin of the 'grey gneiss' complex of the southern Outer Hebrides, Scotland. *J. Geol. Soc. London*, Vol.131, 213–222.

— Stewart, A. D., Lawson, D. E., and Williams, G. E. 1967. Geochronological studies in the Torridonian sediments of northwest Scotland. *Scott. J. Geol.*, Vol.3, 389–412.

— and TAYLOR, P. N. 1974. Lewisian age for the Scardroy mass. *Nature, London*, Vol.250, 41–43.

— WELKE, H. J., and GALE, N. H. 1969. The significance of lead isotope studies in ancient high-grade basement metamorphic complexes, as exemplified by the Lewisian rocks of northwest Scotland. *Earth Planet. Sci. Lett.*, Vol.6, 245–256.

MOORHOUSE, S. J., and MOORHOUSE, V. E. 1977. A Lewisian basement sheet within the Moine at Ribigill, North Sutherland. *Scott. J. Geol.*, Vol.13, 289–300.

— — 1979. The Moine amphibolite suites of central and northern Sutherland. *Mineral. Mag.*, Vol.43, 211–225.

— — 1983. The geology and geochemistry of the Strathy complex of north-east Sutherland, Shetland. *Mineral. Mag.*, Vol.47, 123–137.

MUNRO, M. 1965. Some structural features of the Caledonian granitic complex at Strontian, Argyllshire. *Scott. J. Geol.*, Vol.1, 152–175.

— 1973. Structures in the south-eastern portion of the Strontian Granitic Complex, Argyllshire. *Scott. J. Geol.*, Vol.9, 99–108.

MYERS, J. S. 1970a. Gneiss types and their significance in the repeatedly deformed and metamorphosed Lewisian Complex of Western Harris, Outer Hebrides. *Scott. J. Geol.*, Vol.6, 186–199.

— (with a note by R. J. LISLE). 1970b. Zones of abundant Scourie dyke fragments and their significance in the Lewisian Complex of Western Harris, Outer Hebrides. *Proc. Geol. Assoc.*, Vol.82, 365–378.

— 1971. The Late Laxfordian granite-migmatite complex of Western Harris, Outer Hebrides. *Scott. J. Geol.*, Vol.6, 254–284.

MYKURA, W. 1975. Possible large-scale sinistral displacement along the Great Glen Fault of Scotland. *Geol. Mag.*, Vol.112, 91–94.

— 1976. *British Regional Geology: Orkney and Shetland.* (London: HMSO.)

— 1983a. The Old Red Sandstone east of Loch Ness, Inverness-shire. *Rep. Inst. Geol. Sci.*, No.82/13.

— 1983b. Old Red Sandstone. *In* CRAIG, G. Y. (editor), *The geology of Scotland* (2nd edition). (Edinburgh: Scottish Academic Press.)

— and OWENS, B. 1983. The Old Red Sandstone of the Mealfuarvonie Outlier, west of Loch Ness, Inverness-shire. *Rep. Inst. Geol. Sci.*, No.83/7.

NAUMOVA, S. N., and PAVLOVSKY, E. V. 1961. The discovery of plant remains (spores) in the Torridonian shales of Scotland. *Dikl. Adal. Nauk. SSSR*, Vol.41, 181–182.

NESBITT, H. C. 1961. The geology of North Rona. *Trans. Geol. Soc. Glasgow*, Vol.24, 169–189.

NEVES, R., and SELLEY, R. C. 1975. A review of the Jurassic rocks of north-east Scotland. *Proceedings of the Jurassic Northern Sea Symposium, Stavanger 1975.*, 5-1 to 5-29.

NICHOL, J. 1844. *Guide to the geology of Scotland.* (Edinburgh: Oliver and Boyd.)

NICHOLLS, G. D. 1951. The Glenelg-Ratagain igneous complex. *Q. J. Geol. Soc. London*, Vol.106, 302–321.

OATES, M. J. 1978. A revised stratigraphy for the western Scottish Lower Lias. *Proc. Yorkshire Geol. Soc.*, Vol.42, 143–150.

O'HARA, M. J. 1961a. Petrology of the Scourie dyke, Sutherland. *Mineral. Mag.*, Vol.32, 848–865.

— 1961b. Zoned ultrabasic and basic gneiss masses in the early Lewisian metamorphic complex at Scourie, Sutherland. *J. Petrol.*, Vol.2, 248–276.

— 1962. Some intrusions in the Lewisian complex near Badcall, Sutherland. *Trans. Edinburgh Geol. Soc.*, Vol.19, 201–207.

— 1965. Origin of ultrabasic and basic gneiss masses in the Lewisian. *Geol. Mag.*, Vol.102, 296–314.

— 1977. Thermal history of excavation of Archaean gneisses from the base of the continental crust. *J. Geol. Soc. London*, Vol.134, 185–200.

O'REILLY, K. J. 1983. Composition and age of the conglomerate outliers around the Kyle of Sutherland, Scotland. *Proc. Geol. Ass.*, Vol.94, 53–64.

PALMER, F. K. 1971. A comparative study of two Pre-Cambrian gneiss areas—the Suportog region, East Greenland, and South Harris, Outer Hebrides—and their bearing on Precambrian crustal evolution. Unpublished PhD thesis, University of Birmingham.

PALMER, T. J., McKERROW, W. S., and COWIE, J. W. 1980. Sedimentological evidence for a stratigraphical break in the Durness Group. *Nature, London*, Vol.287, 721–722.

PANKHURST, R. T. 1979. Isotope and trace element evidence for the origin and evolution of Caledonian granites in the Scottish Highlands. *In* ATHERTON, H. P., and TARNEY, J. (editors). *Origin of granitic batholiths*, 18–33. (Orpington: Shiva.)

PARK, R. G. 1961. The pseudotachylite of the Gairloch district, Ross-shire, Scotland. *Am. J. Sci.*, Vol.259, 542–550.

— 1970. Observations of Lewisian chronology. *Scott. J. Geol.*, Vol.6, 379–399.

— 1973. The Laxfordian belts of the Scottish mainland. *In* PARK, R. G., and TARNEY, J. (editors). *The early Precambrian of Scotland and related rocks of Greenland*, 65–76. (Keele: University of Keele.)

— and CRESSWELL, D. 1972. Basic dykes in the early Precambrian (Lewisian) of NW Scotland: their structural relations, conditions of emplacement and orgenic significance. *Proc. 24th Sess. Int. Geol. Congr., 1972*, Vol.1, 238–245.

— — 1973. The dykes of the Laxfordian belts. *In* PARK, R. G., and TARNEY, J. (editors). *The early Precambrian of Scotland and related rocks of Greenland*, 119–130. (Keele: University of Keele.)

PARSONS, I. 1965. The feldspathic syenites of the Loch Ailsh intrusion, Assynt, Scotland. *J. Petrol.*, Vol.6, 365–394.

— 1979. The Assynt alkaline suite. *In* HARRIS, A. L., HOLLAND, C., and LEAKE, B. E. (editors). *The Caledonides of the British Isles—reviewed. Spec. Pub. Geol. Soc. London*, No.8, 667–81.

PEACH, B. N., GUNN, W., and others. 1912. The geology of Ben Wyvis, Carn Chuinneag, Inchbae and the surrounding country. *Mem. Geol. Surv. GB.*

PEACH, B. N., HORNE, J., GUNN, W., CLOUGH, C. T., HINXMAN, L. W., and TEALL, J. J. H. 1907. The geological structure of the north-west Highlands of Scotland. *Mem. Geol. Surv. GB.*

— and HORNE, J. 1892.   The *Olenellus* zone in the north-west Highlands of Scotland.   *Q. J. Geol. Soc. London*, Vol.48, 227–241.

— HORNE, J., and others. 1907.   The geological structure of the North-West Highlands of Scotland.   *Mem. Geol. Surv. GB.*

— and HORNE, J. 1930.   *Chapters on the geology of Scotland.*   (London: Oxford University Press.)

PEACOCK, J. D. 1973.   Sodic rocks of metasomatic origin in the Moine Nappe.   *Scott. J. Geol.*, Vol.9, 96–97.

— 1975.   'Slide Rocks' in the Moine of the Loch Shin area, Northern Scotland.   *Bull. Geol. Surv. GB.*, No.49, 23–30.

— 1977.   Metagabbros in granitic gneiss, Inverness-shire, and their significance in the structural history of the Moines.   *Rep. Inst. Geol. Sci.*, No.77/20.

— 1981.   Report and excursion guide—Lewis and Harris.   *Quat. Newsl.*, No.5, 45–54.

— 1984.   Quaternary geology of the Outer Hebrides.   *Rep. Br. Geol. Surv.*, Vol.16, No.2.

— GRAHAM, D. K., and GREGORY, D. M. 1980.   Late- and post-glacial marine environments in part of the inner Cromarty Firth, Scotland.   *Rep. Inst. Geol. Sci.*, No.80/7.

— and ROSS, D. L. 1978.   Anomalous glacial erratics in the southern part of the Outer Hebrides.   *Scott. J. Geol.*, Vol.14, 3 [letter].

PIASECKI, M. A. J., and VAN BREEMEN, O. 1979a.   A Morarian age for the 'Younger Moines' of Central and Western Scotland.   *Nature, London*, Vol.34–36.

— — 1979b.   The 'Central Highland Granulites' cover-basement tectonics in the Moine.   *In* HARRIS, A. L., HOLLAND, C., and LEAKE, B. E. (editors).   *The Caledonides of the British Isles—reviewed. Spec. Rep. Geol. Soc. London*, Vol.8, 139–143.

— — and WRIGHT, A. E. 1981.   Late Precambrian geology of Scotland, England and Wales.   *In* KERR, J. W., and FERGUSSON, A. J. (editors).   *Geology of the North Atlantic Borderlands. Mem. Can. Soc. Pet. Geol.*, Vol.7, 57–94.

PICKERING, K. T. 1984.   The Upper Jurassic 'Boulder Beds' and related deposits: a fault-controlled submarine slope, NW Scotland.   *J. Geol. Soc. London*, Vol.141, 357–374.

PIDGEON, R. T., and AFTALION, M. 1972.   The geochronological significance of discordant U-Pb ages of oval-shaped zircons from a Lewisian gneiss from Harris, Outer Hebrides.   *Earth Planet. Sci. Lett.*, Vol.17, 269–274.

— — 1978.   Cogenetic and inherited zircon U-Pb systems in granites: Palaeozoic granites of Scotland and England.   *Spec. Issue Geol, J.*, No.10, 183–220.

— and BOWES, D. R. 1972.   Zircon U-Pb ages of granulites from the central region of the Lewisian of north-western Scotland.   *Geol. Mag.*, Vol.109, 247–258.

— and JOHNSON, M. R. W. 1974.   A comparison of Zircon U-Pb and whole-rock Rb-Sr systems in three phases of the Carn Chuinneag granite, Northern Scotland.   *Earth. Planet. Sci. Lett.*, Vol.24, 105–112.

POOLE, A. B. 1966. The stratigraphy and structure of north-eastern Morar, Inverness-shire. *Scott. J. Geol.*, Vol.2, 38–53.

POWELL, D. 1964. The stratigraphical succession of the Moine schists around Lochailort (Inverness-shire) and its regional significance. *Proc. Geol. Assoc.*,Vol.75, 223–246.

— 1974. Stratigraphy and structure of the western Moine and the problem of Moine orogenesis. *J. Geol. Soc. London*, Vol.130, 575–593.

— BAIRD, A. W., CHARNLEY, N. R., and JORDON, P. J. 1981. The metamorphic environment of the Sgurr Beag Slide, a major crustal displacement zone in Proterozoic, Moine rocks of Scotland. *J. Geol. Soc. London*, Vol.138, 661–673.

— BROOK, M., and BAIRD, A. W. 1983. Structural dating of a Precambrian pegmatite in Moine rocks of nothern Scotland and its bearing on the status of the 'Morarian orogeny'. *J. Geol. Soc. London*, Vol.140, 813–823.

PRICE, R. J. 1983. *Scotland's environment during the last 30 000 years.* (Edinburgh: Scottish Academic Press.)

PRINGLE, J. R. 1970. The structural geology of the North Roe area of Shetland. *Geol. J.*, Vol.7, 147–170.

RAMSAY, J. G. 1958a. Superimposed folds at Loch Monar, Inverness-shire and Ross-shire. *Q. J. Geol. Soc. London*, Vol.113, 271–307.

— 1958b. Moine-Lewisian relations at Glenelg, Inverness-shire. *Q. J. Geol. Soc. London*, Vol.113, 487–520.

— 1963. Structure and metamorphism of the Moine and Lewisian rocks in the north-western Caledonides. *In* JOHNSON, M. R. W., and STEWART, F. H. (editors). *The British Caledonides* (Edinburgh: Oliver and Boyd.)

— and SPRING, J. 1962. Moine stratigraphy in the Western Highlands of Scotland. *Proc. Geol. Assoc.*, Vol.73, 295–326.

RATHBONE, P. A., and HARRIS, A. L. 1979. Basement-cover relationships at Lewisian inliers in the Moine rocks. *In* HARRIS, A. L., HOLLAND, C., and LEAKE, B. E. (editors). *The Caledonides of the British Isles—reviewed. Spec. Publ. Geol. Soc. London*, No.8, 101–107.

— — 1980. Moine and Lewisian near the Great Glen Fault in Easter Ross. *Scott. J. Geol.*, Vol.16, 51–64.

RAYNER, D. H. 1963. The Achanarras Limestone of the Middle Old Red Sandstone, Caithness, Scotland. *Proc. Yorkshire Geol. Soc.*, Vol.34, 1–44.

READ, H. H. 1931. The geology of central Sutherland. *Mem. Geol. Surv. GB.*

— 1961. Aspects of the Caledonian magmatism in Britain. *Proc. Liverpool and Manchester Geol. Soc.*, Vol.2, 653–683.

— PHEMISTER, J., and ROSS, G. 1926. The geology of Srath Oykell and Lower Loch Shin. *Mem. Geol. Surv. GB.*

— ROSS, G., PHEMISTER, J., and LEE, G. W. 1925. The geology of the country around Golspie, Sutherlandshire. *Mem. Geol. Surv. GB.*

RICHARDSON, J. B. 1962. Spores with bifurcate processes from the Middle Old Red Sandstone of Scotland. *Palaeontology*, Vol.5, 171–194.

— 1965. Middle Old Red Sandstone spore assemblages from the Orcadian basin, north-east Scotland. *Palaeontology*, Vol.7, 559–609.

— 1967.   Some British Lower Devonian spore assemblages from the Orcadian Basin, north-east Scotland.   *Palaeontology*, Vol.7, 559–605.

RICHARDSON, S. W. 1968.   The petrology of the metamorphosed syenite in Glen Dessarry, Inverness-shire.   *Q. J. Geol. Soc. London*, Vol.124, 9–51.

RICHEY, J. E. 1939.   The dykes of Scotland.   *Trans. Edinburgh Geol. Soc.*, Vol.13, 395–435.

— and KENNEDY, W. Q. 1939.   The Moine and sub-Moine series of Morar, Inverness-shire.   *Bull. Geol. Surv. GB.*, part II, 26–45.

— MACGREGOR, A. G., and ANDERSON, F. W. 1961.   *British Regional Geology: The Tertiary Volcanic Districts*.   (London: HMSO.)

RILEY, L. A. 1980.   Palynological evidence of an early Portlandian age for the uppermost Helmsdale Boulder Beds, Sutherland.   *Scott. J. Geol.*, Vol.16, 29–31.

RITCHIE, W. 1968.   *The coastal geomorphology of North Uist.*   O'Dell Memorial Monograph No.1. (Aberdeen: Aberdeen University Department of Geography.)

— 1971.   *The beaches of Barra and the Uists.* (Aberdeen: Aberdeen University Department of Geography.)

— and MATHER, A. 1970.   *The beaches of Lewis and Harris.* (Aberdeen: Aberdeen University Department of Geography.)

— — 1970.   *The beaches of Caithness.* (Aberdeen: Aberdeen University Department of Geography.)

ROBERTS, A. M., and HARRIS, A. L. 1983.   The Loch Quoich Line—a limit of early Scotland.   *J. Geol. Soc. London*, Vol.140, 883–892.

— SMITH, D. I., and HARRIS, A. L. 1984.   The structural setting and tectonic significance of the Glen Dessary Syenite, Inverness-shire.   *J. Geol. Soc. London*, Vol.141, 1033–1042.

ROBERTSON, R. C. R., and PARSONS, I. 1974.   The Loch Loyal syenites.   *Scott. J. Geol.*, Vol.10, 129–146.

ROBINSON, M., and BALLANTYNE, C. K. 1979.   Evidence for a glacial readvance pre-dating the Loch Lomond Advance in Wester Ross.   *Scott. J. Geol.*, Vol.15, 271–277.

ROCK, N. M. S. 1977.   A new occurrence of fenite in the Loch Borralan alkaline complex, Assynt.   *Mineral. Mag.*, Vol.41, M7.

— 1982.   Petrography and age of agglomeratic vents near Toscaig, Applecross.   *Proc. Geol. Assoc.*, Vol.93, 305–308.

— 1983a.   The Permo-Carboniferous camptonite-monchiquite dyke-suite of the Scottish Highlands and Islands.   *Rep. Inst. Geol. Sci.*, No.82/14.

— 1983b.   A note on the distribution and significance of metamorphic limestones in the Moine and Lewisian of the Scottish Highlands and Islands.   *Geol. Mag.*, Vol.120, 639–641.

— 1984.   New types of hornblende rocks and prehnite-veining in the Moines west of the Great Glen, Inverness-shire.   *Rep. Inst. Geol. Sci.*, No.83/8.

— 1985.   Contributions on the limestones of Scotland.   *Rep. Br. Geol. Surv.*, Vol.16, No.5.

— 1985.   Value of chemostratigraphical correlation in metamorphic terrains: an illustration from the Colonsay Limestone, Inner Hebrides, Scotland.   *Trans. R. Soc. Edinburgh, Earth Sci.*, Vol.76, 463–465.

— In press. A reappraisal of the Glen Urquhart serpentinite-metamorphic complex west of Loch Ness, Scottish Highlands. *Rep. Br. Geol. Surv.*

— 1987. The geochemistry of Lewisian marbles. *Spec. Publ. Geol. Soc. London*, No.27, 109–126.

— MacDonald, R., Drewery, S., Pankhurst, R. J., and Brook, M. 1986. Pelites of the Glen Urquhart serpentinite-metamorphic complex, west of Loch Ness. (Anomalous local limestone-pelite successions within the Moine outcrop: III.) *Scott. J. Geol.*, Vol.22, 179–202.

— Jeffreys, L. A., and MacDonald, R. 1984. The problem of anomalous local limestone-pelite successions within the Moine outcrop, I: metamorphic limestones of the Great Glen area, from Ardgour to Nigg. *Scott. J. Geol.*, Vol.20, 383–406.

— MacDonald, R., Walker, B. H., May, F,, Peacock, J. D., and Scott, P. 1985. Precambrian metabasites intruding the Moine assemblage west of Loch Ness, Scottish Highlands: evidence for modification of metabasite chemistry by interaction with country-rocks. *J. Geol. Soc. London*, Vol.142, 643–661.

— MacDonald, R., Szucs, T., and Bower, J. 1986. Comparative geochemistry of some Highland pelites. (Anomalous limestone-pelite successions within the Moine outcrop: II). *Scott. J. Geol.*, Vol.22, 107–126.

Rollinson, H. R. 1979. Ilmenite-magnetite geothermometry in trondhjemites from the Scourian complex of NW Scotland. *Mineral. Mag.*, Vol.43, 165–170.

Sabine, P. A. 1953. The petrography and geological significance of the post-Cambrian minor intrusions of Assynt and the adjoining districts of north-west Scotland. *Q. J. Geol. Soc. London*, Vol.109, 137–171.

— 1963. The Strontian granite complex, Argyllshire. *Bull. Geol. Surv. GB.*, Vol.20, 6–41.

Salter, J. W. 1859. Durness Limestone fossils. *Q. J. Geol. Soc. London*, Vol.15, 374–381.

Selley, R. C. 1965. Diagnostic characters of fluviatile sediments of the Torridonian formation (Precambrian) of northwest Scotland. *J. Sediment. Petrol.*, Vol.35, 366–380.

— 1969. Torridonian alluvium and quicksands. *Scott. J. Geol.*, Vol.5, 328–346.

— Shearman, D. J., Sutton, J., and Watson, J. V. 1963. Some underwater disturbances in the Torridonian of Skye and Raasay. *Geol. Mag.*, Vol.100, 224–243.

Shand, S. J. 1909, 1910. On borolanite and its associates in Assynt. *Trans. Edinburgh Geol. Soc.*, Vol.9, 202–215 and 376–416.

Shepherd, J. 1973. The structure and structural dating of the Carn Chuinneag intrusion, Ross-shire. *Scott. J. Geol.*, Vol.9, 63–88.

Sheraton, J. W. 1970. The origin of the Lewisian gneiss of north-west Scotland, with particular reference to the Drumbeg area, Sutherland. *Earth Planet. Sci. Lett.*, Vol.8, 301–310.

— Skinner, A. C., and Tarney, J. 1973. The geochemistry of the Scourian gneisses of the Assynt district. *In* Park, R. G., and Tarney, J. (editors). *The early Precambrian of Scotland and related rocks of Greenland*, 13–30. (Keele: University of Keele.)

— TARNEY, J., WHEATLEY, T. H., and WRIGHT, A. E. 1973. The structural history of the Assynt district. *In* PARK, R. G., and TARNEY, J. (editors). *The early Precambrian of Scotland and related rocks of Greenland*, 31–44. (Keele: University of Keele.)

SIBSON, R. H. 1975. Generation of pseudotachylite by ancient seismic faulting. *Geophys. J. Astron. Soc.*, Vol.43, 775–794.

— 1977. Fault rocks and fault mechanisms. *J. Geol. Soc. London*, Vol.133, 191–213.

— 1980. Transient discontinuities in ductile shear zones. *In* CARRERAS, J., COBBOLD, P. R., RAMSAY, J. G., and WHITE, S. H. (editors). *J. Struct. Geol.*, Vol.2, 165–171.

SILLS, J. D., SAVAGE, D., WATSON, J. V. and WINDLEY, B. F. 1981. Layered ultramafic-gabbro bodies in the Lewisian of NW Scotland: geochemistry and petrogenesis. *Earth Planet. Sci. Lett.*, Vol.58, 345–360.

— and WINDLEY, B. F. 1982. Petrogenesis of Lewisian amphibolite dykes from Clashnessie Bay, near Stoer, Sutherland. *Scott. J. Geol.*, Vol.18, 167–176.

SIMONY, P. S. 1973. Lewisian sheets within the Moines around 'The Saddle' of North West Scotland. *J. Geol. Soc. London*, Vol.129, 191–201.

SISSONS, J. B. 1967. *The evolution of Scotland's scenery.* (Edinburgh: Oliver and Boyd.)

— 1974. The Quaternary in Scotland: a review. *Scott. J. Geol.*, Vol.10, 311–337.

— 1976. *The geomorphology of the British Isles: Scotland.* (London: Methuen.)

— 1977. Former ice-dammed lakes in Glen Moriston, Inverness-shire, and their significance in upland Britain. *Trans. Inst. Br. Geogr.*, Vol.2, 224–242.

— 1979a. Palaeoclimatic inference from former glaciers in Scotland and the Lake District. *Nature, London*, Vol.278, 518–521.

— 1979b. The Loch Lomond Stadial in the British Isles. *Nature, London*, Vol.280, 199–203.

— 1982a. A former ice-dammed lake and associated glacier limits in the Achnasheen area, central Ross-shire. *Trans. Inst. Br. Geogr.* (New Ser.), Vol.7, 98–116.

— 1982b. The so-called high 'interglacial' rock shoreline of western Scotland. *Trans, Inst. Br. Geogr.* (New Ser.), Vol.7, 205–216.

— 1983. Quaternary. *In* CRAIG, G. Y. (editor). *Geology of Scotland* (2nd edition), 399–424. (Edinburgh: Scottish Academic Press.)

SMITH, D. I. 1963. Moine–Old Red Sandstone unconformity at Sugar Loaf Island, near Beauly, Inverness. *Bull. Geol. Surv. GB.*, No.20, 1–5.

— 1979. Caledonian minor intrusions of the Northern Highlands of Scotland. *In* HARRIS, A. L., HOLLAND, C., and LEAKE, B. E. (editors). *The Caledonides of the British Isles — reviewed. Spec. Pub. Geol. Soc. London*, No.8, 683–697.

— and WATSON, J. V. 1983. Scale and timing of movements on the Great Glen Fault, Scotland. *Geology*, Vol.11, 523–526.

SMITH, J. S. 1978. The last glacial epoch around the Moray Firth. *In* GILL, G. (editor), *Moray Firth Area geological studies*, 72–82. (Inverness: Inverness Field Club.)

— and MATHER, A. S. 1972. *The beaches of East Sutherland and Easter Ross.*
(Aberdeen: Aberdeen University Department of Geography.)

SMITH, R. L., STEARN, J. E. F., and PIPER, J. A. 1983. Palaeomagnetic
studies of the Torridonian sediments NW Scotland. *Scott. J. Geol.*, Vol.19,
29–45.

SOPER, N. J. 1963. The structure of the Rogart igneous complex,
Sutherland, Scotland. *Q. J. Geol. Soc. London*, Vol.11, 445–478.

— and BROWN, P. E. 1971. Relationship between metamorphism and
migmatisation in the northern part of the Moine nappe. *Scott. J. Geol.*, Vol.7,
305–325.

— and WILKINSON, P. 1975. The Moine thrust and the Moine Nappe at
Loch Eriboll, Sutherland. *Scott. J. Geol.*, Vol.11, 339–359.

SPEIGHT, J. M., and MITCHELL, J. G. 1979. The Permo-Carboniferous
dyke-swarm of northern Argyll and its bearing on dextral displacement on the
Great Glen Fault. *J. Geol. Soc. London*, Vol.136, 3–12.

— SKELHORN, R. R., SLOAT T., and KNAPP, R. J. 1982. The dyke swarms
of Scotland. *In* SUTHERLAND, D. S. (editor) *Igneous rocks of the British
Isles.* (Chichester: John Wiley.)

STEAVENSON, A. G. 1928. Some geological notes on three districts of
Northern Scotland. *Trans. Geol. Soc. Glasgow*, Vol.18, 193–233.

STEEL, R. J. 1974a. Cornstone (fossil caliche)—its origin, stratigraphic and
sedimentological significance in the New Red Sandstone in Western
Scotland. *J. Geol.*, Vol.82, 351–369.

— 1974b. New Red Sandstone floodplain and piedmont sedimentation in the
Hebridean province, Scotland. *Sediment. Petrol.*, Vol.44, No.2, 336–357.

— 1978. Triassic rift basins of Northwest Scotland—their configuration,
infilling and development. In *Mesozoic Northern North Sea Symposium* [MNNS-
77], 7/1 to 7/18.

— and WILSON, A. C. 1975. Sedimentation and tectonism (?Permo-Traissic)
on the margin of the North Minch Basin, Lewis. *J. Geol. Soc. London*,
Vol.131, 183–202.

STEVENS, A. 1913. Notes on the geology of the Stornoway district of Lewis.
Trans. Geol. Soc. Glasgow, Vol.15, 51–63.

STEVENSON, B. A. 1971. Chemical variability in some Moine rocks of
Lochailort, Inverness-shire. *Scott. J. Geol.*, Vol.7, 51–60.

STEWART, A. D. 1963. On certain slump structures in the Torridonian
sandstones of Applecross. *Geol. Mag.*, Vol.100, 205–218.

— 1966a. An unconformity in the Torridonian. *Geol. Mag.*, Vol.103,
462–464.

— 1966b. On the correlation of the Torridonian between Rhum and Skye.
Geol. Mag., Vol.103, 432–439.

— 1969. Torridonian rocks of Scotland reviewed. *In* KAY, M. (editor).
North Atlantic—geology and continental drift: a symposium. *Mem. Am. Assoc. Petrol.
Geol.*, Vol.12, 595–608.

— 1975. Torridonian rocks of western Scotland. *In* HARRIS, A. L. and
others (editors). *Precambrian. Spec. Rep. Geol. Soc. London*, No.6, 43–51.

— 1982. Late Proterozoic rifting in NW Scotland: the genesis of the
'Torridonian'. *J. Geol. Soc. London*, Vol.139, 415–420.

— and IRVING, E. 1974.   Palaeomagnetism of Precambrian sedimentary rocks from north-west Scotland and the apparent polar wandering path of Laurentia.   *Geophys. J. R. Astron. Soc.*, Vol.37, 51–72.

— and PARKER, A. 1979.   Palaeosalinity and environmental interpretation of red beds from the late Precambrain ('Torridonian') of Scotland.   *Sediment. Geol.*, Vol.22, 229–241.

STEWART, M. 1933.   Notes on the geology of Sula Sgeir and the Flannan Islands.   *Geol. Mag.*, Vol.70, 110–116.

STOKER, M. S. 1982.   Old Red Sandstone sedimentation and deformation in the Great Glen Fault Zone, NW of Loch Linnhe.   *Scott. J. Geol.*, Vol.18, 147–156.

— 1983.   The stratigraphy and structure of the Moine rocks of eastern Ardgour.   *Scott. J. Geol.*, Vol.19, 369–385.

STOREVEDT, K. M. 1987.   Major late Caledonian and Hercynian shear movements on the Great Glen Fault.   *Tectonophysics*, Vol.143, 253–267.

STRACHAN, R. A. 1982.   Tectonic sliding within the Moinian Loch Eil Division near Kinlocheil, W. Inverness-shire.   *Scott. J. Geol.*, Vol.18, 187–203.

SUTHERLAND, D. G., BALLANTYNE, C. K., and WALKER, M. J. C. 1982.   A note on the Quaternary deposits and landforms of St Kilda.   *Quat. Newsl.*, No.38, 1–5.

— and WALKER, M. J. C. 1984.   A late Devensian ice-free area and possible interglacial site in the Isle of Lewis, Scotland.   *Nature, London*, Vol.309, 701–703.

SUTHERLAND, D. S. (editor).   *Igneous rocks of the British Isles.*   (Chichester: John Wiley.)

SUTTON, J. 1962.   Torridonian microfossils.   *Geol. Mag.*, Vol.99, 379.

— 1962.   Futher observations on the margin of the Laxfordian complex of the Lewisian near Loch Laxford, Sutherland.   *Trans. R. Soc. Edinburgh*, Vol.65, 89–106.

— 1964.   Some aspects of Torridonian stratigraphy on Skye.   *Proc. Geol. Assoc.*, Vol.75, 251–289.

— 1969.   Scourian-Laxfordian relationships in the Lewisian of north-west Scotland.   *Spec. Pap. Geol. Assoc. Can.*, Vol.5, 119–128.

— and WATSON, J. V. 1951.   The pre-Torridonian metamorphic history of the Loch Torridon and Scourie areas in the northwest Highlands, and its bearing on the chronological classification of the Lewisian.   *Q. J. Geol. Soc. London*, Vol.106, 241–307.

— — 1953.   The supposed Lewisian inlier of Scardroy, central Ross-shire and its relations with the surrounding Moine rocks.   *Q. J. Geol. Soc. London*, Vol.108, 99–126.

— — 1955.   The stratigraphy and structure of the Moine rocks of eastern Ardgour.   *Scott. J. Geol.*, Vol.19, 369–385.

— — 1960.   Sedimentary structures in the Epidotic Grits of Skye.   *Geol. Mag.*, Vol.97, 106–122.

SWETT, K. 1966.   Authigenic feldspars and cherts resulting from dolomitisation of illitic limestone: a hypothesis [abstract].   *Geol. Soc. Amer. Prog., 1966 Annu. Meet.*, San Francisco, p.216.

— 1969. Interpretation of depositional and diagenetic history of Cambro-Ordovician succession of North-west Scotland. *In* KAY, M. (editor). *North Atlantic—Geology and continental drift—a symposium.* *Mem. Amer. Assoc. Pet. Geol.*, Vol.12, 630–646.

— KLEIN, G. DE V., and SMITH, D. E. 1971. A Cambrian tidal sand body—the Eriboll Sandstone of north-west Scotland: an ancient-recent analog. *J. Geol.*, Vol.79, 400–415.

SYKES, R. M. 1975. The stratigraphy of the Callovian and Oxfordian stages (Middle–Upper Jurassic) in northern Scotland. *Scott. J. Geol.*, Vol.11, 51–78.

SYNGE, F. 1978. Land and sea level changes during the waning of the last regional ice sheet in the vicinity of Inverness. *In* GILL, G. (editor). *The Moray Firth area geological studies*, 83–102. (Inverness: Inverness Field Club.)

TAFT, M. B. 1978. Basic minor intrusions in the Lewisian gneisses of southern Lewis, Outer Hebrides. *Scott. J. Geol.*, Vol.14, 185–190.

TAIT, D. 1910. On a large glacially transported mass of Lower Cretaceous rock at Leavad in the county of Caithness. *Trans. Geol. Soc. Edinburgh*, Vol.10, 1–9.

TALBOT, C. J. 1983. Microdiorite sheet intrusions as incomplete time and strain markers in the Moine assemblage NW of the Great Glen Fault, Scotland. *Trans. R. Soc. Edinburgh*, Vol.74, 137–152.

TANNER, P. W. G. 1965. Structural and metamorphic history of the Kinloch Hourn Area, Inverness-shire. Unpublished PhD thesis, University of London.

— 1971. The Sgurr Beag Slide—a major tectonic break within the Moine of the Western Highlands of Scotland. *Q. J. Geol. Soc. London*, Vol.126, 435–463.

— 1976. Progressive regional metamorphism of thin calcareous bands from the Moinian rocks of NW Scotland. *J. Petrol.*, Vol.17, 100–134.

— JOHNSTONE, G. S., SMITH, D. I., and HARRIS, A. L. 1970. Moinian stratigraphy and the problem of the Central Ross-shire inliers. *Bull. Geol. Soc. Am.*, Vol.181, 299–306.

— and TOBISCH, O. T. 1972. Sodic and ultra-sodic rocks of metasomatic origin from part of the Moine Nappe. *Scott. J. Geol.*, Vol.8, 151–178.

TARNEY, J. 1963. Assynt dykes and their metamorphism. *Nature, London*, Vol.199, 672–674.

— 1973. The Scourie dyke suite and the nature of the Inverian event in Assynt. *In* PARK, R. G., and TARNEY, J. (editors). (Keele: University of Keele.)

— SKINNER, A. C., and SHERATON, J. W. 1972. A geochemical comparison of major Archaean gneiss units from north-west Scotland and east Greenland. *24th Sess. Int. Geol. Congr., Canada 1972*, Sect.1, 162–174.

TEALL, J. J. H. 1885. The metamorphosis of dolerite into hornblende-schist. *Q. J. Geol. Soc. London*, Vol.41, 133–145.

THOMPSON, R. N. 1982. Magmatism of the British Tertiary Volcanic Province. *Scott. J. Geol.*, Vol.18, 49–105.

TILLEY, C. E. 1936. Eulysites and related rock types from Loch Duich, Ross-shire. *Mineral. Mag.*, Vol.24, 331–342.

TOBISCH, O. T., FLEUTY, M. J., MERH, S. S., MUKHOPADHYAY, P., and RAMSAY, J. G. 1970. Deformation and metamorphic history of Moinian and Lewisian rocks between Strathconon and Glen Affric. *Scott. J. Geol.*, Vol.6, 243–265.

TRAQUAIR, R. H. 1890. On the fossil fishes found at Achanarras Quarry, Caithness. *Ann. Nat. Hist.*, Vol.6, 479–486.

— 1895. The extinct vertebrata of the Moray Firth area. *In* HARVIE-BROWN, J. A., and BUCKLEY, T. E. (editors). *A vertebrate fauna of the Moray Basin*, Vol.II, 235–285. (London, Cambridge and Glasgow.)

TREWIN, N. H. 1976. Correlation of the Achanarras and Sandwick Fish Beds, Middle Old Red Sandstone, Scotland. *Scott. J. Geol.*, Vol. 12, 205–208.

VAN BREEMEN, O., AFTALION, M., and PIDGEON, R. T. 1971. The age of the granite injection complex of Harris, Outer Hebrides. *Scott. J. Geol.*, Vol.7, 139–152.

— AFTALION, M., and JOHNSON, M. R. W. 1979. Age of the Loch Borrolan Complex, Assynt and late movements along the Moine Thrust Zone. *J. Geol. Soc. London*, Vol.16, 489–495.

— — PANKHURST, R. J., and RICHARDSON, S. W. 1979b. Age of the Glen Dessarry syenite, Inverness-shire: diachronous Palaeozoic metamorphism across the Great Glen. *Scott. J. Geol.*, Vol.15, 49–62.

— PIDGEON, R. T., and JOHNSON, M. R. M. 1974. Precambrian and Palaeozoic pegmatites in the Northern Moines of Scotland. *J. Geol. Soc. London*, Vol.130, 493–508.

VAN DER VOO, R., and SCOTESE, C. 1981. Palaeo-magnetic evidence for a large (2000 km) sinistral offset along the Great Glen Fault during Carboniferous time. *Geology*, Vol.9, 583– 589.

VON WEYMARN, J. 1979. A new concept of glaciation in Lewis and Harris, Outer Hebrides. *Proc. R. Soc. Edinburgh*, Vol.77B, 97–106.

WATERSTON, C. D. 1950. Note on the sandstone injections of Eathie Haven, Cromarty. *Geol. Mag.*, Vol.87, 133–139.

— 1951. The stratigraphy and palaeontology of the Jurassic rocks of Eathie (Cromarty). *Trans. R. Soc. Edinburgh*, Vol.62, 33–51.

WATSON, J. V. 1964. Conditions in the Metamorphic Caledonides during the period of late orogenic cooling. *Geol. Mag.*, Vol.101, 457–465.

— 1968. Post-Scourian metadolerites in relation to Laxfordian deformation in Great Bernera, Outer Hebrides. *Scott. J. Geol.*, Vol.4, 53–67.

— 1969. The Precambrian gneiss complex of Ness, Lewis, in relation to the effects of Laxfordian regeneration. *Scott. J. Geol.*, Vol.5, 268–285.

— 1975. The Lewisian complex. *In* HARRIS, A. L., and others (editors). *Spec. Rep. Geol. Soc. London*, Vol.6, 15–29.

— 1976. The Outer Hebrides—a geological perspective. *Proc. Geol. Assoc.*, Vol.88, 1–14.

— 1983. Lewisian. *In* CRAIG, G. Y. (editor). *The geology of Scotland* (2nd edition). (Edinburgh: Scottish Academic Press.)

— 1984. The ending of the Caledonian orogeny in Scotland. *J. Geol. Soc. London*, Vol.141, 193–214.

— and LISLE, R. J. 1973. The pre-Laxfordian complex of the Outer Hebrides. *In* PARK, R. G., and TARNEY, J. (editors). *The early Precambrian of Scotland and related rocks of Greenland*, 45–50. (Keele: University of Keele.)

WESTBROOK, G. K. 1972. Structure and metamorphism of the Lewisian of east Tiree, Inner Hebrides. *Scott. J. Geol.*, Vol.8, 13–30.

— 1974. The South Harris magnetic anomaly. *Proc. Geol. Assoc.*, Vol.85, 1–12.

WESTOLL, T. S. 1937. The Old Red Sandstone fishes of the north of Scotland, particularly Orkney and Shetland. *Proc. Geol. Assoc.*, Vol.48, 13–45.

— 1951. The vertebrate-bearing strata of Scotland. *Rep. 18th Sess. Int. Geol. Congr., Part II, London 1948*, 5–21.

— 1977. Northern Britain. *In* HOUSE, M., and others (editors). *A correlation of Devonian rocks in the British Isles. Spec. Rep. Geol. Soc. London*, No.7.

WILKINS, D. A. 1984. The Flandrian woods of Lewis (Scotland). *J. Ecol.*, Vol.72, 251–258.

WILKINSON, P., SOPER, N. J., and BELL, A. N. 1975. Skolithus pipes as strain markers in mylonites. *Tectonophysics*, Vol.38, 143–157.

WILKINSON, S. B., TEALL, J. J. and PEACH, B. N. 1907. The geology of Islay, including Oronsay and portions of Colonsay and Jura. *Mem. Geol. Surv. GB.*

WILLIAMS, G. E. 1969. Petrography and origin of pebbles from Torridonian strata (late Precambrian), northwest Scotland. *In* KAY, M. (editor). *North Atlantic—geology and continental drift: a symposium. Mem. Am. Assoc. Pet. Geol.*, No.12, 609–629.

WILLIAMS, A., STRACHAN, I., BASSETT, D. A., DEAN, W. T., INGHAM, J. K., WRIGHT, A. D., and WHITTINGTON, H. B. 1972. A correlation of Ordovician rocks in the British Isles. *Spec. Rep. Geol. Soc. London*, No.3.

WILSON, D., and SHEPHERD, J. 1979. The Carn Chuinneag granite and its aureole. *In* HARRIS, A. L., HOLLAND, C. H., and LEAKE, B. E. (editors). *The Caledonides of the British Isles—reviewed. Spec. Publ. Geol. Soc. London*, No.8, 669–675.

WILSON, G. V., EDWARDS, W., KNOX, J., JONES, R. C. B., and STEPHENS, J. V. 1935. The geology of the Orkneys. *Mem. Geol. Surv. GB.*

WINCHESTER, J. A. 1972. Pattern of regional metamorphism suggests a sinistral displacement of 160 km along the Great Glen Fault. *Nature Phys. Sci.*, Vol.246, 81–84.

— 1971. Some geochemical distinctions between Moinian and Lewisian rocks and their use in establishing the identity of supposed inliers in the Moinian. *Scott. J. Geol.*, Vol.7, 327–344.

— 1974. The zonal pattern of regional metamorphism in the Scottish Caledonides. *J. Geol. Soc. London*, Vol.130, 509–524.

— 1976. Different Moinian amphibolite suites in northern Ross-shire. *Scott. J. Geol.*, Vol.12, 187–204.

— and LAMBERT, R. St J. 1970. Geochemical distinctions between the Lewisian of Cassley, Durcha and Loch Shin, Sutherland and the surrounding Moinian. *Proc. Geol. Assoc.*, Vol.81, 275–302.

— LAMBERT, R. ST J., and HOLLAND, J. G. 1981.   Geochemistry of the western part of the Moine Assemblage.   *Scott. J. Geol.*, Vol.17, 181–294.

WOOD, B. J. 1965.   The influence of pressure, temperature and bulk composition on the appearance of garnet in orthogneisses—an example from South Harris, Scotland.   *Earth Planet Sci. Lett.*, Vol.26, 299–311.

WOOLLEY, A. R. 1970.   The structural relationships of the Loch Borralan complex, Scotland.   *Geol. J.*, Vol.7, 171–182.

— 1973.   The pseudoleucite borolanites and associated rocks of the south-eastern tract of the Borralan complex, Scotland.   *Bull. Br. Mus. Nat. Hist. (Mineral.)*, No.2, 287–333.

ZHANG, Z. 1982.   Upper Proterozoic microfossils from the Summer Isles, NW Scotland.   *Palaeontology*, Vol.25, 443–460.

Page numbers in italics refer to illustrations.